The Church in Devon

400–1560

The Church in Devon
400–1560

Nicholas Orme

IMPRESS BOOKS

To my friends in the Nether Exe parishes

First published 2013
by Impress Books Ltd
Innovation Centre, Rennes Drive,
University of Exeter Campus, Exeter EX4 4RN

Typeset in 10/14 Palatino by Swales and Willis Ltd, Exeter, Devon

Printed and bound by Short Run Press, Exeter, Devon

British Library Cataloguing in Publication Data
A catalogue record for this book is available from the British Library

ISBN: 978 1 9076054 1 3

Contents

List of Illustrations and Maps vii
Preface ix

1. From the Romans to Domesday Book 1
2. From 1086 to 1300 31
3. The Later Middle Ages: the Clergy 69
4. The Later Middle Ages: the Laity 109
5. The Reformation 151
6. A Thousand Years of Christianity 191

Guide to Technical Terms 197
Notes and Abbreviations 205
Bibliography 223
Index 231

List of Illustrations and Maps

The author and publishers are grateful for permission to reproduce illustrations from The Bodleian Library (Oxford), the Dean and Chapter of Exeter Cathedral, the Dean and Chapter of Wells Cathedral, the Royal Albert Memorial Museum and Art Gallery (Exeter), and the clergy and churches of Ashton, Doddiscombsleigh, and Ottery St Mary.

1 The former church of St Mary Major, Exeter by George Townsend (Royal Albert Memorial Museum and Art Gallery, Exeter) 3
2 Braunton parish church 7
3 Crediton parish church 10
4 The Exon Domesday (Exeter Cathedral Library) 14
5 Minsters in Devon before 1086 17
6 St Martin's parish church, Exeter 21
7 Lesser churches in Devon before 1086 24
8 Rogationtide processions (C. Wordsworth, *Ceremonies and Processions of the Cathedral Church of Salisbury*, Cambridge, 1901) 28
9 Bishop's Tawton parish church 34
10 The effigy of Walter Bronescombe, Exeter Cathedral 38
11 The diocese of Exeter 42
12 Exeter Cathedral, the north tower and north elevation 46
13 Religious houses in Devon 50
14 Parishes north-west of Exeter 54
15 St Mary Arches parish church, Exeter, arcading 58
16 Down St Mary parish church, tympanum 62
17 List of members of the Guild of Kalendars, Exeter (Exeter Cathedral Archives, D&C 3675, f. 7v) 66
18 Roof-boss of a bishop, Exeter Cathedral 73
19 Confirmation (Doddiscombsleigh parish church) 79
20 Ottery St Mary parish church 84
21 St Mary Magdalene chapel, Taddiport in Little Torrington 90

22 Ordination (Doddiscombsleigh parish church) 95
23 A priest and clerk at the altar (Bodleian Library, MS Douce 245 f. 264v) 101
24 The Hailes Psalter (Wells Cathedral Library) 106
25 Ashburton parish church before the Reformation 112
26 Ashton parish church, the roodscreen 117
27 Baptism (Doddiscombsleigh parish church) 121
28 The eucharist (Doddiscombsleigh parish church) 126
29 The chapel of St Anne, Barnstaple 130
30 Confession (Doddiscombsleigh parish church) 135
31 Wax images from the tomb of Bishop Lacy, Exeter Cathedral (Exeter Museum) 139
32 St Anne teaching the Virgin Mary (Bodleian Library, MS Douce 231 f. 3r) 144
33 An English grammar school from the *Hymnal* (Richard Pynson, 1497) 148
34 The effigy of Bishop Oldham, Exeter Cathedral 155
35 The Greenway chapel, St Peter's parish church, Tiverton 161
36 The Dorset aisle, Ottery St Mary parish church 166
37 Frontispiece of *The Byble in Englyshe* (Richard Grafton, 1539) 172
38 Sampford Courtenay parish church 177
39 The Commotion of 1549 183
40 The city walls of Exeter 188
41 The ruins of Frithelstock Priory 193
42 St Nicholas Priory, Exeter 195

Preface

This book is a sequel to a similar volume, *Cornwall and the Cross* (2007), which I wrote about Devon's neighbour to the west. Its purpose is twofold: to give a broad account of English Church history, centred on Devon, for local historians and general readers, and to provide a resource for scholars who wish to know what the county's history reveals about topics in which they are interested. It is not an archaeological study of buildings and artefacts, although I hope that it will be useful in recreating the religious and social context to which they belonged. For reasons of space, it has been necessary to restrict the coverage of Exeter Cathedral, which has already been explored in another of my books, *Exeter Cathedral: the first thousand years* (2009).

I began to research and write on the Church history of Devon in the early 1970s, since when I have incurred debts to many people, including my colleagues in the Department of History at Exeter University and the librarians and archivists of the University Library, the Devon and Exeter Institution, the Devon Record Office, and the Library and Archives of Exeter Cathedral. I have also greatly benefited from the help and advice of John Allan, Julia Crick, Robert Higham, Jeanne James, David Lepine, Joanna Mattingly, Michael Williams, and the Historic Environment Services of Cornwall and Devon. John Thurmer taught me Church history. I am grateful to all of them and especially to my publishers, Impress Books, who are also responsible for much of the photography. This is the fourth book that they have kindly and efficiently produced for me.

Nicholas Orme
Oxford
March 2013

Chapter 1

From the Romans to Domesday Book

Concerning Devon

In 1328–9, John Grandisson, who had just become bishop of Exeter, wrote to the papal court at Avignon about the region in which he had lately arrived. 'I am not only at the ends of the earth, but – I may say – at the ends of the ends thereof.' The region, he said, was well provided with wine from Gascony, and produced plenty of meat but rather less corn. It was linked with England on only one side; the rest of its edges were surrounded by the ocean, and the ocean was seldom navigable save by local people. In this brief sketch, the bishop identified several of Devon's essential features. It is a peripheral part of England, it has long coast-lines, its seas are dangerous but make possible trade with other shores, and it has a great deal of pasture for stock-raising as against grain-growing arable land. All these elements have helped to shape its history and that of its churches.[1]

Grandisson could have added that Devon is large: the third biggest of the ancient English counties.[2] It takes a crow 70 miles (112 kilometres) to fly from Ilfracombe to Salcombe. The land is not only extensive but varied. It spans the line that runs roughly speaking from Exeter to York, dividing England into highland and lowland zones. The lowland zone extends into the east and south of Devon. In the Middle Ages, much of this was studded with villages where people lived close together. It also contained one major English city (Exeter), two leading ports (Plymouth and Dartmouth), and some thriving inland towns such as Honiton and Tiverton. The highland zone covers the north and west of the county with the eastern fringes. In medieval times, this had one significant urban centre and port at Barnstaple with Pilton, and there was mining on the edges of Dartmoor which gave prosperity to Ashburton, Chagford, and Tavistock. The majority of the north and west, however, was upland where people lived in scattered farms and hamlets. This highland terrain gave rise to one of Devon's distinctive religious features: the large number of free-standing chapels, although they were also to be found in the lowland areas.

As the bishop was also aware, Devon is an outlying part of England. But even when Cornwall is added, the South-West is not one of England's largest peripheries or, historically, one of its most important. Wales and the North are bigger and have always been weightier in political terms. Monarchs rarely came to the South-West in the Middle Ages. They had no need except in times of civil war or war with France. Devon did not possess much influence outside its borders. It absorbed what happened elsewhere, but the rest of England was rarely affected by events in Devon. Perhaps the only exception, in the thousand-odd years to which this book relates, was the Prayer-Book rising of 1549 which helped to bring down the leader of the English government, the duke of Somerset.

This does not mean that Devon was rustic and backward: impoverished in its life and history. It has been fully part of England in terms of government and law ever since England became a unity in the tenth century. It traded by land and sea. Its people travelled out to work, study, or go on pilgrimage. It received the Christian faith at an early date, before the end of Roman Britain, and nearly all the great religious movements and institutions of the Middle Ages and the Reformation took root in its soil. It acquired a rich array of monasteries, parish churches, church furnishings, books, and saint cults. It produced Church leaders and scholars, church builders and craftsmen, devout lay people, and those who resisted the Church's claims on their lives. Devon's Church history, like its landscape, is as varied, complex, and worth studying as that of any other English county.

The Roman and Post-Roman Periods

It is an example of 'the law of unintended consequences' that the Roman Empire, having brought about the execution of Jesus, enabled his teachings and followers to spread across its territories. From Palestine where Christians first appeared, peace and transport within the empire allowed them to take their faith to the most distant provinces, including Britain. We do not know when they reached Devon, except that it was probably a good deal earlier than the oldest evidence for Christianity in the region. This is a piece of pottery from the fourth century, found in Exeter and rudely scratched with the letters XP: the first two letters of 'Christ' in Greek.[3] At first, the empire's leaders repressed the new faith but eventually they came to allow and embrace it. Toleration was granted in AD 313 by the Emperor Constantine, and in 391 his successor Theodosius forbade pagan worship, making Christianity the only lawful religion of the empire.

The administrative centre of the South-West of Britain in Roman times was Exeter, and one would expect a church to have existed there with a measure of public status by at least the end of the fourth century, now that the empire was officially Christian. This expectation gained support in the 1970s with the discovery of a

Figure 1 The old church of St Mary Major, Exeter, formerly opposite the cathedral. It probably began its life as part of the late Anglo-Saxon minster and stood near the oldest recorded Christian site in Devon.

cemetery in the area of the forum (the civic centre of Roman Exeter), at the south-western corner of the present cathedral Close.[4] Its burials appear to be Christian and to date from the end of the Roman period or soon afterwards: say 400–500. They also imply the presence of a church, since Christians by this time liked to be laid to rest near such places, unlike earlier pagan Romans who preferred to lie in cemeteries outside towns.

The period during which Christianity enjoyed official status in Roman Britain was brief. Effective rule from Rome came to an end round about 410, and the city of Exeter fell into decay. Nevertheless, that period laid foundations for the future. Christianity survived after Roman rule died out. Exeter, even in ruins, remained as a symbol of authority and civilisation, ensuring its revival as the county's centre of government and religion in later times. The cathedral is only a few yards away from the site of the likely Roman church. After the evaporation of Roman power, the people of the South-West, the Dumnonii, who shared a Brittonic (i.e. ancient British) language and culture akin to that of the rest of Roman Britain, acquired their own local rulers. But there is no sign of a relapse into paganism, although it must be admitted that we know little of the politics or religion of the region for the next two centuries.

The aristocracy at least remained Christian. This is suggested by the survival in Devon of some seventeen stones of a pillar type, bearing inscriptions in Latin to named people, usually men. Most of the names are Brittonic, two Irish, and one or two Latin (Nepos, Sabinus). They are modelled on a kind of monument that arose in south Wales and spread to Cornwall and Devon, although in the latter they are only found on Lundy (four examples), the north coast (two), and the south of the county (eleven).[5] The use of Latin on the monuments indicates that those who commissioned the monuments felt themselves as still belonging to Roman civilisation and hence to Christianity. An attack by the British writer Gildas in the middle of the sixth century on the ruler of the Dumnonii, Constantine, points to the same conclusion. Gildas portrayed this man as a wicked ruler. He had killed two royal youths and their guardians at an altar while under the protection of a holy abbot. If he did not turn to the Lord, God would punish him.[6] Yet sinful though he was, Gildas did not describe him as a pagan and there seems to have been at least one monastery in his territory. His name was that of Roman emperors.

The kingdom of the Dumnonii probably included the whole of Devon for at least two hundred years until the middle of the seventh century. That being the case, with the region's leaders as Christians, one would anticipate the laying of some permanent Christian foundations. There was once an assumption that the faith was brought to Devon by missionaries from Wales, and contacts between the two lands are likely in view of the diffusion of the inscribed stones, especially on the north coast of Devon. But we should also envisage the county's early Christianity as inherited from Roman times and nurtured by contacts with the rest of southern Britain and with the continent of Europe. A basic building block would have been the creation of churches, perhaps at first in the form of monasteries. Sherborne in Dorset appears to have had an early church with a Brittonic name, later recorded as *Lamprobi* (probably meaning the 'lann' or religious site of Probus, a saint recorded in Cornwall), and the church may have fallen within the territory of the Dumnonii.[7] It later became the seat of an Anglo-Saxon bishop responsible in part for their welfare. Other signs of monasteries appear in north Devon, where Braunton (Figure 2, p. 7) and Hartland are recorded as churches served by groups of clergy, although the records of this post-date the conquest of Devon by the Anglo-Saxons.

Such monasteries may have been modest in numbers and scattered in distribution. Cemeteries would have been more common, no doubt often inherited from pagan times but now Christianised to the extent that burials took place with Christian rites, while the sites might include a Christian symbol such as a cross or an inscribed stone honouring an important person. One such cemetery has been excavated one kilometre east of Kenn, to the south-west of Exeter. It contained at least 111 burials of a Christian character, chiefly dating from the sixth and seventh centuries. The graves were arranged in rows and groups, a few of them being surrounded by small ditches, and the cemetery had a defined area.[8] Two place-names in north Devon, Landcross and Landkey, include the Brittonic word 'lann', perhaps originally in the sense of an enclosed cemetery but one that eventually acquired a church. The fact that Landkey also contains the name of Kea, the patron saint of churches in Brittany, Cornwall, Somerset, and Wales, suggests more strongly that a church was built there and dedicated to the saint while north Devon was still Brittonic in culture.[9] The other site worth mentioning is Chittlehampton in the same area, the church of which honours a saint called Urith whose name appears to be Brittonic rather than Anglo-Saxon.[10]

These indications of Dumnonian religious sites are scanty, but their rarity is likely to reflect changes of settlements and place-names that followed the Anglo-Saxon conquest after 650, particularly when new villages arose in about the tenth century. Even the cemetery at Kenn is some way from the later, modern settlement. The lack of evidence probably disguises a substantial development of Christianity in the South-West between 400 and 650, based on churches and cemeteries.

The Anglo-Saxon Period: Church Government

During the early seventh century, the South-West began to come under pressure from the kings of the West Saxons, who ruled southern England from Somerset and Dorset to Berkshire and Hampshire. In 614 and 658, according to the later Anglo-Saxon Chronicle, the West Saxons gained victories over the *Walas* (Welsh, meaning Britons) at *Beandune* and *Peonnan*, perhaps in Dorset and Somerset or Devon respectively.[11] This opened the way for English penetration into Devon during the second half of the seventh century. In 682, the Chronicle states that Centwine, the West Saxon king, 'drove the *Bretwalas* [Brittonic *Walas*] as far as the sea',[12] and within a few years of this, in about 685, there was a monastery in Exeter, ruled by an abbot with an English name, when an English boy called Winfrith entered it: a boy later to be known as St Boniface.[13] In 693 Centwine's successor-but-one, King Ine, issued a code of laws for his subjects who included a number of 'Welsh', some paying tax to the king and others riding on his errands.[14]

There was still an important Brittonic ruler in the South-West during the years around 700: a king named Gerent with whom Ine fought at least one battle. But by the middle of the eighth century, the West Saxon kings were claiming authority well inside Devon. Ine's successor, King Æthelheard, felt able to grant land near the River Torridge in north Devon to the church of Glastonbury in 729, and an estate on the River Creedy near Exeter to the bishop of Sherborne ten years later.[15]

Most of Devon was probably under his rule by this time. The political conquest was followed by the Anglicisation of Devon in terms of the language spoken. This process may have been due in part to immigration by Anglo-Saxons but also (perhaps chiefly) to the adoption of the English language by the Brittonic peoples of Devon. The change was relatively rapid, and was probably completed during the eighth and early ninth centuries, unlike western Cornwall where the Brittonic language lingered for another nine hundred years.

Once the West Saxon kings were in command of parts of Devon, they wished to control its religious affairs as well. At first there was only one bishop of the West Saxons based at Winchester, but in about 705 Ine created a second diocese to serve Somerset, Dorset, and Devon. The bishop of this diocese was placed at Sherborne perhaps because, if it had been a Brittonic church centre, it had a resonance for people of that language and culture. The first bishop, Aldhelm, had personal links with the Brittonic lands. He was the author of a letter to King Gerent, asking him and his clergy to adopt the current practices of the western Roman Church with regard to the calculation of the date of Easter and the shape of the clerical tonsure.[16] He also made at least one journey through Cornwall and Devon which he described in a poem, recounting how he sheltered from bad weather in an unidentified church and attended a service there.[17]

By about the 880s, the Christians in the diocese of Sherborne appear to have been too many for one bishop to supervise, especially since Cornwall was now falling under West Saxon rule. Asser, a Welsh bishop who came to King Alfred's court and wrote his biography, tells us in the work that the king gave him the church at Exeter 'with all its *parochia* in the Saxon lands [*Saxonia*] and Cornwall', probably during the 880s.[18] Historians usually interpret *parochia* as lands which the Exeter church held in Devon and Cornwall, and presume that Asser received them to support him in some leading role in the Church of the two counties. This was very likely as a bishop, perhaps as an assistant to the bishop of Sherborne. In fact, the Exeter minster is not known to have held any property in Cornwall until the twelfth century; its possessions were in east and south Devon.[19] Asser is probably simplifying matters here; it is more likely that Alfred gave him Exeter and other properties, including the church of Plympton which Asser is known to have held.[20]

Nevertheless, the conclusion that he was endowed with local lands in order to underpin his work as a Church leader seems likely. As a Welshman loyal to Alfred, he was both trustworthy and able to reach out to English and Cornish speakers. The link with Exeter is also significant. It was a place that Alfred was trying to revive (he strengthened its defences against the Vikings),[21] and it was the old Roman capital of Devon: the only Roman city of the two South-Western counties. As such it was the obvious place for Asser to operate from, as bishops did from other Roman

Figure 2 Braunton parish church, named after a Brittonic saint Brannoc and probably a Christian site before the Anglo-Saxon conquest of Devon.

cities: Canterbury, London, Winchester, York, and so on. The Anglo-Saxons had an understanding that the building of Christianity involved rebuilding Roman civilisation, and that the old Roman sites were appropriate places to found churches and bishoprics.

In the late 890s, Asser was also made bishop of Sherborne, but when he died in 909 the next king of the West Saxons, Edward the Elder, decided to make a permanent division of the Sherborne diocese. Sherborne was left only with Dorset; Somerset was given a new bishop based at Wells and Devon one located at Crediton.[22] The question arises why Crediton was chosen rather than Exeter. One possibility is that Asser had found Exeter a difficult church to work with: its clergy may have been resistant to sharing their resources and labour with a bishop. Another is that King Edward, unlike Alfred, did not wish to give up the minster of Exeter to the bishop, since the minster belonged to the king and probably originated as a royal foundation. Edward's son and successor, King Æthelstan, seems to have taken a similar view to his father, since he did much to enhance the wealth and status of the Exeter minster. Crediton offered an alternative. It lay on the estate by the Creedy which King Æthelheard had given to the bishop of Sherborne in 739, it may already have had a church although this is not certain, and it was available for the bishop of Devon now that Sherborne no longer had a responsibility for that area.

We think of Crediton and Exeter as separate places. However, the Creedy estate, at least by the tenth or eleventh century, came very close to the northern edge of Exeter, and the bishop was probably thought of as living as near to the city as possible. Crediton is the only site of an Anglo-Saxon bishopric that was based just outside, rather than inside, an old Roman city that was also a reviving town. It was evidently chosen not so much for its own significance but for its proximity to Exeter, so as to be closely in touch with that city's growing importance. Eventually, in 1050, Edward the Confessor, now king of England, proved willing to give up the Exeter minster to the bishop of Crediton.[23] Accordingly the bishop, Leofric, moved his seat to Exeter, the minster became his cathedral, and he the first bishop of Exeter (1050–72).

Minsters: Dates and Numbers

The establishment of an Anglo-Saxon bishop with control of Devon in about 705 was accompanied by the appearance of Anglo-Saxon churches in the county. Some of these may have been Brittonic creations which became English in terms of the vernacular language of their clergy and congregations and in their similarity to churches in southern England. Others were new foundations by Anglo-Saxon kings, bishops, or lords. It is difficult to know which churches belonged to each category. Those mentioned in north Devon – Braunton, Chittlehampton, Hartland, Landcross, and Landkey – are the only ones with signs of a history before the Anglo-Saxon conquest.

The earliest churches of Anglo-Saxon Devon of which we have records were minsters.[24] 'Minster' was the Anglo-Saxon word for a monastery, and in the seventh and eighth centuries the Devon minsters were probably staffed by groups of monks living communally although not always equally: monks might have private wealth. Later, in the ninth century, communal life declined. Most minster clergy divided the property of their church into individual portions, rather than sharing it in common. They often moved to live in private houses, married, and passed on their posts and revenues to their sons. But whether married or not and living together or not, the purpose of minster clergy was to worship God by reciting a series of daily services known as the 'divine office' and to pray for their founders and patrons. They also had a public role, even if they were monks: providing masses, baptisms, and funerals for a surrounding area, and allowing lay people to visit their churches for private devotion or to attend services.

The first minster of which we hear in Devon is the one at Exeter recorded in the earliest Life of St Boniface in relation to the year 685 or thereabouts, at which time it was governed by an 'abbot' named Wulfhard and was presumably monastic in its way of life.[25] In the eleventh century, charters were produced to validate claims by the Exeter minster to certain of its lands, and five of these charters bear the date 670 which suggests a tradition to this effect about the founding of the minster.[26] The date falls in the reign of Cenwealh, king of the West Saxons from 642 to 672, and he is a likely founder. He was probably the first such king to hold power in the Exeter region; other kings had already placed churches in old Roman cities; and the Exeter minster was later regarded by the West Saxon kings as their possession (Figure 1, p. 3). Excavations in the cathedral Close at Exeter have revealed a cemetery of the late seventh century that was probably linked to this monastery, but the exact site of the church and its ancillary buildings has not yet been located.[27]

Other minsters make their appearance in documents after 700. We have seen that King Æthelheard of the West Saxons gave land beside the River Creedy to the bishop of Sherborne in 739 'to found a minster'.[28] This grant, like the creation of the bishopric in 909, looks like a plan to give the bishop a base close to Exeter without giving him control of the minster in the city. It is not known if the minster was founded in the 700s, but it must have come into existence by about 909 at the latest when the new bishopric was founded at Crediton, the principal settlement on the Creedy estate (Figure 3, p. 10). Meanwhile, we hear of Axminster in 786, *Brannocmynstre* meaning Braunton in 839–855, Exminster in about 881, and Plympton as a minster in 899–909.[29] Tavistock acquired a minster in 981 and Buckfast one in 1018: these were more strictly monastic foundations.[30] Finally, there are two churches that were

Figure 3 Crediton parish church, the successor of a minster founded by about 909 which became the seat of the bishop of Devon from then until 1050. Later it was a minster church of canons and vicars choral.

given to Battle Abbey by William the Conqueror. One is Cullompton, a church said to have supported five clergy before 1066.[31] The other is St Olave in Exeter, which Gytha countess of Wessex endowed with a valuable estate at Sherford in 1057–1065.[32] Her gift was probably necessary because churches in Exeter (other than the minster) did not have parishes and therefore revenues, but it was on a generous scale for a single priest and may have been intended for a small group of clergy.

The documentary evidence improves with the help of Domesday Book, compiled in 1086 and extant in two versions: the regional and more detailed 'Exon Domesday' (Figure 4, p. 14) and the general and simplified 'Exchequer Domesday'.[33] Domesday Book was concerned to record major holdings of land with the names of those who held them, their value, and the tax that they paid to the crown. Accordingly it contains entries for Buckfast Abbey, Tavistock Abbey, and five other churches staffed by groups of clergy holding land: Hartland and Plympton, where the clergy are described as canons, South Molton as priests, and Totnes and Yealmpton as clerks.[34] Two other churches of canons, Exeter Cathedral and Crediton, existed in 1086 and might be expected to figure in Domesday Book, but the property of the cathedral canons was subsumed within that of the bishop of Exeter.[35] As a result, they were mentioned only in passing as receiving benefits from him, while the canons of Crediton were omitted altogether because they were supported by tithes which fell outside the concern of the Domesday survey.[36] Domesday also mentions some churches holding land without describing the type or number of their clergy. Woodbury had a substantial estate of just over one hide of land, and three churches owned smaller properties: Pinhoe one virgate of land (about 30–40 acres) and Colyton and Kingskerswell each half a virgate.[37] A fifth property of one and a half virgates called *Jacobescherche* lay just outside Exeter to the south-east. This became the site of a priory of St James in the twelfth century, but in 1086 the land belonged to a woman named Alveva and whether the church had ever possessed it is not revealed.[38]

The Exon Domesday preserves some additional taxation records known as the 'Geld Rolls', which sometimes seem to preserve material about land ownership predating 1086. These rolls mention churches holding land at *Alentona* in Plympton Hundred (meaning Yealmpton, one hide), Modbury (one hide), *Niuuentona* in Alleridge Hundred (signifying Newton Ferrers, half a hide), and Plympton (two hides), as well as priests with land at Hartland (one hide), Newton St Petrock (one hide), and South Molton (one virgate), and clerks with land at Hollacombe (one virgate).[39] A hide was large enough to maintain a group of priests, so it is possible that Modbury at least can be added to the minsters. A virgate was not sufficient by itself, but since clergy also received tithes which were more valuable, it is possible that even the churches with only one virgate supported such a group, as we know to have been the case at South Molton. From a contrary point of view, properties of a virgate or less were no larger than the glebe lands of some ordinary parish churches in later times, so that Colyton and Kingskerswell in particular may have been such churches whose land, for some reason, was reported to the Domesday survey. It should also be noted that Hollacombe and Newton St Petrock belonged to the Cornish minster of Bodmin, raising the possibility that the priests and clerks associated with them were the clergy of Bodmin rather than separate religious communities.

The documentary references to minsters may be supplemented by the evidence of parish sizes and boundaries. This evidence is much later than the Norman Conquest, indeed most of it comes from the tithe maps compiled in about 1840, but it often matches what we would expect of parishes in the tenth and eleventh centuries. Because minsters were early foundations, they acquired large parishes and often (although not always) retained them to an extent above the average even when other churches came into existence nearby. It is possible to reconstruct an approximate map of the parishes in Devon in 1291, using the tithe maps and taking out parish boundaries that are known to have solidified after that date.[40] At that time, the minster churches of Crediton, Hartland, and Plympton all had territories much larger than those of normal later parishes, apart from those in moorland areas where populations were thinner. A further example is Tiverton whose parish also covered an extensive tract. Its church is not recorded until after 1086, but in the thirteenth century it was staffed by four clergy: a situation that must have been far older but was not recorded in Domesday Book, probably because the clergy were supported by tithes rather than land.[41]

It follows that some other churches with large parishes are strong candidates to have been minsters before the Norman Conquest. One is Stokenham, which used to include the modern parishes of Chivelstone and Sherford, so that it covered most of the terrain to the east of the Avon estuary. Another is West Alvington, which once incorporated Malborough, South Huish, and South Milton on the west side of the same estuary. On similar grounds one might propose Lydford. Its core parish was not unduly large, but it was technically the parish church of Dartmoor, and if that is included, the parish was very extensive. Chulmleigh was a parish of moderate size but had, like Tiverton, a group of clergy in the thirteenth century. However, they held a significant amount of land which does not appear in their hands in the Domesday survey, suggesting that the group was formed or at least endowed at some time after 1086.[42]

Three other kinds of context are worth considering as evidence for minsters. One is the presence of a major royal estate. We know that Anglo-Saxon kings were important, indeed crucial, in the adoption of Christianity in their kingdoms and were active in encouraging the growth of churches. Exeter seems to have begun as a royal minster, and Axminster had early royal links. Its first appearance in a document relates to the burial of a West Saxon prince, and it was eventually granted to York Minster by Edward the Confessor in the early 1060s.[43] King Alfred held property at Cullompton, Exminster, and Tiverton, where there were minsters, as well as at Lifton, a candidate to have had such a church.[44] By 1086, the crown owned several estates containing minsters, including Axminster, South Molton, Plympton, Totnes, and Yealmpton,[45] as well as such contenders to be minsters as Stokenham on the royal estate of Chillington, West Alvington, and Woodbury.[46]

Another likely pointer to minster locations is the location of *burhs*: places fortified against the Vikings by Alfred and his successors, some of which grew into towns. There were four *burhs* in Devon: Exeter, Halwell, Lydford, and Pilton.[47] Exeter already had a minster by this time, and Lydford may have possessed a large parish, while Halwell lies close to Totnes where a minster is later recorded. None is known in Halwell itself, either because it lost its minster to Totnes or never had one due to their proximity. There was a church in Pilton by the twelfth century which was important enough to become a monastery, and Pilton adjoins Barnstaple which developed as a significant town with defences in the late-Saxon period. A large cemetery of this period has been identified in Barnstaple, probably indicating a church but not the present parish church which lies some distance away from the cemetery.[48] A minster in Pilton, Barnstaple, or both looks very likely, given their importance at a major landing-place in north Devon.

A third sign of a minster is one that post-dates the Norman Conquest, and must therefore be read with caution lest it be anachronistic. In the twelfth century, when a new wave of monasteries was founded in Devon, three of these (Hartland, Plympton, and Totnes) were re-foundations of existing minsters and six others were sited at churches that are candidates to have been minsters. They were Barnstaple, Exeter (St James), Exeter (St Nicholas Priory, which incorporated the church and property of St Olave), Modbury, Pilton, and Totnes. There must have been something special about these churches that caused them to be turned into monasteries, and it may have consisted of buildings, properties, or status that had been shaped by earlier life as a minster. Finally, it has been observed that many minsters in England possessed the body of their own saint. Six churches in Devon were dedicated to unique saints and probably claimed to possess their remains: Braunton, Chittlehampton, St Sidwell (Exeter), Hartland, Stoke Fleming, and Stokenham.[49] Braunton and Hartland were minsters and Stokenham, as we have seen, has a claim to be one from the size of its parish, but there are no other signs that the other three were minsters. The church of St Sidwell was a chapel-of-ease of Heavitree church by the thirteenth century, and although the Heavitree parish was quite large, it looks more like the rural part of the ancient minster parish of Exeter than the parish of a separate minster.[50]

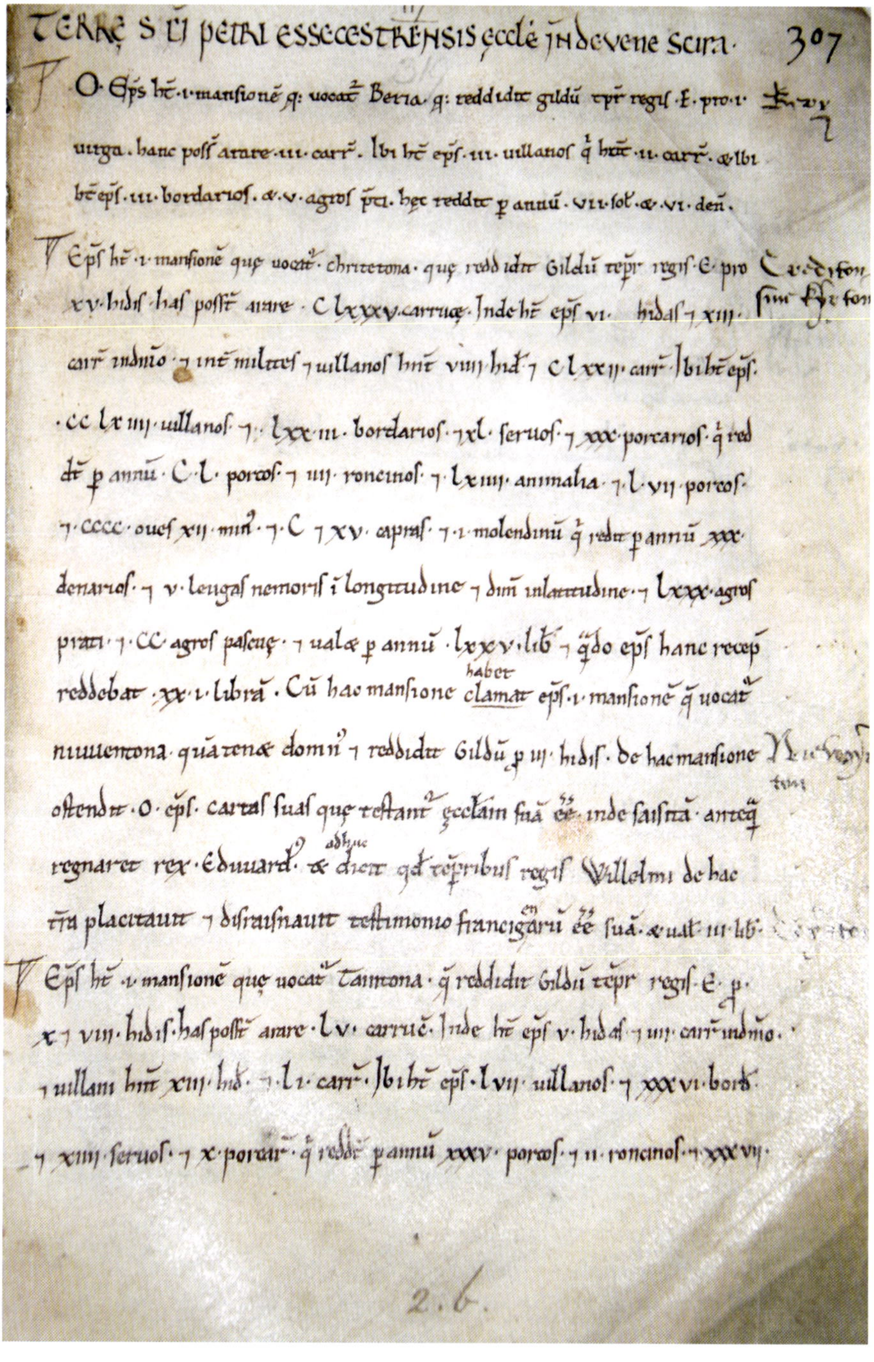

Figure 4 The Exon Domesday. This regional record, part of the process of compiling Domesday Book in 1086, is a valuable source for early churches in Devon. The page begins the inventory of the lands of the bishop of Exeter.

Building all this evidence into a definitive list of minsters is a difficult task (Figure 5, p. 17). Documentary sources and place-names give us the names of fourteen that are reasonably certain to have had this status and to have been served by groups of clergy: Axminster, Braunton, Buckfast, Crediton, Cullompton, Exeter, Exminster, Hartland, Plympton, South Molton, Tavistock, Tiverton, Totnes, and Yealmpton. Five others look likely from their sites, parish sizes, royal connections, *burh* status, land holdings, or more than one of these: Barnstaple/Pilton, Lydford, Stokenham, West Alvington, and Woodbury. The objection might be made that if such churches were minsters, they would have left more records of the fact. However, there is no evidence for Exminster as a minster apart from its name, and although it might be judged to have lost this status at an early date (say the tenth century), there is still the example of Tiverton whose clergy have left no trace before 1100, even in Domesday Book. A further eleven churches are possible minster candidates on similar (but less compelling) grounds or because of equivocal references in documents. These are Chittlehampton, Colyton, Exeter (St Olave), Exeter (St James), Hollacombe, Kingskerswell, Lifton, Modbury, Newton Ferrers, Newton St Petrock, and Stoke Fleming. Several of these, however, may only have ever been churches of a single priest. In later times, the parishes of Hollacombe and Newton St Petrock were modest in size with no sign of a minster past, and Kingskerswell was merely a chapel of St Marychurch.[51]

Minsters: an Analysis

The places where minsters were founded probably reflect some planning on the part of the kings of Wessex. At the same time, it is not clear that the minsters ever formed a neat geographical system. We know of none at present in the triangle between Lydford, Barnstaple, and Crediton, while elsewhere there were minsters fairly close together, notably Plympton and Yealmpton, Exeter and Exminster, Crediton and Exeter. It would appear from the laws of King Ine of Wessex (688–726) that everyone was regarded as belonging to a church, since they had to pay it a due called 'church-scot' each November.[52] How widely this was paid, and how much of Devon the minsters could serve with baptisms, worship, and burials, it is impossible to say. Until other churches began to appear in the tenth century, access to spiritual services may have varied greatly. Ine had to allow a month for a new-born child to be baptised.[53]

The foundation role of the kings of Wessex is most likely at Axminster and Exeter. The bishops of Sherborne or Crediton must have been responsible for the creation of Crediton, although it too was based on a grant by a king. The lay nobility were involved at Tavistock, the foundation of Ordgar, ealdorman of Devon, in the late tenth century and at Buckfast, that of a nobleman named Æthelweard although

King Cnut was given the honour of being its founder.[54] Those who made foundations and their heirs would undoubtedly have had a strong influence on the later history of the minsters concerned, including their staffing. Nearly all clergy in English minsters during the tenth and eleventh centuries followed the more worldly way of life that has been outlined above, in separate houses with families. Such clergy came to be known as clerks, priests, or canons: the last of these terms being used in the larger and more prestigious foundations. In the middle of the tenth century, there was a monastic revival in England which sought to replace clerks with monks in some minsters or to found new houses for monks. But this revival had only a modest impact on Devon. In 968 King Edgar appointed Sideman 'to rule as abbot the monks gathered at Exeter', thus turning (or trying to turn) the Exeter minster into a monastery,[55] and this initiative was followed within the next fifty years by the foundation of Tavistock and Buckfast. But Exeter reverted to being a minster of clerks within a generation or so, leaving the other two as the only true houses of monks in Devon at the Norman Conquest.

Minsters varied much in terms of their wealth, possessions, and organisation. Wealth is difficult to estimate. Our only source is Domesday Book which, as previously mentioned, listed lands not the tithes that often provided the bulk of a church's income. The richest Devon minster according to Domesday was Tavistock Abbey with lands of about 19 hides and an income of about £70, but 5 of these hides and about £12 of the income were held by lay tenants of the abbey, reducing the value available to the monks.[56] Moreover, it is probable that Tavistock's wealth was exceeded by that of the Exeter minster, whose ancient lands amounted to over 27 hides in Domesday with an income of £35 plus a good deal more from the tithes of the churches that it owned.[57] Buckfast owned 15 hides worth about £18,[58] but Crediton's income is not recorded for the reason already explained. The other minsters had more modest resources in 1086. Hartland held 2 hides with an income valued at about £2, Plympton 2 hides supposedly worth £1 15*s*., Yealmpton one hide of 10*s*., and Axminster a half hide not valued.[59] The virgate of the priests of South Molton was said to produce £1 and a similar virgate of the clerks of Totnes 10*s*., while a priest at Braunton, who may have possessed the ancient property of the minster there, received £2 10*s*. from one hide.[60] The locations of the lands of these lesser minsters are not identified, but they were probably close to the church; only Buckfast, Exeter, and Tavistock had more widely scattered possessions. And, with the exception of the last three foundations, minster lands were worth far less than the tithes which the clergy took from their parish but of which, in the period of Domesday, there are no valuations.

Wealth determined the numbers of minster clergy. Exeter's total is not known until well after it became a cathedral in 1050; it had grown to twenty-four canons by the mid thirteenth century.[61] Crediton had eighteen canons in the early twelfth century, at which time they were reduced to twelve by the bishop of Exeter because of limited resources.[62] Hartland was staffed by twelve canons at the time of Domesday Book.[63] Numbers at Tavistock and Buckfast are not recorded, but Tavistock had thirteen monks on the eve of the Black Death, so that a complement of at least twelve looks likely before the Conquest.[64] The lesser minsters had fewer clergy in line with their endowments. Traditions about Axminster in the fourteenth century credited it with seven,[65] and the Tudor antiquary John Leland recorded a document or belief to the effect that Plympton had included a dean or provost and four colleagues.[66] Cullompton supported five clergy up to the reign of William the Conqueror,[67] while South Molton was served by four priests in 1086[68] and Tiverton probably likewise.[69]

In terms of internal government, a division opened up in the tenth century between the monasteries and the non-monastic minsters. Buckfast and Tavistock were founded in an era when monasteries were adopting the Rule of St Benedict. They would have modelled their practices on that rule, including obedience to an abbot with strong authority, and Exeter may have done so for a period after 968. The

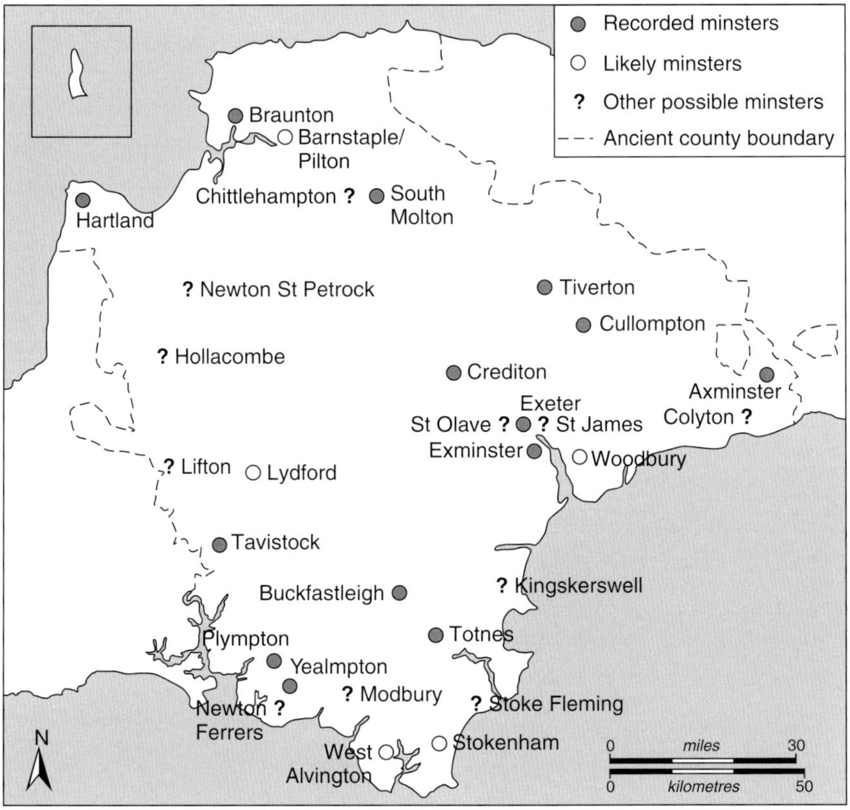

Figure 5 Minsters in Devon before 1086.

minsters served by canons and clerks had no uniform rule of life, although Exeter followed a Continental one during the second half of the eleventh century, now known as the 'Enlarged Rule of Chrodegang'.[70] Some non-monastic minsters had a presiding officer entitled the dean or provost, and this appears to have been the case at Crediton and Plympton, at least by the early twelfth century, but the authority of these figures is likely to have been less than an abbot's.[71] Exeter indeed lacked a head except for its bishop from when it became the cathedral in 1050 until the 1220s. Its affairs were managed by two canons elected to handle finance, a precentor in charge of the choir, and a treasurer with the care of vestments and ornaments.[72]

As such arrangements show, minster communities tended to be oligarchies rather than autocracies. The clergy would have decided their affairs among themselves, and their worship and duties would have followed local custom: unique to their church and difficult to change. Usually, the clergy divided up the church's resources so that each one held a prebend (a personal endowment) consisting of land, tithes, or both. At Plympton, one of the clerics was later believed to have held the church of St Andrew (Plymouth) as a prebend, presumably receiving its tithes and offerings. This prebend was stated to have passed by hereditary succession through two families from the late 930s until its last holder surrendered it towards the end of the twelfth century to the rest of the Plympton community which, by that time, was a monastery.[73] At Cullompton, each of the five clergy appears to have held the lands or tithes of one of the five local estates that belonged to the church.[74] At the smaller minsters, the land may have been too tiny to divide and was more likely to be used as a common source of food. The clergy would then share out the tithes as personal incomes. This was also the case at Crediton, whose canons were each allotted the tithes of a part of the church's extensive parish, although the details of this are not recorded until the later Middle Ages.[75] Divisions of minster revenues could be unequal and complicated. Some clergy might get a bigger portion than others, and a man might hold one source of revenue alone while sharing other sources with one or more of his colleagues.[76]

The minsters also varied in terms of their other possessions and status. Here the Exeter minster was probably the leader, in that it was the chief royal minster in Devon and probably the best endowed of all the county's churches. It appears to have been refounded by King Æthelstan in 932, with a confirmation of its lands or a grant of new ones plus a gift of a third of his collection of relics. These included such choice items as parts of Christ's manger and cross, parts of the hair and clothes of the Virgin Mary and St Peter, and a neck-bone of St Paul, as well as relics of a long list of Biblical, Roman, and French saints.[77] The Exeter minster also owned manuscripts, several of which survive including liturgical books and the famous Exeter Book of Anglo-Saxon poems.[78] At Crediton, Ælfwold the bishop (perhaps the man of that name who died in the 1010s) bequeathed a missal, a benedictional, an epistle-book, and a set of mass vestments to the church, as well as leaving a work by Hrabanus Maurus and a martyrology (a calendar of saints) to a personal friend.[79] The other minsters were probably less well-endowed with spiritual and scholarly resources, but Tavistock had the shrine of St Rumon and even the poorer foundations may have attracted devotees to a relic or a statue of a saint.

Lesser Churches

It is the view of historians at present that England changed in about the tenth century from being a country with a limited number of minsters to one with many churches: those that we now think of as parish churches.[80] There may have been smaller churches alongside the minsters in earlier centuries, but they seem to have become more common at this time. An important document in this respect is the 'Laws of King Edgar', issued between 959 and 972. Edgar was concerned about how people should pay tithes from their agricultural produce. Normally they were to pay tithes to the 'old minster' which had rights over them. But if a thegn (meaning a landed gentleman) had a church with a graveyard on his property, he needed to pay only two thirds of his tithes to the minster and might give the rest to his own church. If he had a church without a graveyard, he might pay a priest to staff it, but he had to do so out of the resources left after paying all his tithes to the minster.[81] This shows us that lesser churches had appeared or were appearing alongside the minsters. Some of these were already acquiring rights and privileges: graveyards and at least a share of tithes. Others existed, but did not yet have privileges.

The evidence for lesser churches in Devon, like that for minsters, comes from a variety of sources. Documents provide little information before 1066 because more of them relate to the affairs of kings or bishops than to those of thegns, but there are a few apposite references in charters. One of 974 mentions Copplestone: originally the name of a boundary stone at the meeting place of the later parishes of Colebrooke, Crediton, and Down St Mary, raising the question whether these met as parishes with churches or only as estates.[82] More reliably, we hear of 'the church way' at Meavy in 1031,[83] and of (St) 'Michael's church' at East Teignmouth in 1044.[84] Domesday Book and the Geld Rolls, as we have seen, refer to some other churches with very small land-holdings which were not or may not have been minsters, such as Colyton, Kingskerswell, and Pinhoe. In Exeter, the city church of St Martin (Figure 6, p. 21) is recorded as having been dedicated in 1065,[85] and this church still possesses some Saxon masonry as does the ruin of a nearby church: St George. Sidbury too has a crypt of the same period.

Place-names are another helpful source, and Domesday greatly enhances the other documentary records in this respect. Five places in its pages contain the name of a saint: Bridestowe (Bridget), Instow (John, probably the Baptist), *Jacobescherche* near

Exeter (James), St Marychurch, and Petrockstow (Petroc), indicating the presence of churches at these places. Eight other place-names include the word 'church' without a saint's name: Charford in South Brent (the 'church ford', presumably on the way to that church), Cheriton (Bishop), Cheriton (Fitzpaine), Cheriton in Brendon (the 'settlement or farm' of the church there), Churchill in East Down (the 'church hill' there), Churston (Ferrers), Honeychurch, and Whitchurch.[86]

Finally, there is indirect evidence from church dedications.[87] This is a delicate matter for several reasons. Many dedications in use today are inventions of the eighteenth and nineteenth centuries, so that it is important to restrict one's attention to those recorded before the Reformation, and they comprise only about two thirds of the ancient parish churches of Devon. Most of the pre-Reformation evidence comes from after 1300, which raises the question whether dedications changed during the Middle Ages: the answer appears to be that in most cases they did not. Very few dedications are mentioned before Domesday Book except for those of minsters, and the most common parish church dedications in later records were to Mary, Michael, and the apostles, who were perennially popular and are difficult to link with any one century.

There are three groups of parish church dedications in Devon, however, which plausibly arose in the late Anglo-Saxon period. The first is to Swithin, bishop of Winchester, who died in 862 but whose cult received an impetus in 971 when his tomb was moved into his former cathedral. He is represented at Woodbury which had a church by 1086, Littleham near Bideford, and Sandford. The second is to King Edward the Martyr, murdered in 978, whose cult is likely to have been at its most popular during the next hundred years. He, rather than the Confessor, must be the Edward recorded as the patron saint of Egg Buckland, St Mary Steps (Exeter, shared with Mary), Holne, and Shaugh Prior.[88] The third is to Petroc, which probably stems from the English conquest of Cornwall and the adjacency to Devon of Bodmin where the saint had his shrine. He had been adopted at Petrockstow by 1086, and some of his other churches were in existence by then, including Hollacombe, Newton St Petrock, and probably Lydford and South Brent. Accepting his dedications adds another fourteen churches to the list, and possibly three chapels where he was later venerated.[89]

Putting all these sources together gives us a list of 45 lesser churches in existence by 1086, including the 11 least likely candidates for minster status (Figure 7, p. 24).[90] They are widely spread across the county and incorporate some churches which did not become fully independent in later times but were technically under the jurisdiction of another neighbouring church and came to be known as chapels. Churches of this kind included Dartmouth (St Petrox), Shaugh Prior, and East Teignmouth. The geographical range of the 45 and the modesty in size and wealth of some of their later parishes suggest that their existence by 1086 was not unusual

Figure 6 St Martin's parish church, Exeter. One of many small parish churches in the city, it existed by 1065 and served a tiny parish between the High Street and the cathedral Close.

but representative of a much larger number of churches that have left no verifiable record of their presence. It may indeed be the case that most of the ancient parish churches of Devon were in existence by Domesday Book, although others were added later.[91]

These churches were typically founded by landlords on their estates: landlords who probably included the king and bishops as well as lay lords or ladies. Whitchurch belonged to King Alfred, while Colyton and Kingskerswell were both royal properties in 1086.[92] Such people had the authority to allocate a piece of land for the church and churchyard, arrange for their construction, and provide a house and some fields (known as a glebe) for the support of a priest to serve the church. Once a landlord established a church for the tenants on an estate, neighbouring lords were likely to follow because they did not wish their tenants to go to another church and form bonds with its lord. As the Laws of Edgar indicate, such churches often arose within the territories of existing minsters and they did not always become fully parochial until about the twelfth century. Nevertheless, most churches of whatever status must have had recognisable territories from the beginning, because they served particular estates. Their later parish boundaries would have been influenced by the boundaries of these estates, and even those that remained as chapels often had a recognised area of activity within a larger parish. Thus the boundaries of an estate near Brampford Speke in 944 resemble those of the later parish of Upton Pyne, and may well have determined them.[93]

The founding of lesser churches affected the minsters. The latter lost worshippers, tithes, and eventually territory to their newer rivals, and often ceased to have the resources to support a group of clergy. Two managed to survive in forms that owed something to their Anglo-Saxon origins: Exeter as a cathedral and Crediton as a collegiate church. Buckfast and Tavistock remained as monasteries, and at least three and possibly eight other minsters were converted into monasteries, as has already been noted. The rest of the minsters lost their clergy communities and turned into ordinary parish churches served by a single clergyman. This was the fate of Axminster, Braunton, South Molton, and Yealmpton, as well as those contenders for minster status (if they acquired it) such as Lydford, Stokenham, and West Alvington. Devon, like the rest of England, entered the twelfth century with a relatively small number of minsters and monasteries and a vastly larger cohort of lesser parish churches served by a single priest, with parishes that stretched for only a couple of miles in each direction.

Churches exist in the landscape, and the relationship between the two is a large subject that has been studied in specialised works.[94] Exeter's minster is the only certain example of a church re-established on or near a Roman site; whether this is true of any other churches in Devon is not yet known. Most of the Devon minsters were sited by rivers, and two were named after them, Axminster and Exminster, as were others elsewhere in England. Crediton, Plympton, Totnes, and Tiverton had similar locations. A riverside situation brought with it fertile ground and fisheries, but perhaps the river was less important than the presence of a ford or bridge across it, conveying a major road. The road would offer good communications, and the river crossing would encourage the growth of a settlement, either before the minster was founded or afterwards. The minster could serve the settlement spiritually and be served in return by its traders and craftsmen. Many of the lesser churches were probably placed at convenient points within their founders' estates, but one or two may have been deliberately planted at ancient holy or significant sites such as Halwell and Halwill, meaning 'holy well'. Generally, churches came to take the name of their adjoining estate, but a sprinkling of church-names refer to the patron saint. These lie in the western half of the county, from Christow ('St Christina's holy place') westwards to Bridestowe, Marystow, and Virginstow, and north-westwards to Instow and Jacobstow. Similar names are found in Cornwall as far west as Padstow.

Little can be said about early church buildings because they have not survived, having been rebuilt under the Normans and again at the end of the Middle Ages. St Andrew (Plymouth) was a wooden building in the tenth century, or so it was later believed,[95] but stone was in use at the two Exeter churches already mentioned and at Sidbury by the time of the Norman Conquest. Whitchurch was evidently white-washed and, like other churches with this name, was regarded as unusual in being so. More certainly, some of these early churches have left us the names of their patron saints. Very few Devon churches apparently had their own saint buried in the church and took their dedications from that saint. Most of England differed from Cornwall and Wales in this respect, where many churches were not only dedicated to unique local saints but named after them like St Austell and St Ives. As has been stated, only six examples of churches with unique saints are recorded in Devon: Braunton (Brannoc), Chittlehampton (Urith), Hartland (Nectan), Stoke Fleming (Earmund), Stokenham (Humbert), and St Sidwell (Exeter, Sidwell). Most churches in the county with a likely pre-Conquest origin were dedicated to the well-known international saints: Mary, Peter, Andrew, Michael, George, and All Saints, as well as the saints already mentioned as popular in the late Anglo-Saxon period.

However, Devon had a minority of dedications which were unusual by English standards, because they were to Brittonic saints from Cornwall, Brittany, and Wales. These do not date from pre-Anglo-Saxon days before AD 700, as Victorian writers thought, but constitute a later wave of Brittonic influence during and after the tenth century. This was partly due to the conquest and absorption of Cornwall into the kingdom of Wessex in the ninth and early tenth centuries. After Tavistock Abbey

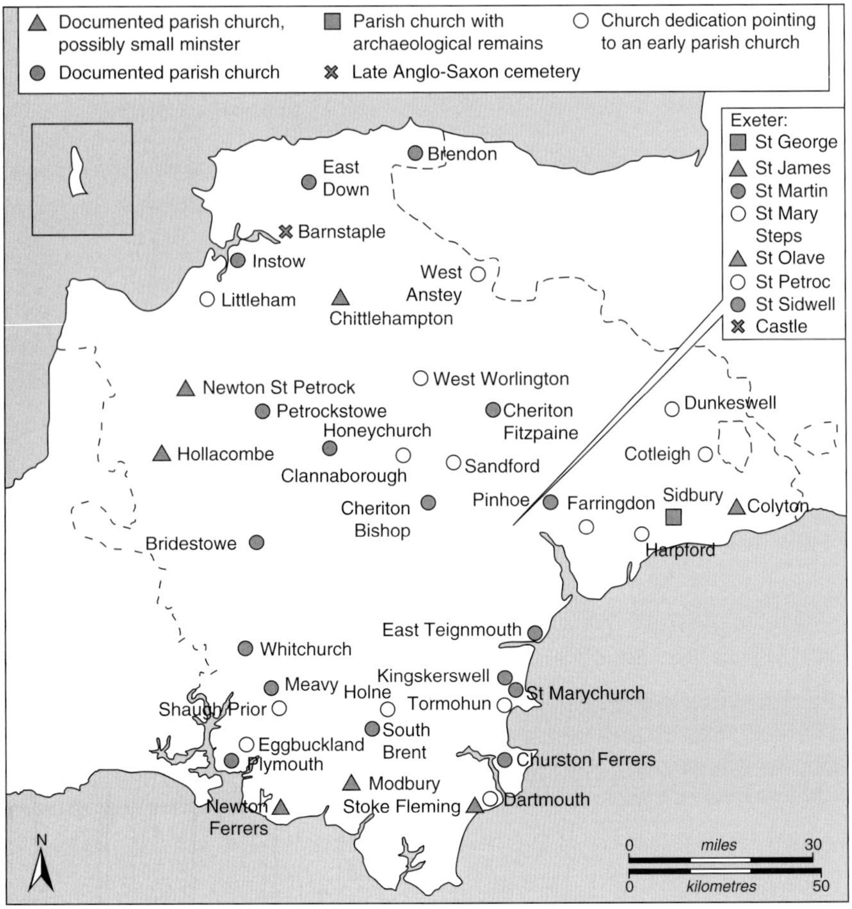

Figure 7 Lesser churches in Devon before 1086.

was founded in 981, its founder or clergy wanted a saint's body to confer holiness and bring pilgrims, and between that date and about 1031 the body of St Rumon was procured for that purpose from its previous resting place at Ruan Lanihorne in west Cornwall.[96] Romansleigh may also contain his name. The most important Cornish saint was Petroc, whose body lay at the minster of Bodmin; as we have seen, at least fourteen Devon churches came to be dedicated to him.[97] Two of these, Hollacombe and Newton St Petrock, belonged to Bodmin minster, and the others may have procured small relics of the saint from Bodmin, since church altars were required to contain a relic or two. A third Cornish saint, Piran, may have given his name to the church of St Kerrian in Exeter,[98] while Winwaloe of Brittany, who had eight churches and chapels in Cornwall, inspired the dedication of East Portlemouth in the South Hams.[99] David, a Welsh saint uncommon in England, also acquired churches in Exeter and at Dotton in east Devon, but in his case and those of Piran and Winwaloe the date of the acquisition is not clear: it could have been as late as the twelfth century.[100]

These borrowings of British saints by Devon churches constitute an interesting example of cultural interchange. On the one hand the Church in Cornwall was made to conform to the Church in England and adopted English usages, including some English saints. On the other hand, the Anglo-Saxons respected the holiness of the Cornish saints and wanted to import them to England. There was even a church of St Petroc in Winchester, one of the chief cities of the Anglo-Saxon kings.[101]

Church Life

Listing and categorising churches takes us only a little way towards understanding Christianity in early medieval Devon. We would like to know how people practised religion, how far this practice was enforced, and how far voluntary. Most of the evidence for this is limited to the tenth and eleventh centuries, the end of the Anglo-Saxon era. By that time, the proliferation of churches, and the development of villages which is thought to be linked to this proliferation, made it possible for the Church to reach and influence more people for more of the year and for more of their lives.

There was now a significant body of parish clergy, far in excess of the minster clergy: usually one cleric to each church who was preferably (but not necessarily always) a priest. By about 1000, he had the help of a clerk, typically a young man and often an aspirant to be a priest, who prepared the altar, rang the church bell, and said the responses at services.[102] With a priest close at hand, the baptism of children which Ine wanted within a month of birth could happen far more quickly, and by the Norman Conquest, the rite was moving towards the day of birth itself.[103] The presence of the priest also made it possible for people to have a Christian funeral and burial close to their death: normally on the next day in the local church and graveyard. Church attendance became easier and could be done each Sunday and festival day. We do not know how often people went to church, but great festival days were likely to be popular and Rogationtide processions in late spring began to take place (Figure 8, p. 28). At the same time, Church obligations increased, especially the duty to fast during Lent and render tithes to the parish priest. Other small annual payments were also required: church-scot (a render of grain in November), church-bot (a contribution to maintaining the church building), soul-scot (a payment in return for burial), and Rome-scot (a penny per household, sent to the pope).[104]

These duties involved all adults and the monetary ones all heads of households, but there was also scope for individual piety. The first recorded examples of guilds are found in the tenth century: voluntary societies that promoted worship and supported their own members. The statutes have survived of such a guild in Exeter. It was dominated by wealthy men who were expected to contribute money and resources for the guild's activities. They met at Michaelmas (29 September), Candlemas (2 February), and after Easter. At each meeting, a priest said a mass for the living members and a mass for the dead ones, after which there was probably a drinking session since the guildsmen were required to contribute malt and honey. When a member died, the others were bound to contribute towards the cost of six masses for the soul of the dead person. If one of them went on pilgrimage to Rome, each was to pay five pence, and if anyone's house was burnt, a penny.[105] By the Conquest or soon afterwards, guilds were common. The outer leaves of the Exeter Book contain lists of fourteen from about the year 1100 in what were or became nine parishes in the vicinity of Exeter, stretching from Axmouth in the east to Bridford in the west. Most parishes were represented by a single guild, but Woodbury had three as well as a fourth based within its parish at Nutwell, Colaton Raleigh two, and Whitestone a second at Halsford.[106]

The name of each guild is followed by those of its members: sometimes one or two clergy first, next men, and finally a few women who were doubtless wives or widows of the men. Three of the guilds – at Bridford, Colaton Raleigh, and Nutwell – had twelve members each, while two others – at *Lege* (probably Doddiscombsleigh) and Halsford had twenty. These numbers are significant ones and suggest a closed circle to which people were admitted only when vacancies happened.[107] The rest of the guilds returned more names, either because they were more open or had existed for longer and included the dead in their list as well as the living. Altogether these records demonstrate that parish society was approaching, or had even achieved, the complex form that it would retain until the Reformation. Each parish was a single religious community supporting the church, but the community was now dividing itself into subsets which could be exclusive to people of a distinctive social rank, place of residence, or perhaps devotion to a particular saint. The guild at Nutwell may even have tried to express its distinctiveness from Woodbury which was, or would become, its parish church.

Rank was as important inside church as outside, and most of the records of religion up to 1100 relate to wealthy and influential people. Lords and ladies of estates regarded the churches they founded as their own possessions. They appointed the clergy, invested them with the church's property when they arrived, and might take the property back in time of need. In the twelfth century, the Church objected to this degree of lay control and restricted it, but that was not the case in earlier times. Lords and ladies probably had special privileges to sit or kneel in the chancel with the priest rather than in the nave with the laity, and to be buried inside the church. Only they could have afforded to go on a pilgrimage as far as Rome. Clergy could also be rich. Bishop Ælfwold bequeathed substantial sums of money in gold as well as horses, armour, weapons, and even a ship.[108] Domesday Book lists twelve priests who held personal pieces of land in Devon, perhaps having inherited property from their families after the deaths of older brothers.[109] Some wealthy people owned slaves, and when a lady named Hunnaflæd purchased a woman called Wulfgyth in about 1000, she had the fact inscribed in the 'Leofric missal' later owned by Exeter Cathedral.[110] Even Ælfwold bought slaves, although he liberated all those on his estates in his will. Freeing slaves was regarded as an act of charity that benefited one's soul, and the act was sometimes written down in liturgical books. The Leofric missal includes several such records including the fact that Ordgar, for example, freed nine at Bradstone 'where he lay in sickness'.[111]

We know virtually nothing of the spiritual life of lesser folk, and much can only be guessed from conditions in England as a whole. By the late Anglo-Saxon period, people were expected to know by heart the Latin versions of the Lord's Prayer and the Apostles' Creed, and to say them devoutly.[112] There were places in Devon to which one could make pilgrimage more easily than travelling abroad. The Exeter minster had its array of Æthelstan's relics and Tavistock its shrine of St Rumon, while other churches with saints buried in them may have attracted local devotees. Wells were already regarded as holy and probably resorted to for healing, as we have seen from the place-names Halwell near Totnes, recorded by the tenth century, and Halwill, which is mentioned in Domesday Book along with a place called Halwell in Brixton.[113] Human nature suggests that people varied widely in their religiosity and in the ways that they expressed it or avoided doing so.

A Retrospect

This chapter has addressed a span of nearly seven hundred years, and it is hard to sum up concisely the character of such a long and changing period. Evidence increases as time progresses, especially after about AD 900, which produces a foreshortening effect by which Christianity appears to be stronger and more developed the later the date. There is a danger of underestimating its power and support in the earlier centuries of which we know so little, and we should certainly be aware of the difficulties that it faced in subsequent ones. Wars between kingdoms and later Viking raids must sometimes have caused disruptions. The Vikings seized Exeter twice, in 875 and 1003, with the likelihood that its minster and other churches suffered in consequence.

Nonetheless, there was certainly development. An age of mission, in which the Church had a pioneering presence, evolved into an age of consolidation when society was becoming more thoroughly Christian. The greatest and most enduring achievement of the period was arguably the creation of parish churches and

Figure 8 Rogationtide processions began in Anglo-Saxon times and remained popular until well after the Reformation. This woodcut shows the order of the procession for Rogation Wednesday, including banners, a dragon, and the eucharist in a portable shrine flanked by incense bearers.

boundaries, most of which were probably in place in Devon by 1086 and remain as a network today. At the same time there were continuities. The doctrines and practices of Christianity were broadly similar. Even the differences that used to be characterised as 'Roman' and 'Celtic' were limited to the calendar, the clerical tonsure, and some matters of Church organisation caused by the lack of much of an urban tradition in Wales and Ireland. Throughout the period, the role of lay people was constant and crucial. Church history is often thought as a procession of famous clergy like Augustine of Canterbury, Aidan, Cuthbert, Theodore, Aldhelm, Dunstan, and (in Devon) Bishop Leofric. Such people were indeed important as leaders, organisers, and writers, but Christianity could not have been preached without the permission of kings. Nor could it have been furnished with cathedrals, minsters, and parish churches unless these kings and their nobility had endowed it with property and enforced its claims with laws. They continued to intervene in Church affairs thereafter: appointing bishops, changing the nature of religious houses, and even retaking Church property. Beyond them, is the great unrecorded contribution of the rest of the lay population. Without their willingness to be baptised, learn prayers, attend church, pay church dues, and be buried in church-yards, there would have been no Church at all.

CHAPTER 2

From 1086 to 1300

Normans and Bishops

The Norman Conquest of 1066 made its first impact on Devon at the top of lay society, rather than on the Church and ordinary people. The lands of the English king and his chief subjects passed to the hands of a Norman king and his leading followers. The major religious landholders, in contrast, kept most of their possessions. This was the case with the bishop of Exeter, the cathedral, the minster of Crediton, the monasteries of Tavistock and Buckfast, and (as far as we know) the parish clergy with their glebe lands and tithes.[1] Indeed, the long-term effect of the Conquest was to increase the strength of the Church. During the century that followed it, the Norman kings and aristocracy gave lands and churches in Devon to abbeys with which they had links in France. The abbeys then established small monasteries to administer these possessions. Later, from the middle of the twelfth century to the end of the thirteenth, the aristocracy (now Anglo-Norman rather than purely Norman) endowed new English monasteries such as Dunkeswell, Forde, and Torre. By 1300, there was vastly more property in the hands of the clergy in Devon than there had been in 1066.

There were changes in the leadership of the Church after the Conquest, but these were of a gradual nature. The Conqueror did not replace the bishop of Exeter, Leofric, until his death in 1072. After that, the king appointed Osbern, who was one of his relatives but had lived in England serving Edward the Confessor.[2] Osbern held office for thirty years from 1072 to 1103, ruling in a quiet way that grew quieter after about 1093 from his poor health and eventual blindness. When Osbern died, the diocese remained vacant for four years, and it was not until 1107 that Devon gained a dynamic Norman bishop in the person of William Warelwast who headed the diocese until 1137. Even he was not an outsider, since he had apparently been archdeacon of Exeter under Osbern. William got to work on what he considered to be the shortcomings of the diocese. He began the rebuilding of the cathedral, increased the number of archdeacons, and set about turning three of the largest minsters in the diocese into monasteries. These were Plympton in Devon and Bodmin and Launceston in Cornwall, his intention being to make their clergy more pious and regulated, with less involvement in the everyday world.

Thirteen bishops of Exeter held office from Osbern in 1072 until 1307. In theory, they were elected by the canons of the cathedral. In practice, they were usually men who were close to the king and of whom he approved. William Warelwast served William Rufus and Henry I. Bartholomew (1161–84) did judicial work for Henry II. Henry Marshal (1194–1206) was a brother of William Marshal, a close associate of Richard I. William Brewer (1224–44) was a strong adherent of Henry III. The Norman and Angevin kings needed their bishops to be their trustworthy supporters, as the Anglo-Saxon kings had done, although the bishops of 1072–1307 were not as closely involved with royal administration as some of their later successors. Like the governing class in England as a whole, they imperceptibly evolved from being Normans to being English. William Warelwast, his nephew and successor Robert (1138–55), and Bartholomew were all born in France. Henry Marshal, on the other hand, came from a family long domiciled in England, and William Brewer and his successors must have been wholly English except in terms of speaking French as well. An oddity among the bishops is Simon de Apulia (1214–23), whose tomb is in the cathedral. He was an Italian, although he had been dean of York, and owed his promotion as bishop to an alliance which King John made with the pope in 1213 to try to outwit the English barons. He was thus in part a royal appointment and partly a papal one: a sign of the growing ambition of the popes to be involved with the choice of bishops. As we shall see in another chapter, however, that ambition was hardly ever effective.[3]

The bishops from Leofric onwards were wealthy landowners, the wealthiest in the South-West of England. Leofric inherited the lands and churches of the bishops of Cornwall and Crediton, as well as those of the minster that became the cathedral. Legally, the property of the cathedral belonged to the bishop and it is credited to him in Domesday Book, but in practice it formed a separate body of endowments devoted to maintaining the cathedral clergy and gradually came under their sole control. Putting aside those endowments and omitting the bishop's properties in Cornwall,[4] his principal Devon possessions were as follows. In Exeter, he owned the palace, the cathedral Close, and a number of tenements within the city. These constituted 'St Stephen's fee' and claimed exemption from the control of the city authorities.[5] Elsewhere he held Crediton in mid Devon, Bishop's Clyst in east Devon, Bishopsteignton, Chudleigh, and Paignton in south Devon, and Bishop's Tawton (Figure 9, p. 34) and Bishop's Nympton in north Devon. Leofric, Osbern, and their successors gained other possessions in return for their work for the king. These included Bampton (Oxon.), Bosham (Sussex), Faringdon (Hants.), and Morchard Bishop (Devon).[6]

The bishops' wealth and royal connections dictated that they should be travellers. They were needed at London and Westminster to advise the king or take part in Church councils, and on their estates to do their duties as landowners and, at first, to consume the produce of these estates. A new bishop was expected to make a visitation of his diocese, to inspect its religious houses and churches, and to make rulings and corrections where necessary. This process was to be repeated every three years, but it is doubtful whether the repetitions were done so often, at least in a systematic way. At times in the twelfth and thirteenth centuries, the bishops went to France or Rome on business for the king or the Church, and William Brewer even reached the Holy Land in 1227–9. All the bishop's major estates in Devon and Cornwall had a manor house at which he and his household could stay, and Henry Marshal acquired land in Longditch Street, Westminster, by 1200 for a dwelling to use while in the capital.[7] Later, the residence moved further east to the Strand. To some extent, one can trace the bishops' movements from the documents they issued, but that is difficult until the thirteenth century. However, it looks likely that they all made journeys around the diocese and to London unless they were ill or old, visiting Cornwall and north Devon occasionally but staying for the most part on their estates in and around Exeter, especially Bishopsteignton, Chudleigh, Crediton, and Paignton.[8]

Church Development and Administration

We imagine the medieval Church as a powerful organisation led by popes, bishops, and theologians: often (it is alleged) a repressive body, imposing its beliefs and morals on people. That was scarcely the case in 1100. At that date, the pope had hardly any power in England, and even bishops not much more. A cleric had to go to his bishop to be ordained, but we know little about the vetting procedures that were employed. When a cleric became rector of a parish, the bishop was unlikely to be involved unless he was the patron of the parish and selected the clergyman. In the majority of parishes, a local lay lord chose the rector and put him in possession of his benefice, meaning the rights, property, and duties belonging to his post, without involving the bishop. In some of the minsters that existed in 1100, such as Hartland and Plympton, the clergy who ran the church were still married and passed down their posts to their sons. This may have been true in some parishes too, since many parish clergy had wives despite the dislike of the more rigorous Church leaders for such arrangements.

During the twelfth and thirteenth centuries, these leaders extended their powers. Church councils were held, both international and national, which passed laws regulating the way that the Church operated, the behaviour of the clergy, and that of the laity. Such laws came to be known as canon law, meaning Church law, and

Figure 9 Bishop's Tawton, one of the bishop's parish churches. It stood near a manor house that formed a base for his activities in north Devon, and its parish was a peculiar under his control.

grew into a subject of detailed study, leading to degrees in universities. The popes began to claim their right to issue dispensations from the new laws, so that one had to apply to them for privileges such as the power to choose one's own confessor, marry a cousin (which was strictly speaking against canon law), or be released from the duty of fasting in Lent. The bishops followed the popes and the councils in enforcing canon law upon their dioceses. Between 1225 and 1237, Brewer convened a synod of his clergy which laid down procedures relating to worship, the sacraments, and moral behaviour.[9] Walter Bronescombe (1258–80, Figure 10, p. 38) held a similar synod, apparently of clergy and laity, although its decisions have not survived.[10] Finally, in 1287, Peter Quinil called a synod which enacted a comprehensive code of instructions covering worship, the duties of the clergy, and the conduct of the laity. The code extends to seventy-four pages in the modern edition, with a further document of sixteen pages containing a guide for the clergy when hearing confessions. These initiatives brought the Church closer to everyday life.[11]

One aspect of the new emphasis on canon law was that bishops began to impose more control on their churches and clergy. During the twelfth century, the Church cut down the freedom of lay lords and monasteries who owned churches to appoint whom they wished as parish clergy. The owner of a church was redefined as its 'patron' or 'advocate', from which comes the word 'advowson' meaning the right to choose a church's clergyman. The patron now had to 'present' his chosen candidate to the bishop, who examined the man to ensure that he was qualified in terms of age, ordination, and celibacy – because the marriage of clergy was coming to be forbidden. On being found suitable (which was usually the case), the candidate had to swear an oath of obedience to the bishop who then formally 'instituted' or 'admitted' him to the church. In 1258, Bronescombe began to keep a register of this and others of his activities.[12] It records the churches he dedicated, the clergy he instituted, and the dates on which he held ordinations. This practice was followed by his successors, although the register of Thomas Bitton (1292–1307) has been lost, and by the time of Walter Stapledon (1308–26), the registers contain many other items such as licences to found chapels, permissions for clergy to be absent from their parishes, and the names of all those whom the bishop ordained.[13] Meanwhile his deputies, the archdeacons, were visiting the parish churches to see if their structures were sound and if they possessed all the furniture and equipment needed for conducting services.[14]

As Church leaders extended their authority, it became necessary for them to know what churches they had in their dioceses. There must have been detailed knowledge of this in Devon by about 1180 because by this date, as we shall see, there was a system of rural deaneries in which churches were put together in groups for administrative purposes. No lists of churches have survived before the middle of the thirteenth century, however, when taxation of the clergy was introduced:

originally to finance crusades but before long to benefit the papacy and the crown. Taxing the clergy required all those with significant incomes to be identified and their incomes to be estimated. The first attempt to do so in England was the 'Valuation of Norwich' made in 1254–5, but the definitive assessment was that which Pope Nicholas IV ordered to be compiled in 1291, now known as the 'Taxation of Pope Nicholas'. It valued the annual incomes of all bishops, cathedrals, monasteries, and parish benefices, and was used as the basis for the taxation of the clergy by both the pope and the king of England until 1535.

The valuations were made by assessors who were clergy, and because all taxation involves an element of negotiation, the valuations were set on the low side. How low can be seen by comparing the figures of 1291 with those reported ten years earlier for some of the parishes belonging to Exeter Cathedral (Table 1).[15] These show that the real figures were two or three times higher than those of 1291, the information of which is therefore unreliable, except perhaps for comparing one church with another. Still, it is better than nothing, and the Taxation provides us with a virtually complete list of monasteries and parish churches in England and Wales, including Devon. Only the two crusading orders, the Knights Templars and the Order of St John, were exempted, along with the friars who had no property and the hospitals that cared for the sick and for travellers.[16]

Table 1 Estimated rectory income, 1281 and 1291

	1281			*1291*		
	£	*s.*	*d.*	£	*s.*	*d.*
Ashburton	26	16	8	10	0	0
Branscombe	22	0	0	8	0	0
Clyst Honiton	5	0	0	2	3	4
Colebrooke	13	6	8	5	6	8
Colyton	46	13	4	10	13	4
Culmstock	20	0	0	8	0	0
Dawlish	30	0	0	9	6	8
Salcombe Regis	14	13	4	5	6	8
Sidbury	22	0	0	10	0	0
St Marychurch	40	0	0	13	6	8
Staverton	16	0	0	7	6	8
Upottery	21	6	8	10	0	0

The Taxation of 1291 arranged the churches of the diocese under its four archdeaconries. These date back to the early twelfth century. The bishop employed one or more archdeacons to assist him as early as 1083, and during the 1120s William Warelwast established a group of four: three for Devon and one for Cornwall.[17] The archdeaconry of Exeter comprised east Devon and the Exeter region, Totnes included the south and west of the county, and Barnstaple covered the north (Figure 11, p. 42). The archdeacons had seats in the choir of the cathedral and houses in the cathedral Close, where they usually lived.[18] They acted for the bishop in their territories, made an annual visitation of every church therein, and held courts at which offences against canon law were judged and wills were proved. There is one surviving record of their visitations, relating to the Totnes archdeaconry in 1342,[19] but much of their work is rather obscure and it is not clear what they did themselves or where their courts met. References are frequently made to the archdeacon's 'official', a deputy appointed by him from among the clergy, who probably carried out most of the local duties.[20]

Within the archdeaconries, the Taxation of 1291 listed the rural deaneries: groups of parish churches that varied in number from ten in the deanery of Dunkeswell to twenty-nine in that of Shirwell.[21] The deaneries are first mentioned in Devon between 1174 and 1184, their alternative title being 'deaneries of Christianity' (meaning Christian people), which has led to an erroneous belief that the rural deanery of Exeter alone had this name; in fact the name was common to all. How the groups were formed and how they got their names are unknown. Some deaneries were named after the principal church of the area, such as Barnstaple, Plympton, and Totnes, but in other cases, like Cadbury, Dunkeswell, and Shirwell, the naming church was of no significance and not always in a central location. The two earliest references to rural deans are to those of Modbury and Virginstow, which were not the subsequent names of the deaneries in question and imply that, at first, the dean took his title from his own church.[22] Perhaps a list of deaneries was made at some point in which the current dean's church was sometimes designated as the title of the deanery. The rectors and vicars of each rural deanery formed a chapter or meeting, but this body seems to have had little importance. The significant person was the dean himself, who served for a year at a time. Sometimes the clergy in a deanery took turns, one church after another, and sometimes they elected a dean from among their members.[23] His duties were to 'induct' new clergy to their churches, thereby giving them local possession after the bishop had instituted them, and to carry out tasks for the bishop or archdeacon in the deanery.

This account of a diocese ruled by a bishop and neatly divided into archdeaconries and rural deaneries is not complete, however. Medieval society was full of legal exemptions. Kings, noblemen, and towns gained special privileges for themselves, their households, and property, and this process extended to the Church. Several

Figure 10 The effigy of Walter Bronescombe (died 1280) in Exeter Cathedral. An active bishop, he was the first to keep a register of his acts and began the rebuilding of the cathedral into its present form.

of the new religious orders of monks and friars that appeared in the twelfth and thirteenth centuries were given immunity by the popes from the power of local bishops. In Devon, this involved the five Cistercian monasteries, the Premonstratensian abbey of Torre, the four friaries in Exeter and Plymouth, and the house of the Order of St John at Bodmiscombe. Tavistock Abbey gained a similar exemption in 1193, but this lapsed and the abbey remained subject to the bishop until 1517 when it gained a new papal grant for itself and its daughter house of Cowick Priory.[24] In all these cases, the bishop and his deputies could not exert authority over the house concerned or its clergy.

Certain parishes had special status as well. Those on the bishop's estates and some (but not all) of those belonging to the cathedral were removed from the archdeaconries and rural deaneries during the late twelfth or early thirteenth centuries, and placed under the supervision of special officials directly responsible to the bishop and the cathedral respectively. Such parishes were known as 'peculiar jurisdictions' or 'peculiars', and had their own church courts and probate of wills (Figure 11, p. 42). The bishop's peculiars consisted of thirteen parishes in north Devon, mid Devon, and the Torbay area. The cathedral's peculiars fell into three categories. The dean and chapter acting together controlled twenty-three parishes and sub-parishes in east, mid, and south Devon. The dean alone was in charge of Braunton, and the vicars choral of the cathedral had power over Woodbury.[25] All the peculiars remained in being until the nineteenth century.

By 1300, therefore, the Church had grown into a more complex organisation in western Europe and in Devon particularly than had been the case in 1100. There were more officers and institutions to administer its affairs, more detailed laws for its government, and more precise definitions of its beliefs. One of the most important definitions was the doctrine of transubstantiation: that when a priest consecrated the communion bread and wine at mass, the substances turned into the physical body and blood of Christ and only retained the appearance of bread and wine. This belief determined which people were allowed to share in the communion (children were excluded), when they did so (which was normally limited to Easter Day, after a long period of preparation in Lent), and what they could receive (the bread alone, in case the wine was spilt). Inevitably, the result of more laws and doctrines was to make some people dissent from them, or appear to do so, and the Church authorities became more intolerant of such dissent, real or imagined. The worst examples of intolerance, such as the 'Albigensian Crusades', included the execution of 'heretics', but these affected mainland Europe rather than England until the 1380s when England developed its own 'heresy' in the beliefs of John Wycliffe and his Lollard followers.[26]

There was some persecution in England during the twelfth and thirteenth centuries, but it chiefly affected the Jews, who settled in England after the Conquest and became important figures in trade and money-lending. Their only significant community in the South-West was based in Exeter. It is first mentioned in 1181 and maintained organised Jewish worship, since we hear of what Christians referred to as two 'bishops' and a 'chaplain' or 'priest'. There were probably a synagogue and a burial ground, although neither has been recorded.[27] Jews received protection from the crown for which they paid handsomely in the form of special taxes. This did not save them from clergy disapproval or popular prejudice. Very soon after their arrival in Exeter, Bishop Bartholomew wrote a work criticising them, and in 1287 Quinil's synod forbade Jews to employ Christian servants, Christians and Jews to meet at social occasions, or sick Christians to receive medicines from Jews.[28] In the following year, a leading Exeter Jewess named Henna had stones thrown at her in South Street by a boy from the grammar school which lay in that part of the city.[29] However, the relationship of Jews and Christians was not uniformly hostile. The attack of 1288 got as far as the mayor's court, and the synod would have not have issued its condemnations unless it believed that people of both faiths were interacting. We know of two Jews in Devon who converted to Christianity, despite the fact that the king seized the possessions of anyone who did so. In the end it was not local prejudice that drove the Jews from Exeter but a decision of Edward I in 1290 that they should all be expelled from the kingdom.

Jews could be targeted because they were relatively few in number and easily visible. The power of the Church to enforce its rules more widely was much weaker. Even in 1300, after two centuries of administrative development, bishops still had little contact with most of their clergy, let alone the laity. A cleric still normally encountered his bishop only when he was ordained and, if he became a parish rector or vicar, at his institution to his church post. Otherwise, bishops rarely meddled with clergy or parishes, and their courts affected most lay people only at times of the probate of wills. Archdeacons were expected to visit churches annually, but as we shall see, this did not always result in well-kept buildings and contents. In theory, a lay person who committed sins such as refusing to pay tithes, attend church, or observe the Church's code of sexual behaviour would be summoned before a Church court, either that of the bishop or the archdeacon. He or she might then be fined or made to carry out a humiliating public penance. Those who defied the court would be excommunicated and reported to the king for arrest until they complied.[30] But as with all legal systems, it is likely that only the most flagrant or unpopular offenders were brought to justice. Many ordinary people avoided their responsibilities and the Church was hampered in bringing them into line.

Minsters and Monasteries

Another feature of the period 1100–1300 was a great change in the number and character of the religious houses of England in general and Devon in particular. At the time of the Conquest in 1066, the religious houses in Devon consisted of the cathedral, two monasteries at Buckfast and Tavistock, and a number of minster churches of which only Crediton, Hartland, and Plympton were relatively large and wealthy bodies. The next hundred years were a bad period for minsters. Crediton alone survived in its ancient form, albeit with some loss of clergy. Hartland and Plympton were both turned into monasteries, as were St James (Exeter) and Pilton if these were ever minsters. Tiverton survived as a 'portionary' church of four clergy, the chapel of Exeter Castle (perhaps a late Saxon, perhaps a Norman, foundation) with another four, and Chulmleigh (which appears mysteriously during the thirteenth century) with six. But none of these three seems to have had a communal life of any significance after the Conquest. The other lesser minsters, as we have seen, shrank to be ordinary parish churches.

The one exception to this 'decline of the minsters' was the cathedral, which developed in a spectacular way after 1066.[31] When Leofric moved his seat to the Exeter minster in 1050, the place was moderately well endowed with estates in east and south Devon. Its church (or possibly two churches) was a building of about the tenth century, and probably modest in size. Rebuilding began under William Warelwast in 1114 and was finished towards the end of the twelfth century. This created a much larger church with the two great towers that are still to be seen today (Figure 12, p. 46). The endowments of the cathedral also increased. Domesday Book mentions only four of the bishop's estates as supporting its clergy, but as time went on more properties were added, some in the form of lands and others in that of parish churches whose tithes could be exploited.

The Taxation of 1291 credits the cathedral with an astonishing income of about £567 per annum, of which about £140 came from lands and £427 from churches and their tithes. This was four and a half times as much as that of Tavistock Abbey, the richest monastery in Devon. It enabled the clergy of the cathedral to grow in number and wealth. By the middle of the thirteenth century they included eight dignitaries (dean, precentor, chancellor, treasurer, and four archdeacons) and twenty-four canons, but what with doubling of posts and absences, there were usually about a dozen resident dignitaries and canons. The residents lived in individual houses around the cathedral Close with substantial wealth, households of servants, and exemption from attending most cathedral services. By 1200, they employed twenty-four vicars choral to take their places in the daily worship, and these vicars came to be joined by twelve adolescent clerks known as 'secondaries', fourteen choristers, and a growing number of privately endowed 'annuellars' or chantry priests. In 1300, the resident staff of the cathedral stood at about seventy clergy plus lay servants, occupying a building with many treasures in terms of vestments, ornaments, relics, and books. Indeed, by that date rebuilding was in progress on an even larger scale, to which we shall return in the following chapter.

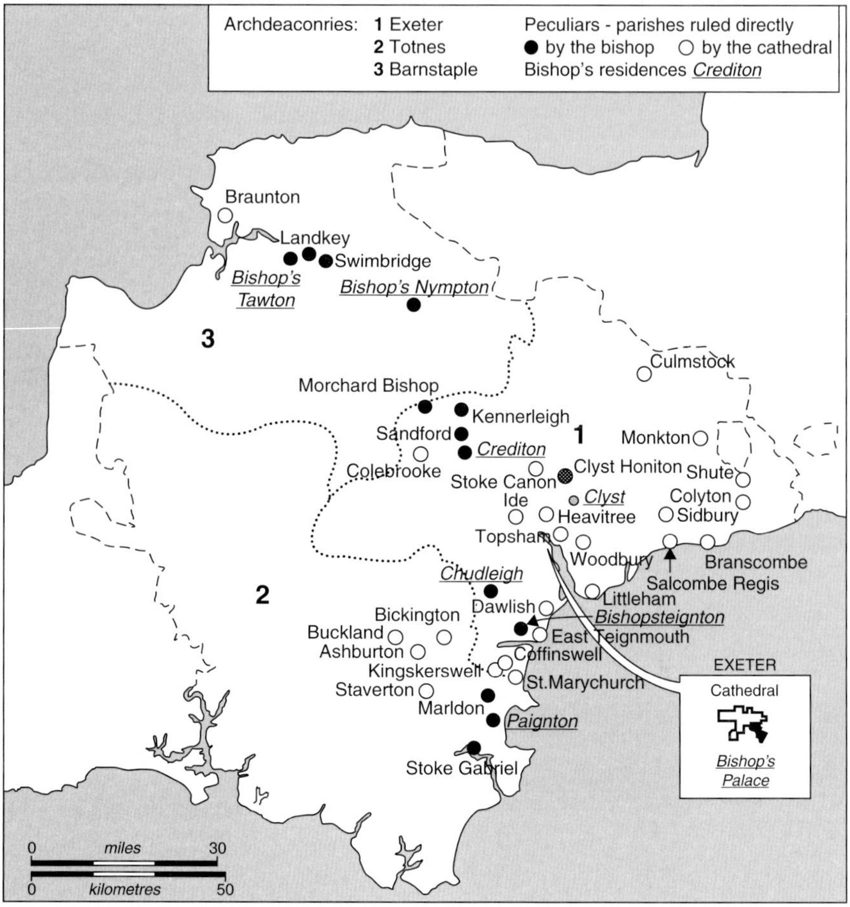

Figure 11 The diocese of Exeter in the Middle Ages, showing the bishop's major residences, the archdeaconries, and the peculiar jurisdictions.

The greatest expansion was that of monasteries.[32] This began as a result of the Norman Conquest. France contained more abbeys and priories than England, and the Norman aristocracy had close relationships with them. The aristocracy soon began to grant some of the lands that they acquired in Devon to French religious houses; indeed, Edward the Confessor gave Ottery St Mary to Rouen Cathedral even before the Conquest. By 1086, Mont St Michel had acquired Otterton, St Stephen (Caen) Northam, and Holy Trinity (Caen) Umberleigh, while William the Conqueror had given Cullompton and St Olave (Exeter) to his own new monastery at Battle in Sussex. Later on, Norman lords gave property to St Serge (Angers), Bec-Hellouin, Cluny, St Martin-des-Champs (Paris), St Pierre-sur-Dives, and St Pierre-Rillé, as well as to Malmesbury (Wiltshire). When a monastery outside Devon held substantial property in the county, it founded a daughter house or 'cell' to administer the property. In this way, the priories of Barnstaple, Cowick, St Nicholas (Exeter, Figure 42, p. 195), St James (Exeter), Ipplepen, Kerswell, Modbury, Otterton, Pilton, and Totnes came into existence between about 1087 and 1150. Most of them were staffed by French monks, and this continued to be the case until the fourteenth century.

A wider enthusiasm for founding monasteries and entering the monastic life swept through western Europe during the twelfth century, independently of the Conquest. More people came forward to make such foundations and to enter them as monks than had done before, or would do again in English history. The framework of monastic life that had been most popular since the tenth century was the Rule of St Benedict, whose followers, the Benedictines, wore black robes and have come to be known as 'black monks'. The pre-Conquest monasteries of Buckfast and Tavistock were Benedictine, as were most of the small dependent priories mentioned above. Apart from having the Rule in common, Benedictine houses were independent of one another, but in the thirteenth century their leaders in England began to meet together in a 'general chapter' and make laws for their own government. Most Benedictine houses were also subject to the authority of the local bishop, including Tavistock until the eve of the Reformation.

The growing enthusiasm for the monastic life, however, led to many monastic founders and monks criticising the Benedictine framework and seeking for alternatives. As early as the tenth century, the great monastery of Cluny in France had developed a reformed version of Benedictine life, and Cluniac houses were founded in western Europe which came closer to forming a religious organisation. Each house owed allegiance to Cluny and their heads went there for regular meetings under the leadership of the abbot. The priories of Barnstaple, St James, and Kerswell were Cluniac houses. Another variant of the Benedictine rule was that of Cîteaux in France, which introduced a strict and austere way of life that came to be followed widely in Europe, symbolised by the wearing of undyed white cloth, hence the name 'white monks'. Cistercian monasteries, as they are known, formed a more regular and centralised organisation than that of Cluny. Each house was usually dedicated to St Mary, laid out on similar plans, and sent its abbot to Cîteaux every year for a general chapter which made laws for the order and supervised its affairs. Four Cistercian houses were founded in Devon: Buckland, Dunkeswell, Forde, and Newenham, while Buckfast, originally Benedictine, became affiliated first to the abbey of Savigny in France and later to the Cistercians.

Although the strict Cistercian model of monasticism gained popularity in some circles, there was also a desire for a simpler and more flexible model. This was provided by the Rule of St Augustine, which became popular on the Continent in the eleventh century and reached England in the early twelfth. It was considered especially suitable for minsters, which Norman Church leaders found unsatisfactory in form and wished to make more monastic. William Warelwast introduced the Rule to Plympton in 1121 and Bartholomew to Hartland in the 1160s. Later, a small cell of Plympton was established at St Mary Marsh (Alphington) and two little independent priories at Canonsleigh (Burlescombe) and Frithelstock (Figure 41, p. 193), although Canonsleigh, as we shall see, did not endure. Meanwhile, during the twelfth century, St Norbert founded an Augustinian house at Prémontré in France which combined elements of the Rule with those of the Cistercians, and in due course this house generated a family of 'Premonstratensian' communities of canons, which was represented in Devon by the abbey of Torre, established in 1196.

Augustinian and Premonstratensian clergy were technically canons not monks, and historians call them 'regular canons' to distinguish them from the 'secular canons' who ran the cathedral and minsters such as Crediton. Augustinians resembled the Benedictines in wearing black and in having houses that were independent of one another. However, like the Benedictines, the Augustinians eventually created a general chapter in England which enacted laws and arranged visitations of houses. The Premonstratensians followed the Cistercians in wearing white and developing an international organisation with regular meetings at Prémontré and similar methods of government. Apart from differences of detail, the regular canons did not differ greatly from monks in their way of life. So whereas it is sometimes assumed that they had more scope to work in the outside world, in running parish churches for example, there is little sign that this took place. Indeed the introduction of Augustinians to Hartland and Plympton led to the creation of two churches, one for the canons and one for parishioners, in place of single churches for both parties. Frithelstock and Torre likewise had separate churches, and in all four places the parish churches were generally served by chaplains rather than canons.

Nearly all this monastic expansion was powered by men, who came forward in substantial numbers to become monks and regular canons. Far fewer nunneries were founded. The earliest in Devon was Polsloe in about 1160, a priory of Benedictine nuns, which was followed much later by two Augustinian houses: Cornworthy in the early thirteenth century and Canonsleigh, which was transformed from a male to a female house in about 1285. Nuns faced problems not encountered by monks or canons. They could say the daily services, but they were not allowed to be priests and celebrate mass, so that they needed chaplains for that purpose. They did not carry out medical or social work like modern nuns, and their teaching was restricted to a few boys under the age of seven and girls under that of twelve, whom they accepted as boarders. Nuns tended to be from wealthy families, and the equivalent of a dowry was usually required from would-be entrants. This, along with the narrowness of the life beyond daily worship, kept the numbers of nuns and nunneries at a low level across the whole of England.

Friars, Military Orders, and Hospitals

A monastery was a place apart from lay society. It could never be totally separate because of its need to manage its property and its obligation to provide hospitality and charity, but its clergy did not have much of a public pastoral role. During the twelfth and thirteenth centuries, however, several organisations were formed that combined the monastic model of a disciplined community with the provision of services to the outside world. Two of them arose from the Crusades. The Knights Templars were established in 1118 as a celibate order of warriors for the defence of the Holy Land; they adopted a rule similar to that of the Cistercians. At about the same time, the Order of St John, or the Hospitallers, came into being for the protection of pilgrims to Jerusalem. They followed the rule of St Augustine and gradually evolved into a military force like the Templars. The Hospitallers obtained land at Bodmiscombe in Uffculme parish by about 1200 and built a small 'preceptory' there, staffed by two of their brothers with a chaplain and a clerk.[33] The Templars acquired some manors in mid Devon, including Clayhanger and Templeton which takes its name from them, but they never founded a house in the county.[34] In 1312, the pope suppressed their order, and their property passed to the Hospitallers.

More influential were the friars. Their principal founders were the Spaniard St Dominic (died 1221), whose background was that of the Augustinian canons, and the Italian St Francis of Assisi (died 1226), who set himself to live as much like Christ as possible. Both men gathered followers who lived in religious communities and said daily prayers, but spent much of their time in the world by ministering spiritually to lay people through hearing confessions and preaching. The communities did not possess estates and tithes like monasteries, but lived by seeking donations from other clergy and laity in the manner of Christ and his apostles, hence the word 'mendicant' ('beggar') which is often applied to their members. Four major orders of friars came into existence during the thirteenth century: Dominicans or Black Friars, from the colour of their dress; Franciscans or Grey Friars; Carmelites or White Friars; and Augustinians or Austin Friars. All were highly organised bodies like the Cistercians, with international and national leaders, and they took their organisation a step further in that a friar belonged to his order not to his friary. He could be moved about by his leaders for education or deployment, so that a man recruited in Devon might be sent out of the county, and conversely somebody working there might come from elsewhere in England or even from the Continent.

The dependence of friars on charity led them to the larger towns, where charity was most plentiful and where there were more opportunities for pastoral work. Exeter was the first place in Devon to receive them, the Dominicans arriving in about 1232 and the Franciscans soon afterwards, not later than 1240.[35] Plymouth acquired a friary of Carmelites in about 1289 and one of Franciscans much later in

Figure 12 Exeter Cathedral, the north tower. Norman bishops and lords were responsible for much church building in Devon, including the enlargement of the cathedral. Its two towers are the largest surviving remains of Norman church architecture in the county.

1383.[36] The Austin Friars attempted to join the other orders in Devon during the fourteenth century. They started a house at Dartmouth in 1331 but this did not take root: partly, it seems, through the opposition of Torre Abbey which was a major power in that town.[37] Later, in 1348–53, they tried to establish themselves at Barnstaple but this was also a failure, perhaps because of the disruption caused by the Black Death of 1349.[38] All four orders of friars enjoyed a good deal of support, especially from men and women of the gentry and the wealthy urban classes. At the same time they provoked hostility, notably from other clergy. Friars were exempt from the control of bishops; they criticised the endowments enjoyed by monasteries, and competed with the parish clergy in pastoral work. Their claim to be able to hold funerals and arrange burials of people in their churches and cemeteries was particularly unpopular, because it deprived the parish clergy of the offerings made on such occasions. Even among lay people, their practice of begging gave rise to some cynicism.

Finally, there were religious houses providing services for the public in the form of hospitals. Devon seems to have acquired about fifteen of these by 1300.[39] They fell into two categories, the majority caring for lepers and a few others ministering to other kinds of people. Leprosy began to be perceived as a serious problem in the late eleventh century; it could not be cured and seemed to require the isolation of lepers into separate communities. Many of these communities were probably informal and consisted of lepers who retreated or were driven to live in cottages on the margins of society.[40] Others were formally established with buildings, a chapel, and the help of a priest to lead worship. Such hospitals rarely possessed significant endowments, however, and they relied on donations like friars. Exeter supported a leper hospital outside the city walls well before 1184, and others came into existence at Barnstaple, *Clony* (possibly Ivybridge), Honiton, Okehampton, Pilton, Plymouth, Plympton, Taddiport (Little Torrington, Figure 21, p. 90), Tavistock, and Totnes. It is likely that the organised leper hospitals catered for men and women of the middle ranks of society. Lepers in wealthy families could be supported from their own resources, while the very poor lacked the status and influence to enter the hospitals.

Hospitals for others than lepers were uncommon. Exeter acquired one dedicated to St Alexius in about 1170 and another to St John the Baptist by 1184, which later absorbed St Alexius. Crediton had a hospital of St Laurence by 1249, and Totnes one of the Holy Ghost and St Katherine from 1271. The work of these houses is poorly recorded, but it probably included hospitality to travellers and the maintenance of infirm or elderly people rather than medical care of the kind that we associate with hospitals, which went on in as far as it could in people's homes. St John, Crediton, and Totnes were each staffed by a small body of clergy who said daily services as well as ministering to the inmates. The clergy of St John observed the Rule of St Augustine, while those of Crediton and Totnes were Trinitarian friars who followed a similar way of life. Trinitarians were not mendicants and were allowed to hold property, but neither Crediton nor Totnes was well endowed. St John's alone in Devon functioned on a substantial scale, with buildings like those of a small monastery and a good deal of backing from the citizens of Exeter.

The Religious Houses: an Assessment

The monastic revival in Devon between 1066 and 1300 was an impressive one. It brought into existence about twenty-five significant institutions, not counting the tinier hospitals (Figure 13, p. 50). Most of the major religious orders established bases in Devon: Benedictines, Cistercians, Augustinians, Premonstratensians, Trinitarians, Dominicans, Franciscans, and Carmelites. Devon lacked only Austin Friars, Templars, and Carthusians – the latter a very strict order of monks who lived in separate cells, meeting only in church for worship. However, there were only two Carthusian houses in England before the 1340s, both in Somerset, and Devon nearly acquired the third such house to be founded. In 1331 Sir Richard Stapledon gained permission to found a priory of Carthusians on his lands in Devon as a memorial to his murdered brother, Bishop Walter Stapledon, but the project was never accomplished.[41]

Most of the houses were located in east and south Devon, counting Tavistock as lying within the south. They hardly spread into the highland zone and only reached four places in the north: Barnstaple, Frithelstock, Hartland, and Pilton, of which Hartland alone was a substantial foundation. Many were in or near towns, either because a town grew up around an ancient house, as happened at Plympton and Tavistock, or through a choice to settle in a town as was so with the friars. The greatest concentration of houses was around Exeter. It came to have a cathedral, four monasteries, a nunnery, two friaries, and a large hospital, five of which were within the city walls and the others in the nearby countryside. Wholly rural sites were also chosen, Hartland being one of the oldest since it descended from the ancient and probably pre-Saxon minster in an isolated 'Celtic' setting. Cistercian houses were often located in remote places where land was cheap and the surroundings fitted the austere lifestyle of the order. Brightley in 1136 was such a place, north of Okehampton, but the monks found it too challenging; they left and were offered the site at Forde instead. The other three new Cistercian foundations were comparatively late ones, when the order was spreading into more favourable areas, but Buckland and Dunkeswell were still in peripheral places. Newenham alone was close to a market town: that of Axminster.

Only the wealthiest people could afford to found a monastery in view of the large endowments that it needed, although once it was founded, lesser people could make smaller gifts. Three kings had founding roles in Devon. William the Conqueror's grants of lands enabled the foundation of St Nicholas (Exeter) and Otterton, Stephen gave the monastery of Buckfast to Savigny by which it eventually became a Cistercian house, and John founded or refounded Otterton. William Warelwast and Bartholomew, as we have seen, were involved at Plympton and Hartland. Otherwise it was the barons and greater knights of Devon who had the resources to bring houses into existence. Thus Juhel of Totnes was responsible for Totnes and Barnstaple; William Fitz Baldwin for Cowick; his brother Richard for Brightley, later Forde; Baldwin de Redvers for St James (Exeter); Geoffrey of Dinham for Hartland; William Brewer for Dunkeswell and Torre; and Reginald de Mohun for Newenham. Noblewomen were also involved: Matilda Peverel at Kerswell, Amice de Redvers at Buckland, and Matilda de Clare at Canonsleigh.

Founders of monasteries – the king, bishop, nobleman, or noblewoman – expected privileges in return for their generosity. They were remembered in the daily prayers and masses and consulted about the choice of a new abbot or prior. They were received as honoured guests, could send superannuated servants to be cared for, and were granted burial in the monastic church. These privileges duly passed to their heirs, who were recognised as the 'patrons' of the house like the patrons of parish churches and continued to act as such right down to the Reformation. The stamp of noble families was deeply impressed on monasteries. Family coats of arms were blazoned on the floor tiles of the church or in the stained glass windows. Family tombs were given an honoured place. At Newenham Abbey, for example, they occupied the floor of the presbytery immediately in front of the high altar. Reginald de Mohun, the founder, was more or less in the centre, with his brother William on his right, the heart of his son John on his left, and his son William beyond John. Two other knights who gave property to the abbey lay outside them, to north and south.[42]

A wealthy founder was needed because monks, regular canons, and nuns required a substantial and regular income to maintain their buildings and worship, feed their members, provide hospitality and alms, and pay for servants and estate workers. This income came from two major sources: temporal and spiritual, in other words lands and tithes. Founders always gave some land and this was plentiful in the aftermath of the Conquest, but later it became harder to provide because it robbed the founder's family of its property. Tithes were an attractive alternative. Founders were usually patrons of parish churches, but all that this allowed them to do was to choose the clergyman. Granting such churches as endowments cost them little personally but enabled their monasteries to receive the tithes of the churches through a practice known as 'appropriation', which will be explained in the following section. Consequently, most monasteries ended up with more income from tithes than land, with some exceptions like Tavistock which was an ancient

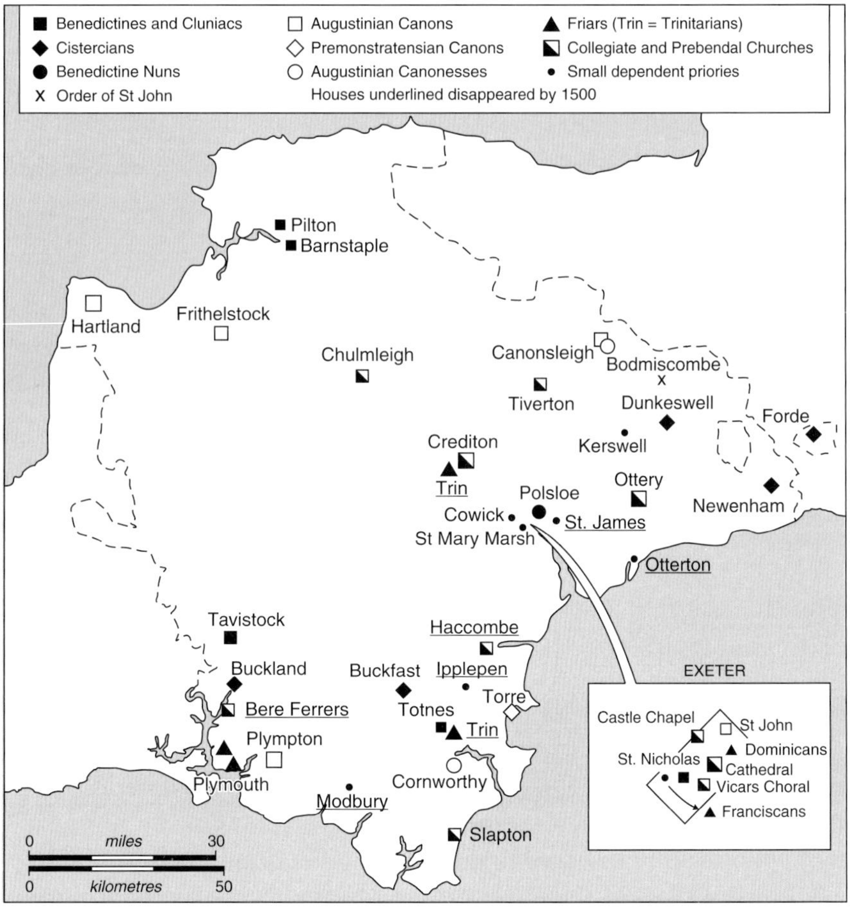

Figure 13 Religious houses in Devon at the height of their prosperity in about 1300. Several of the smaller ones were to disappear during the fourteenth and fifteenth centuries.

landed foundation and the five Cistercian houses. The early Cistercians disliked reliance on tithes, but all those in Devon came to have some income from this source by 1291 except for Newenham, and even Newenham later acquired the tithes of Luppitt.

The income totals of the religious houses in Devon given in Table 2 are derived from the Taxation of 1291 with its greatly undervalued figures, so that the totals are chiefly of use for comparing one house with another. The cathedral, as has been mentioned, was credited with the largest income, £567, although that money was shared among many people and did not exist as a single resource. Only two other houses were appraised at more than £100: Plympton with £145 and Tavistock with £124, followed by Torre with £85. Torre was actually the richest Premonstratensian

Table 2 Approximate annual incomes of religious houses in Devon, 1291, according to the 'Taxation of Pope Nicholas IV'

House	*Spiritual income*			*Temporal income*			*Total*		
	£	*s.*	*d.*	£	*s.*	*d.*	£	*s.*	*d.*
Cathedral									
Exeter Cathedral	427	12	4	139	18	6	567	10	10
Minsters and prebendal churches									
Crediton	57	6	8	—			57	6	8
Tiverton	25	14	10	—			25	14	10
Exeter Castle	20	16	8	—			20	16	8
Chulmleigh	8	13	4	—			8	13	4
Benedictines									
Tavistock	51	10	4	72	10	0	124	0	4
St Nicholas (Exeter)	21	9	8	16	0	0	37	9	8
Pilton	13	0		4	11	8	5	4	8
Cistercians									
Dunkeswell	10	0	0	64	12	0	74	12	0
Buckfast	18	13	4	37	0	5	55	13	9
Buckland	6	13	4	39	13	8	46	7	0
Forde	10	13	4	31	3	4	41	16	8
Newenham	—			26	0	4	26	0	4
Augustinians									
Plympton	91	13	4	53	6	8	145	0	0
Hartland	51	0	4	22	13	9	73	14	1
Frithelstock	4	13	4	4	10	11	9	4	3
St Mary Marsh	—			6	7	1	6	7	1
Premonstratensians									
Torre	62	1	7	23	11	0	85	12	7
Alien Priories									
Otterton	30	6	8	46	13	8	77	0	4
Totnes	41	18	8	5	3	4	47	2	0
Cowick	19	15	4	16	5	8	36	1	0
Modbury	10	0	0	2	3	4	12	3	4
Barnstaple	4	17	0	3	5	0	8	2	0
St James (Exeter)	—			5	15	4	5	15	4
Kerswell	—			4	2	8	4	2	8

Table 2 Continued

House	*Spiritual income*			*Temporal income*			*Total*		
	£	*s.*	*d.*	*£*	*s.*	*d.*	*£*	*s.*	*d.*
Nunneries									
Polsloe	16	1	8	9	14	0	25	15	8
Canonsleigh	2	11	0	13	6	10	15	17	10
*Cornworthy	—			10	0	0	10	0	0
Others									
*Order of St John	25	0	0						
*St John(Exeter)	15	0	0						
*Trinitarian Friars	3	0	0	3	0	0	6	0	0

* indicates a conjectured amount

house in England, while Plympton stood about third among the Augustinian houses. Next in order of rating were the priory of Otterton belonging to Mont St Michel, the Cistercian abbey of Dunkeswell, and the Augustinian abbey of Hartland. At the lower end of the scale, six houses were assessed as worth less than £10: Frithelstock, Barnstaple, St Mary Marsh, St James (Exeter), Pilton, and Kerswell, but most of these were cells of houses elsewhere. The friars, Trinitarians, military orders, and hospitals were exempt from the Taxation of 1291, so that their incomes cannot be calculated.

Economic wealth dictated numbers of clergy. These are difficult to estimate before 1300 because statistics are rarely available, and the following calculation is both rough and confined to the very end of the period: the late thirteenth century. There were probably then about 85 clergy in minsters: 50 at the cathedral (discounting clerks and choristers) and about 35 at Crediton and elsewhere. Monks may have numbered about 175, divided into about 75 Benedictines and Cluniacs, and 100 or more Cistercians, assuming at least twenty men in each of their houses. The regular canons may be reckoned at about 95, consisting of 67 Augustinians and 26 Premonstratensians. There were about 100 friars, 45 nuns, and a miscellaneous group of about 20 Hospitallers, Trinitarians, and hospital clergy. This produces a total of 520 or perhaps 550. The total was higher in 1300 than it would ever be again, because the population of England fell during the fourteenth century and with it that of the clergy. At the same time, the total was lower than that of the parish clergy of Devon, which may have reached 800–1000. Clergy who lived on their own always outnumbered those who dwelt in communities.

The twelfth and thirteenth centuries are not well provided with records of the religious houses, apart from charters relating to property. We know little of their internal life, and it is unwise to assume that the period was their golden age from which they declined in later times, when there is more evidence about their shortcomings and problems. The main work of a religious house was to hold daily services and to pray for the souls of founders and benefactors. Heads of houses and their chief officers had to administer property, provide hospitality to important people, and keep equable relationships with local communities. Monasteries encouraged their members to study, and they gradually acquired books, chiefly works of theology and canon law. Most such study was basic and practical, however, and not much has survived in terms of original writings by monks or regular canons. Five houses are known to have produced historical records in the twelfth and thirteenth centuries. Plympton and Tavistock kept annals of events from Christ to recent times, Hartland and Tavistock wrote lives of their patron saints (Nectan and Rumon respectively), while Forde and Newenham produced accounts of their founders and abbots.[43] Forde had other scholarly members. Baldwin, its abbot in the 1170s, was a notable writer whom we shall consider among the parish clergy. His successor-but-one, Abbot John (died 1214), wrote commentaries on the Song of Songs and Jeremiah, as well as a Life of St Wulfric of Haselbury. A third monk of the house, Roger of Forde, who left it to work in Europe, collected and edited the visions of the German abbess Elizabeth of Schönau.[44]

Roger's career reminds us that the foundations of the twelfth and thirteenth centuries greatly increased the ties between England and the Continent, beyond their extent before the Norman Conquest. The Benedictine alien cells, the Cluniacs, Cistercians, Premonstratensians, military orders, and above all, the friaries, generated comings and goings of clergy across the English Channel to France and beyond. There even came to be a link with Ireland. Two of the Anglo-Norman lords who conquered the island in the late twelfth century, Robert FitzStephen and Miles de Cogan, granted churches in Leinster to the monks of St Nicholas (Exeter) between 1177 and 1182. The grants included an old monastic site at Begerin in Wexford harbour, and a brother named Adam appears to have been sent to found a priory there. The outcome of the mission is obscure, but St Nicholas continued to own four churches in the province until the Reformation.[45]

Parish Churches and Parishes

Parish churches, as we have seen, increased in number from about the tenth century. Most of those that we regard as ancient in Devon probably emerged in that century or the eleventh, and the last ones arrived in the twelfth. The patron saints of churches throw some light on this process. Newton St Cyres and South Pool, which chose Cyr or Cyricus, and Bradninch and Walkhampton, which adopted Denis, may be new churches of the twelfth century because these saints were popular with the

Figure 14 Parishes north-west of Exeter, showing the locations of churches and chapels. The old minster parish of Crediton is clearly visible, and some of the parishes include detached portions.

Normans. Dodbrooke and St Thomas (Exeter) must date from after 1170, because they were dedicated to Thomas Becket who died in that year.[46]

How many churches there were by 1100 is impossible to state, because so few are mentioned in documents. More have left traces during the twelfth century, but even in the thirteenth it is not easy to make a complete list because the Church authorities themselves had not yet perfected systems for recording them. The first bishop's register, that of Bronescombe, which covers the period from 1258 to 1280, includes institutions of clergy to only 264 Devon churches: about two thirds of the total. Whether he instituted the clergy of the other third is not known. The papal Taxation of 1291 made a more determined attempt to track down churches in England, and in so doing compiled the fullest list that had yet been achieved for

Devon. It identified 394 rectories and vicarages, including Ashford, Haccombe, and Shillingford which it described as chapels but which in later times were regarded as parish churches.[47]

Nonetheless, even the Taxation fell short of completeness. Three churches that we know existed (Bishop's Nympton, Chudleigh, and Stoke Gabriel) do not appear in its lists and are only alluded to in relation to Exeter Cathedral. Eight others are completely absent: Bishop's Tawton and Bishopsteignton which belonged to the bishop, Braunton – the property of the dean of Exeter, and Highampton, Newton Tracey, Trusham, Upton Hellions, and Virginstow which were ordinary country churches. All these churches were in being by 1291 because there are earlier references to their clergy in the bishops' registers. They were probably left out of the Taxation either because they were counted as part of the property of the bishop and cathedral or, in the case of the country churches, because they were relatively poor. We also need to include the church of Lundy, which was too remote and probably too impoverished for anyone to bother with. Adding these twelve places to those of the Taxation, we reach a total of 406 parish churches in Devon by the end of the thirteenth century.[48]

The Taxation distinguished between rectories and vicarages. In principle, every church was a rectory and the Latin word often used for a rectory was *ecclesia*, meaning 'a church'. Its clergyman was the rector, a term indicating that he had the rule of the church, its parish, and its people, and thereby the right to the revenues of the church including its tithes. In practice, this right was not always complete because lords of manors in the twelfth century sometimes diverted the tithes of their lands to other churches, but such arrangements were unusual. As early as the tenth century, however, the cathedral and other religious houses which owned parish churches on their estates drew off some of the rectors' revenues for their own benefit. This practice greatly increased in the twelfth century, when bishops and lay lords founded monasteries and gave them parish churches as part of their endowments. It was known as 'appropriation'. At first it probably happened unofficially, but by the early twelfth century the bishop insisted on approving it, and after 1279 the king did so as well. A parish church could be appropriated only to a bishop or a religious house; the right was not available to lay people until the Reformation.

When a church was appropriated, the bishop or the house concerned became rector of the church. This allowed them to take the revenues of the church, but in practice the revenues taken were usually limited to the tithes of grain, known as the 'great' or 'garb' tithes, consisting of every tenth sheaf at harvest time. These were usually the most valuable produce of a parish as well as the easiest to identify, store, transport, and use or sell. Of course, the appropriator was unable to carry out the rector's spiritual duties, because the parish often lay a long distance away.

Accordingly, another clergyman was appointed to run the parish, who came to be known as the 'vicar' (a term meaning 'deputy') and his church and house as a 'vicarage'. The vicar had to be given an income, and this usually included the profits of the church's lands, known as the glebe, and the 'small' tithes due from hay, young animals, vegetables, and dairy produce. These tithes were less valuable and more difficult to identify, so that they were best collected by somebody locally based who could keep track of them.

In 1291, the vast majority of churches in Devon were still rectories, especially in north Devon. A minority of about 72 (18 per cent) were appropriated parishes run by vicars or, in a few places very close to monasteries, by hired chaplains. Except in the ways that they got their income, there was no difference between a rector and a vicar. By the thirteenth century, both kinds of parish clergyman were chosen by the patron of the church (king, bishop, monastery, nobleman, or lord of the manor), presented to the bishop, and instituted. Once instituted, they had tenure for life unless they chose to resign, and could only be removed by the bishop for very grave crimes and with much difficulty. Rectors and vicars had similar duties: providing church services, pastoral care, hospitality to travellers, and alms for the poor, and had complete right to rule the parishes and people attached to their churches in spiritual matters. One cannot even say that rectors were richer than vicars, because although rectors owned all the parish revenues and vicars only a part, every church differed in the amount of its income. Some rectors of poor churches earned less than vicars of wealthier ones.

These differences of income reflected differences between parishes: the districts belonging to each church. Whether churches had such districts in early Anglo-Saxon times is unclear, but by the tenth century when there came to be many churches, there had to be a means of defining the territory that belonged to each one. The history of parish boundaries is even worse documented than that of parish churches. Some attempts to record them were made in what are known as 'terriers' in the early seventeenth century, but it was not until the nineteenth that they were properly mapped: first in the tithe surveys carried out after the Tithe Act of 1836, and subsequently in the large-scale maps of the Ordnance Survey. This Victorian information has to be 'read back' to earlier times, with the risk that there may have been changes to boundaries, but the information (however problematical in detail) seems to preserve a great deal of the structure of parish boundaries that emerged in the tenth and eleventh centuries. One can also remove the subdivisions of some parishes that are known to have taken place after 1291, and produce a creditable map of the 406 parishes of Devon at the time of the papal Taxation.[49]

Mapping the parishes reveals a wide variation in their sizes (Figure 14, p. 54). Most, especially those in the south and east of Devon which were more fertile and populous, covered from about 3 to 6 square miles. This grew to as much as 14 in the larger parishes of the uplands, like Bishop's Nympton, Bradworthy, and South Brent, and to 26 in the case of North Molton (with Twitchen) on Exmoor. Some of the early minster churches also managed to hold on to spacious parishes, although not necessarily as spacious as they were in 900 or 1000. Tiverton owned 27 square miles, Crediton 32, Hartland 37, and Plympton 44, although the latter two included daughter churches. Scattered here and there were some very small rural parishes of only half a square mile or so, such as Landcross in the north and Dotton and Rousdon in the east, which were early churches, small early estates, or later subdivisions of larger estates. The range of sizes was equalled by that of shapes. Chudleigh and Kenn were compact in form, while Clannaborough and Lympstone were long and narrow. Numerous parishes had detached areas beyond their borders, in the manner of Brampford Speke and Chittlehampton, or an insulation within their borders like the outlier of High Bray in North Molton and that of Peter Tavy in Whitchurch. These features probably descended from the manorial churches founded in and after the 900s, and represented the manorial estates on which the parishes were based.

The smallest parishes lay inside the city walls of Exeter. One can still walk round the parish of St Martin (Figure 6, p. 21) in five minutes, for it consists chiefly of the block between High Street, St Martin's Lane, and the cathedral Close. Here the minster, later the cathedral, began its life as the parish church of the whole city. This status survived until 1637 in the rule that all local people must have a funeral in the cathedral and a burial in its churchyard unless they gained permission otherwise. However, during the tenth and eleventh centuries, about 26 other churches came into existence in or close to the city, probably to serve the tenants of particular landlords, groups of neighbouring people, or devotees of particular saints. At first they were not fully independent, and as late as the Taxation of 1291 they were still referred to as 'chapels', but in 1222 Simon of Apulia turned about 24 of them into parish churches by giving them each a territory from which they were to receive people's tithes and offerings.[50] These territories, however, were often too small to be viable, and three churches (St Cuthbert, St John by the Eastgate, and St Mary Minor) were united with larger neighbours in the 1270s. Their buildings disappeared apart from St John, which also served as the church of the main city hospital.[51]

Variations in parish size meant that the income of the churches received by the rector or vicar, the 'benefice income', also ranged widely. The Taxation throws light on these differences, provided that we take account of its low valuations. Thirty-seven churches in Devon had a benefice income valued at less than £1 per annum, and Lundy would doubtless have come within this group. They included all but one of the nineteen churches in Exeter, two of which (St James and St Laurence) were claimed to be worth 'nothing, because of poverty', and most of their neighbours

Figure 15 St Mary Arches parish church, Exeter. Five churches were dedicated to Mary in Exeter, of which this church was built or rebuilt in Norman times with arcades typical of the period.

'scarcely sufficient to support a chaplain'. In the countryside, Clannaborough and Satterleigh were also assessed at nothing, Blackborough at 4*s*., Oldridge at 5*s*., and Huxham and Stockleigh English at 6*s*. 8*d*. each. In truth, the clergy of these 37 churches (nearly all rectors) were probably receiving nearer £2 a year (the minimum living wage for a priest), but they were certainly poorly rewarded.

The largest categories of churches were 147 that were valued as worth between £1 and £4, and 119 that were estimated at between £5 and £9. Making adjustments for under-assessment suggests that the commonest benefice incomes lay between about £5 and £15. Above this average, there were 54 parishes valued at £10–£14, 18 at £15–£19, and 20 at £20 or more. The wealthiest were Crediton (rated at £35), Kenton (£36), Stokenham (£37), and Axminster (£51). In these four instances, however, not all of the income went to the clergyman, because the church either supported several clergy as was the case at Crediton or had most of its income appropriated to a cathedral or monastery elsewhere. The clergyman with the largest income under his own control was the rector of North Molton, whose church was valued at £33. Given the shortcomings of the valuation system, his income was considerably higher than that.

Church Buildings and Their Contents

The focus of the parish was the church. Here all parishioners were required to come for baptism, confession, and funerals, and expected to attend worship on Sundays and festival days. Sometimes the church stood in the centre of the parish, sometimes off centre, and sometimes close to the parish boundary, depending on the history of the estate on which the parish was based and the locations of people's dwellings. The landscape settings of churches included their placement on a hilltop as at Cadbury and Churchstow, in a valley like Offwell and Thorverton, on a main road in the case of Alphington and Newton St Cyres, or in a remote and secluded place such as Abbot's Bickington and Bulkworthy. Churches were usually spaced at least two or three miles apart, but sometimes closer together as with Peter and Mary Tavy or East and West Worlington, perhaps because a former estate became divided which brought about the creation of two parishes.

Far more survives of the church buildings of the period 1100 to 1300 than before the Conquest. It is clear that stone churches were common by this era, and perhaps universal. The 'Norman' or 'Romanesque' style of architecture, with massive features and round arches, was normal up to about 1200, by which time pointed arches were coming into fashion, producing what historians call the 'Transitional' style. During the thirteenth century, this turned into a fully pointed or Gothic style using fairly simple geometrical forms, known as 'Early English'. Churches were designed in two parts: a chancel towards the east where services were performed, and a nave towards the west where lay people were baptised and from whence they watched the services in the chancel. A basic structure of this kind can still be seen at Honeychurch. Chancel and nave were divided visually by a large archway, the 'chancel arch', and were regarded as separate areas for legal purposes. It was an established principle of canon law by the early thirteenth century that the rector of the church should maintain the fabric of the chancel and the lay parishioners that of the nave or, as it was also called, the 'body' of the church. In the case of an appropriated parish, the appropriators looked after the chancel although this duty was sometimes passed to the vicar.

The basic church plan could be embellished by adding aisles, transepts, or a tower. An early example of aisles on both sides of the nave may be seen at St Mary Arches (Exeter), where they date from the mid twelfth century (Figure 15, p. 58). Such aisles were narrower than they became in later centuries, and often only the aisle on the north side, or a trace of it, survives today, as is the case at Farway, Hawkchurch, and Salcombe Regis. There are so many examples of aisle survivals on this side in England that it is possible that some churches in the twelfth and thirteenth centuries had only north aisles. This raises the question of their function. They certainly gave extra dignity and status to a church and they could have been used for processions within it. Another conjecture, although it remains to be confirmed, is that they provided a place for women to stand or sit during services, giving them partial seclusion from the men.

Transepts seem to have been a later feature than aisles, and were typically built in the thirteenth and fourteenth centuries. Some churches may have been designed in the shape of a cross, but often a single transept was built on one or other side of the nave at its eastern end, and sometimes a second transept was added on the opposite side. This makes it appear that the church was planned to look like a cross, whereas it grew by accretion. Braunton appears to be such an example. Transepts were probably private areas for people of knightly rank or prosperous members of guilds. Adding such an area allowed them to have mass celebrated by a priest at a side altar and provided space for their burials inside the church.

Other typical features of churches were decorative doorways and towers. The principal entrance to a cathedral or monastery was at the west end, but in parish churches a south door into the nave was common, sometimes matched by a less important door on the north side. Some doorways in the twelfth century were beautified with zigzag carving or projecting 'beak heads', as at Bishopsteignton, and others had a semicircular tympanum above the door bearing a religious motif. Such a motif might be that of Christ in majesty (like that on a carving at Chulmleigh), Christ as the Lamb (Bondleigh), the Magi (Bishopsteignton), or Daniel and the lions (Down St Mary, Figure 16, p. 62). In later centuries, it became common to add a porch outside the door, but it is not clear how common this was before 1300. Towers were added to naves to give visual impressiveness to the building and to carry bells, important for ringing for services, before funerals, and on festival days. They might be built at the west end of the church, as at Holbeton, Sidbury, and Sampford Courtenay (Figure 38, p. 177); on the north side of the church in the case of Ilfracombe; on the south in those of Barnstaple and Braunton (Figure 2, p. 7); or over the central crossing as at Axminster, Branscombe, Crediton, and elsewhere (Figure 3, p. 10).

As has been mentioned, the archdeacons were in charge of visiting churches to ensure that they were properly maintained and equipped for services. The Totnes visitation of 1342 is the only one to have left any record, but it is preceded by a series of reports by the cathedral clergy on the churches belonging to them, made between 1281 and 1330.[52] In 1281, two of the canons toured sixteen churches in Devon for which they and their colleagues bore responsibility, to check the state of the chancels and the equipment needed for worship. In five parishes (Clyst Honiton, Colebrooke, Colyton, Culmstock, and Topsham) no comment was made on the chancels, presumably because they were in a sound condition. Ashburton, Heavitree, St Marychurch, and Staverton were commended for their roofs, but Branscombe, Dawlish, East Teignmouth, Littleham (Exmouth), Salcombe Regis, Upottery, and

Winkleigh were badly roofed or unroofed. Staverton's chancel was criticised for being small and narrow: only sixteen feet long and twelve wide. Chancels were required to have satisfactory windows of glass, and here Ashburton, Branscombe, Dawlish, Salcombe Regis, Staverton, and Winkleigh were found wanting, while at St Marychurch the glass in one window was frail and badly set. At Culmstock, the bell tower was almost roofless. If we had records of the archdeacons' visitations, no doubt other churches would have been found with similar defects.[53]

The fittings and equipment of churches were precisely set down at Quinil's synod of 1287, but this was a refinement of existing practices rather than a new departure, because many of its details are already apparent in the visitations of 1281. At the east end of the chancel, the high (or chief) altar was to stand under a canopy, with images of the patron saint and the Virgin Mary on the north and south sides of the altar respectively. The font, probably always at the west end or near the principal door, had to be of stone and provided with a cover that could be locked, since holy water was always kept in its basin for christenings. The nave, like the chancel, was to have glass in its windows.[54] It is often assumed that churches were rather empty places before 1300, without a roodscreen between the chancel and the nave[55] or any seating other than a stone bench along the inside walls. It is indeed the case that neither screens nor seats survive from before 1300, but that does not mean they were absent. The word 'chancel' comes from the Latin *cancellus* meaning a screen, and *cancellus* was in use well before 1300, so screens may be older than the evidence about them. Seats certainly existed by 1287 on a scale sufficient to bring them to the notice of Quinil and his synod. Observing that 'many times, parishioners come to blows in church on account of seats', the synod ordered that no-one should claim a place in a church except for church patrons or people of noble rank, but that those who first entered the church should choose where they sat.[56] This ruling looks sensible and modern, but it was doomed to failure. In later centuries, seating was allocated according to wealth and rank, as we shall see in another chapter.[57]

Finally, churches needed books, ornaments, vestments, and linen for service, and Quinil's synod listed these in detail.[58] For the mass or communion service, there must be a silver chalice for communion, a silver or ivory pyx (a small locked cup or box) in which to place a consecrated wafer to hang above the altar, and a silver or tin cup for giving communion to the sick. For the clergy, there were to be two surplices (linen garments with wide sleeves), a rochet (similar but with tight sleeves) for the parish clerk, and two sets of vestments: one for ordinary days and one for festivals. Linen and vessels were to be provided for the altar, and eleven books containing the Latin services. The synod did not say so, but the service books by this time followed the 'Use of Sarum' or practices of Salisbury Cathedral, at least in the parishes belonging to the cathedral.[59] Other requirements included a large veil to hang in the chancel during Lent, a small veil for brides, a bier to carry and

Figure 16 Down St Mary parish church. Here Norman work survives in the tympanum remounted above the south door of the church. It depicts Daniel in a den of two lions.

a pall to cover bodies or coffins during funerals, a chrismatory to hold holy oil, a thurible for incense, a big candlestick for Easter, a processional cross, small bells for ringing at the consecration of the bread and wine in the mass, an offertory box, and a chest to hold the books and vestments. All these things were to be provided by the parishioners, except for the chancel windows, the altar canopy, and two of the service books which were the responsibility of the clergy.

Inevitably, the provision of these things was subject to variation in practice, like the maintenance of buildings. The canons of Exeter in 1281 generally found the majority of items in good order but a few required repair or replacement. Thus at St Marychurch, the canons counted 42 items of which the rochet was unsatisfactory, the lock on the font insufficient, and the Lenten veil decrepit. There was no pall to cover the dead, the offertory box had no lock, and two books were missing. The other visitations uncovered similar failings, but the fact that inspections took place shows that attempts were made to supervise how churches worked and to keep their clergy and parishioners up to the mark.

Parish Clergy

The clergy who served the parishes (and also those of the cathedral and minsters) are known as 'secular clergy' because they lived in the world, as opposed to 'regular clergy' who dwelt under Rules in monasteries. Little survives about their biographies before the second half of the thirteenth century, when the bishops' registers begin to list the names of those who were instituted as rectors and vicars. Even then, the records ignore most of the lesser clergy: the chaplains who were employed in subordinate roles. An appraisal of the parish clergy between 1100 and 1300 must therefore be largely based on what appears to have been generally true, rather than on detailed evidence. In theory, they were the first of the three estates of society, taking precedence of those who fought (the knights) and those who worked (the rest of the people). From at least the thirteenth century they resembled knights in being addressed as *dominus* in Latin, 'sir' in English or French. In practice, they ranged widely in social status and wealth, and were fitted into society accordingly. Chaucer illustrates this in the order in which he places his clergy in the prologue to *The Canterbury Tales*. The Prioress follows the Knight, the Monk and Friar (both senior men in their orders) precede the Merchant, while the Poor Parson or rector gives way to the prosperous Wife of Bath.

The sons of noblemen and knights who entered the Church had family resources and influence to support them. They gained lucrative benefices such as archdeaconries, canonries, and the richer parish rectories. William of Eu (d. 1150) was archdeacon of Cornwall and his relative Hugh (d. 1162) of Totnes. Hugh was probably the father of Baldwin, who succeeded him as archdeacon before becoming abbot of Forde, bishop of Worcester, and finally archbishop of Canterbury (1185–90).[60] In the second half of the thirteenth century, we encounter clergy in Devon from knightly families such as Arcevesque, Bolevile, Mohun, Punchardon, Ralegh, Tracy, and Valletort.[61] Most rectors and vicars were probably from the middle orders of society: sons of merchants, wealthy craftsmen, and the most prosperous peasant farmers. Some men of poorer rank, the children of ordinary peasants or craftsmen, also entered the Church, but without patrons and money they were likely to fill the lowest posts in the church as curates, chantry priests, and private chaplains. Such posts had no security of tenure, and their holders were hired and fired at the will of those who employed them.

The education of the clergy reflected their rank and wealth. Sons of the rich could afford to learn Latin at grammar schools, all of which charged fees in this period. The history of these schools is poorly recorded, but Exeter is likely to have had one from about the early twelfth century and we hear of another at Plympton in 1263.[62] If Plympton was so favoured at that date, we can reasonably conjecture that Barnstaple, Dartmouth, and Plymouth had similar schools. Less wealthy parents would have found it hard to forgo a son's labour and pay for him to study for several years. Here, a basic education in learning how to read in an elementary school was more likely, which took less time and cost less money. This might be followed by assisting a priest as a parish clerk in saying the daily services and the mass: a practice that we have seen dates back to the eleventh century.[63] Such assistance would accustom a teenage boy to the forms and ceremonies of church services. By the thirteenth century, every parish was expected to maintain a parish clerk to help the priest in this way, and in 1287 Quinil's synod ordered that the post should be given to poor scholars in all churches 'within ten miles of the city [of Exeter] and the castles of the diocese'.[64] He evidently assumed that there would be schools not only in Exeter but in towns with castles such as Barnstaple, Plympton, and Tiverton to which such boys could go.

For the wealthy, study at a grammar school might continue at a centre of higher education. Paris was a popular destination for this purpose in the twelfth century, and after about 1200 it was supplemented by English universities at Oxford and Cambridge. Oxford was the preferred destination for young men from Devon because it was nearer. The basic degree course at university was the 'arts course': a mixture of grammar, logic, philosophy, and science that led to the degree of master of arts. The course was a lengthy one of seven years, with the obligation to spend two years after graduation as a university teacher. Further studies – civil (Roman) law, canon law, and theology – required additional years of study. Students supported themselves from family wealth or by securing institution to a parish church and using part of its revenues to pay for their education. There was as yet hardly any provision for poor scholars at universities, forming a further barrier to those of such status.

How clergy behaved in their posts has left hardly a trace. When the canons of Exeter Cathedral made their visitation in 1281, only two of sixteen parishes produced allegations against the incumbents, which may mean that the rest met the expectations of their congregations. The two were Colebrooke and Ashburton. At the first of these, the parishioners claimed that the wife of Matthew Bridge had not lived with her husband for four years, that the vicar was maintaining her 'in various remote places', and that he had fathered four children on her. He did not run the church well, or visit the sick. No comment on this was recorded by the visitors, so the charges may not have been proved. At Ashburton, all the local clergy came in for criticism. The vicar was keeping a female relation of his named Mariot, who had a bad reputation. William of Blakepole, chaplain, was supporting a woman by whom he had several children. Sampson the chaplain had had a concubine for two years, and William Prigge, a deacon, had sired children on a woman named Alice. Here the visitors took action, and all four men were ordered to cease their liaisons.[65]

On a more positive note, a few of the secular clergy became Latin authors, and their contributions compare well with those of monks and regular canons. Bishop Bartholomew wrote a treatise on *Free Will and Predestination*, a collection of sermons for Sundays and festivals throughout the year, and a *Penitential* or guide to confession and penance. Baldwin, the archdeacon and later archbishop, compiled a treatise on *The Sacrament of the Altar*, in other words the eucharist, which he dedicated to Bartholomew and which survives in a dozen manuscripts, as well as a number of sermons. Outside the field of theology, Baldwin's nephew, Joseph of Exeter, became a notable Latin poet, famous for his *Ylias* or epic account of the Trojan War. However, Joseph passed most of his life away from Devon and, although he probably had the status of a cleric, he is not known to have entered the priesthood.[66]

The development of royal government and universities in the thirteenth century opened up fresh fields of study and led to two important works by Devon clergy.

John of Seccheville, from a knightly family in Devon, studied and taught at Paris and Oxford from the 1240s to the 1260s. His reputation rests on *The Principles of Nature*, a work on the philosophy of science that circulated in both France and England. Henry of Bratton (now known as Bracton), chancellor of Exeter Cathedral (died 1268), was one of the compilers (but not the only one) of *The Laws and Customs of England* during the 1250s. This is a major account of the English legal system, but it arose from the work of Bratton and others as royal justices elsewhere in England. Like Seccheville's treatise, it could not have been written by someone based solely in Devon.[67]

The Religion of the Laity

For the laity, religion was a mixture of duty and free choice. Everyone was obliged to be baptised and all, on reaching puberty, were expected to attend church on Sundays and festivals, to observe fasting days (Fridays and Lent), to go to confession in Lent, and receive holy communion at Easter. Heads of families were required to pay tithes or offerings, and contribute to the upkeep of the church building and its contents. Everyone had to receive a Christian burial unless death happened through suicide or while excommunicated, in which case burial in a churchyard was refused. Tithes were paid from crops, young animals, and dairy products (milk, butter, cheese, and eggs), and milled grain. In towns they were rendered in cash, according to local custom. Crops could include grain, peas and beans, garden vegetables, and even brushwood and bracken. Fish was also tithed in coastal parishes. These obligations were not always met, of course, and some people avoided as many as they could.

What the laity chose to do in terms of religious practice is hard to detect in this period. On the one hand people varied greatly in wealth and power; on the other they have not left us records of their religious interests and activities as is increasingly common after 1300. The main evidence from the twelfth century comes from grants of property made by barons and knights to monasteries. This shows their sympathy with the monastic organisations of the day and their wish to support monks and canons who would say prayers for their souls. The presence of private chapels in castles indicates a desire to have regular worship on the premises which a nobleman or his family could attend. When such people died, they were buried in their family monastery or (if they did not own one) in a parish church. By the thirteenth century, knights and ladies or their relatives were commissioning raised tombs crowned with painted effigies to perpetuate their memory and the status of their families.

Evidence improves in the middle of the thirteenth century with the first surviving wills. The earliest of these to be made by lay people in Devon belong to citizens

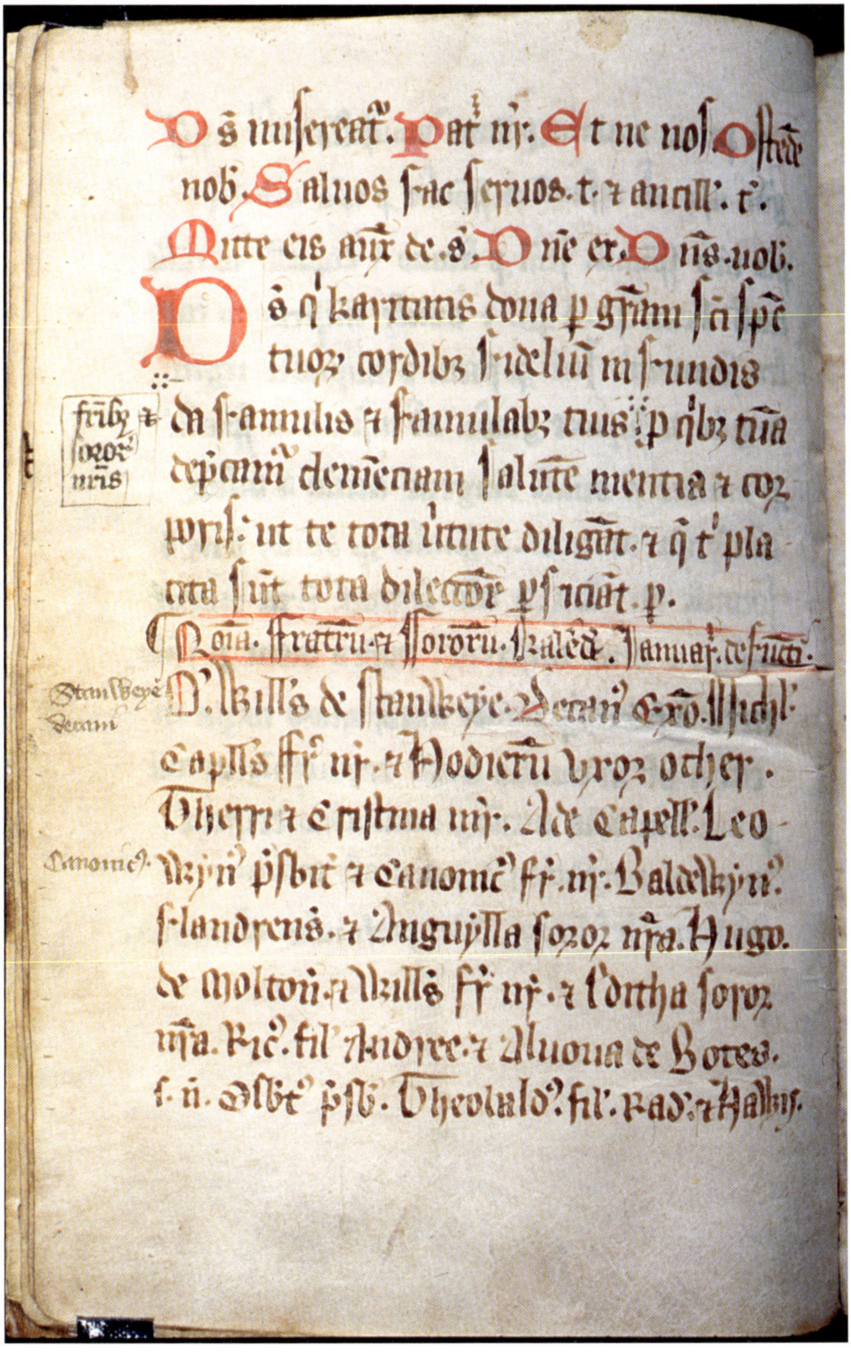

Figure 17 The Guild of Kalendars was the principal religious guild of Exeter in the twelfth and thirteenth centuries. This page includes prayers said at its services, followed by a list of guild members to be prayed for, beginning with the month of January.

and their wives in Exeter, beginning with that of Bartholomew Pinchun in 1244. Medieval wills were formal documents and covered routine matters such as funeral arrangements and family bequests, but they sometimes reveal their makers' particular interests. Pinchun gave much of his property to the hospital of St John in Exeter. Walter Gervas (*c*.1258) bequeathed money to the cathedral, the two Exeter friaries, and the parish church of St James. John de Doulys (1267) left small endowments to the chief religious guild in Exeter, the churches of St Cuthbert and St Kerrian, and the well of St Sidwell, besides assigning the corn on his lands to be distributed to poor people of the diocese. Adam de Collecote (1269) made benefactions to the light in the church of St Mary Steps, the parish clerk of the church, three local bridges, his four godchildren, and poor people on the day of his funeral.[68]

There were other religious activities to which the pious could give their time and money. Chapels were beginning to appear alongside parish churches, attracting some people to attend their worship or venerate their images.[69] Indulgences became available during the twelfth century. These were issued only by popes and bishops, and encouraged people to support a good cause by offering them a remission of part of the penance imposed by their confessor. In Devon, indulgences were granted (for example) to contributors of money to Exeter Cathedral in 1242, supporters of the Trinitarian friars of Totnes in 1259, providers of candles for mass in 1287, and donors to the parish church of North Tawton in 1292.[70] Unfortunately, the practice was sometimes abused. This was the case at Crediton, where the church claimed that worshippers and contributors could gain over forty years reduction of penance. The claim was based on alleged grants by tenth- and eleventh-century popes and bishops that were actually forged documents.[71]

Pilgrimages were another religious activity. As we shall see in a later chapter, most such journeys were made in a day to a nearby church or monastery, but occasionally they took a longer form to pray to a saint at some more famous shrine. In the twelfth century, a knight of Dunster (Somt.) is mentioned receiving a cure for paralysis at Hartland Abbey, while other people found healing from the relics at the cathedral.[72] The extraordinary explosion of devotion to Thomas Becket, after his murder in 1170, brought pilgrims to Canterbury from all over England. Collections of miracles made in the years immediately afterwards mention several involving people from Devon. They included Henry de Pomeroy, lord of Berry Pomeroy; Emma of Halberton, a young girl from an apparently wealthy family; and Osbern, a priest from the neighbourhood of Exeter. Bishop Bartholomew himself vowed a pilgrimage after St Thomas appeared to two local people and told them to pray for the bishop's recovery from illness, which duly took place. Even poor people went, causing Richard, the clerk of the sheriff of Devon, to promise to give to any such person who asked him for alms. When he ran out of money, his purse was miraculously replenished.[73] Further afield, the Hartland records refer to a man who travelled to

St James at Compostella in Spain, and a group of local people who sailed to Jerusalem and escaped from a storm by calling on St Nectan.[74]

Not all religion was personal; lay people joined together in their devotions. We have had a brief glimpse of some guilds of the Exeter district in about 1100, but very little survives about such organisations in Devon during the next two centuries. There were apparently at least two in Exeter in about 1200, when they fused under the name of the Guild of Kalendars: a name that was also adopted by guilds in Bristol and Winchester. Kalendars' guilds were composed of priests, laymen, and laywomen, and took their name from meeting on the first day of each month (the kalends) to hear mass and pray for the souls of their members, living and dead. They kept lists of the dead for this purpose, and we still possess the names for whom prayers were said at Exeter in the early fourteenth century (Figure 17, p. 66). The names include some bishops, several cathedral and parish clergy, and many lay people who were probably wealthier citizens.[75] There is no reason to rule out guilds elsewhere, even in the countryside. The twelfth-century Life of St Nectan of Hartland mentions a guild-house at Hartland where brethren used to meet once a year and hold drinking sessions. Again, the brethren seem to have been of some social standing because they had servants with them.[76] Altogether, there must have been a rich religious culture in the twelfth and thirteenth centuries; it appears poor or simple only because we know so little about it.

CHAPTER 3

The Later Middle Ages: the Clergy

Changes and Crises

We have now reached the period from 1300 to 1500 that historians call 'the later Middle Ages'. During this period, England retained many ties with the Continent. The kings of England and France fought a long intermittent struggle, 'The Hundred Years War', and the English held lands in France until 1558. Edward I, the Black Prince, and Henry IV all visited Devon for reasons linked with their affairs abroad. The Church in England continued to be part of the western Catholic Church, under the headship of the pope. There were trading and cultural ties between England and her Continental neighbours, including ties between Devon and France.

At the same time, the international bonds of the Church were weakening. The power of the popes in England, still strong until about the 1370s, decreased in some respects thereafter. Crusading waned in popularity. The French abbeys lost the lands that the Normans had given them in England and control of the cells that stood upon these lands. New religious orders and fashions no longer spread across the English Channel as easily as they had done in the age of the new monastic orders and the friars. The use of the French language in England fell into decline both in speech and in writing. As a result, the Church in England grew more distinctly English than it had been since the Conquest. The English language (always the spoken tongue of most people) began to invade the sphere of reading and writing at the expense of French and Latin. Architecture developed a distinctive English style that we know as 'Perpendicular'. Education became more insular, with schooling taking on a more local colour (especially in terms of the textbooks that taught boys Latin) while students of higher education now rarely travelled beyond the borders of England.

Another great change of the fourteenth century was a demographic one. In about 1300, the population of England may have reached six million: a higher total than at any time up to the early seventeenth century. By about 1400, this number may have been halved. One reason was the inability of the agricultural system to sustain so many people, leading to famines, notably in 1315–16 when there were two bad harvests in succession. These in turn led to outbreaks of what contemporaries called 'pestilence' and 'dysentery'. At Exeter Cathedral, where most local people had their funerals, funeral offerings increased in these years.[1] Then, in the summer of 1348, the plague that we now call the Black Death came to England, reaching Devon during the early months of 1349. It was to break out again on subsequent occasions, notably in 1361–2. And besides the plague, and perhaps just as significant, many other infectious diseases reduced the population or hindered its recovery.

The impact of the plague in 1349 was probably patchy rather than uniform, but it undoubtedly had dire effects in certain places. At Bodmin Priory (Cornwall), eleven out of thirteen canons succumbed, and at Newenham Abbey the mortality was even higher: twenty out of twenty-three monks.[2] Even in the relatively secluded parish of Witheridge in mid Devon, the mortality in the outlying township of Templeton was so great that corpses were piled on to a cart and driven to the parish church at night. One body fell from the overloaded vehicle and had to be rescued next day.[3] The ravages of the plague are most clearly charted in the little almshouse of Clyst Gabriel on the road from Exeter to Honiton at Clyst St Mary. This was founded by Bishop Stapledon in 1309–12 to provide a home for twelve poor elderly or infirm priests of the diocese. When they celebrated Christmas Day in 1348, there were eleven of them. Guy de Okampton died on 1 January, Richard Artour on the 2nd, and Thomas de Well on the 6th. Three more died in February, and a further three in March. By the time that Easter came on 12 April, only two of the priests were alive.[4]

We can get a broader, but less definite, sense of the plague's effects on the Church in Devon from the register of John Grandisson, the bishop at that time. During the five years from 1343 to 1347, the number of clergy recorded as being instituted by him to rectories and vicarages in the county ranged from 12 to 27 per annum, with an average of 21. The figure for 1348 was 25, which was not out of scale with the previous years, but in 1349 it leapt tenfold to 238. By April 1349, the clerk who kept the register was inserting the name of each month as a heading to subdivide his entries. Within this grievous year, the bishop instituted 21 clergy in January, 27 in February, 39 in March, 36 in April, 28 in May, 29 in June, 18 in July, 4 in August, 11 in September, 4 in October, 9 in November, and 12 in December.[5] Not all these institutions followed deaths. Some were due to clergy moving from poorer to richer benefices, causing a second vacancy, but there were evidently far more deaths than usual. The deaths can probably be backdated from the institutions by two or three months, because it might take that long for the patron of a benefice to find a new candidate, especially if there was a shortage of clergy.

Making that allowance suggests that most of the deaths of rectors and vicars took place in the early months of the year. How many clergy died in Devon cannot be known, and the extent of the mortality among lay people is still obscure. Nor do we know if the plague brought about a religious revival, or a decline of religion due to despair or scepticism. In general the framework of people's religious lives appears to have continued much as before. Changes indeed took place to that framework during the fourteenth and fifteenth centuries, but they were gradual ones caused by various social and cultural processes of which the plague was but one. Some people gained from population decline. Labourers' wages increased as labour grew scarcer. Others lost, especially the clergy. Income from tithes and offerings fell, while wages and prices rose. Monasteries found it harder to get recruits, and even if they found them, to maintain them in their former numbers. Fewer clergy were willing to do lowly paid jobs as chaplains, chantry priests, or vicars choral, and although such posts continued to exist, they were probably less numerous by 1400 than they had been a century before. Indeed it may be that the flourishing of lay activity in the Church, which we shall study in the next chapter, was partly stimulated by a shortage of clergy.

There were some other notable crises in late-medieval England, but these were of less importance for Devon and its churches. The Peasants' Revolt of May and June 1381, which centred on London, has left little trace in the county although it provoked an attack on Bodmin Priory by some local people. The appearance of religious dissent in England in 1382, in the form of Lollardy, appears to have had less impact on Devon than on some other regions.[6] The Wars of the Roses disrupted English political and social life at intervals between the 1450s and the 1490s, and briefly involved some clergy in 1483 when three of them joined in a rising against Richard III, in protest at his seizure of the throne. They were the bishop (Peter Courtenay), the archdeacon of Exeter (David Hopton), and the abbot of Buckland (Thomas Oliver). Their actions forced them to flee abroad until Henry VII defeated Richard in 1485, after which Courtenay rose high in Henry's favour and was made bishop of Winchester.

The Diocese and the Bishops

Fourteen bishops ruled the diocese of Exeter between 1300 and 1500, five of whom (Stapledon, Grandisson, Brantingham, Stafford, and Lacy) filled almost every year from 1307 until 1455 (Figure 18, p. 73). During this period, the popes claimed the right to appoint or 'provide' all bishops in Catholic Europe, in place of the older method of election by the cathedral canons. They first exercised this right at Exeter in 1326. But the popes were not strong enough in England to make it more than a nominal one. In practice, nearly all appointments of bishops in England continued to be made by the king. He simply proposed a candidate to the pope rather than to the cathedral. Like their predecessors before 1300, the king's nominees were clerics who were already in good standing with him and could be trusted to give him support and do duties for him. Thus, when appointed, Walter Stapledon (1308–26) had been in the king's service, Thomas Brantingham (1370–94) the royal treasurer, Edmund Stafford (1395–1419) the keeper of the privy seal, and Edmund Lacy (1420–55) the dean of the Chapel Royal.

There was a single exception to this rule. In 1326, Stapledon, who was then treasurer of England, was murdered by a mob in London after a rising against Edward II. Edward was duly deprived of the throne in favour of his young son Edward III, and a regency government took power headed by Edward's queen Isabel and Roger Mortimer, earl of March. Isabel and Mortimer managed to arrange the papal provision of a new bishop, James Berkeley, whose family supported them, but when Berkeley died three months later, the pope (John XXII) asserted himself, and the queen and Mortimer felt it advisable to placate him to gain his support. It was the only occasion on which a pope has ever made a free choice of a bishop of Exeter. John nominated one of his chaplains, John Grandisson, who belonged to a knightly family in Herefordshire, and Grandisson duly took office in 1327, enjoying a record-breaking reign of over forty-one years. The corollary of this was that he had no royal links and was a political outsider. He never held an office under the king, which left him free to give his time to his diocese. Most bishops of Exeter had to limit their diocesan work because of their other commitments. Grandisson could give all his attention to the Church and its affairs, in ways not always welcome for either clergy or laity.

As in previous centuries, the bishops spent their lives in moving between the houses on their estates. The Bishop's Palace in Exeter was one of these, but it was by no means the most often used. Others in Devon were Bishop's Nympton, Bishop's Tawton, Chudleigh, Bishop's Clyst, Crediton, Paignton, and Peterhayes in Yarcombe parish. Two others, Faringdon (Hants.) and East Horsley (Surrey), acted as staging posts on the road to London, where the bishop's house was now Exeter Inn, opposite St Clement Danes church in the Strand. Bishops differed as to which houses they favoured. Grandisson liked Chudleigh and hardly left it during his last two decades. Brantingham and Stafford preferred Clyst, and both lived there for most of their final years. The extent of their travels also varied. Stapledon was an assiduous traveller throughout both Devon and Cornwall, whereas later bishops tended to restrict themselves to their residences and to journeys to London. Richard Fox (1487–92) never even came to his diocese, preferring to stay in the capital serving the king, and the same appears to have been true of his successor, Oliver King (1492–5).

The relative decline in bishops' movements reflected a more settled and stable Church. After 1287, no diocesan synods appear to have made legislation; the canon law of the Church and diocese was held to be sufficient and complete. The predictability of Church life meant that the bishop could depute many of his duties to others. Spiritual functions were devolved to a suffragan bishop, who ordained clergy when the diocesan bishop was unavailable, and travelled around the diocese confirming young people and consecrating chapels and churchyards (Figure 19, p. 79). There was no national system of suffragans as there is today. Bishops employed them as they wished and paid them by giving them parish benefices. The earliest recorded in Exeter diocese are two Irish bishops, Thomas of Leighlin in 1275 and Robert Le Petit in 1324.[7] Later bishops employed a series of men, some from Ireland and others appointed by the pope with titles taken from extinct dioceses in or around the Mediterranean Sea like Lydda and Tenos.[8] Administrative matters were assigned to a senior cleric known as the vicar-general and official principal. He presided over the bishop's consistory court which dealt with legal cases under Church law; he could institute clergy to benefices and take any kind of action on the bishop's orders or on his own initiative. In the localities, the archdeacons and rural deans continued to carry out their traditional functions and to execute commands when necessary. Only when very serious matters arose, such as attacks

Figure 18 Roof-boss of a bishop, Exeter Cathedral. Dating from the time of Bishop Grandisson, it depicts a bishop of the period wearing mitre, alb, chasuble, and gloves, holding a staff and delivering a blessing.

on clergy and Church property or cases of heresy, did the bishop need to intervene himself to settle the matter through the power of his office.

This top-down government, however, formed a very small part of religious affairs. It impinged on a normal parish only when a new incumbent had to be appointed, or the archdeacon (or his deputy) made the annual visit of inspection. Most Church life was special to each of the parishes: institutions so important and yet so unregarded that, as we have seen, the Church was slow even to keep accurate records of them. The Taxation of 1291 remained the standard list of churches until 1535, when Henry VIII's government carried a new valuation of religious property, the *Valor Ecclesiasticus*.[9] Comparing the two valuations enables us to gauge the continuities and changes in the parochial system during the fourteenth, fifteenth, and early sixteenth centuries. Henry VIII was in a much stronger position to find out the incomes of clergy than Pope Nicholas IV had been in 1291. The data in the *Valor* is fuller. In 1291, we are merely told that the church of Dunchideock, for example, was worth 10*s*. In 1535, not only was the total value estimated, now £15 4*s*. 8*d*., but it was analysed into its main constituents: rent of the glebe land, tithes of corn, hay, wool, lambs, and Easter offerings, together with the dues that had to be paid to the bishop and the archdeacon.[10]

Even so, it would be unwise to regard the *Valor* as wholly correct. Its values were probably a little underestimated, and it does not contain a full account of every Devon church, any more than the Taxation of 1291. Certain churches whose revenues were appropriated to monasteries appear under the heading of the monasteries, rather than being listed with the rest of the churches under the rural deaneries. Thus Plympton and Sutton (St Andrew, Plymouth) are listed among the possessions of Plympton Priory, and Mariansleigh is simply alluded to under its owner, Barlinch Priory, in the section of the *Valor* relating to the diocese of Bath and Wells.[11] There are also one or two omissions. One is Abbot's Bickington, a church belonging to Hartland Abbey, which was probably being served (to save money) by a hired chaplain. Another, inevitably, was Lundy, which had a tiny population by this time and could not support a full-time priest.

Comparing the surveys of 1291 and 1535 reveals that there was very little change in the administrative structure of the diocese between these dates. The archdeaconries, rural deaneries, and peculiars remained unaltered. A few new parishes were created and a few old ones were united, but the numbers involved were so small that we may consider them individually. Two adjoining churches, Knowstone and Molland, shared a rector from at least 1310, although the churches remained in being with separate parishes.[12] The little church of St James (Exeter) was united with its neighbour Holy Trinity after the Black Death, and its rural counterpart at Affeton in mid Devon was joined with West Worlington between 1439 and about

1455. In these two cases, the parishes were amalgamated and one set of church buildings abandoned. A further church, Oldridge in Whitestone, ceased to be independent at an unrecorded date, and its parish became an outlier of St Thomas (Exeter).[13]

In view of the fall in the population during the fourteenth century, it may seem surprising that so few churches disappeared. Affeton, St James, and Oldridge were all reckoned as poor churches in 1291, but others such as Clannaborough and Satterleigh survived along with their parishes. The deciding factor in church closures was not any kind of diocesan planning but the attitude of the person or body possessing the patronage of the church. The patronage of Affeton and West Worlington belonged to the Stucley family, that of St James and Holy Trinity to Exeter Cathedral, and that of Oldridge and St Thomas to Cowick Priory. These patrons evidently felt it more in their interest to have a larger united parish, with a bigger income for the clergyman. Patrons who owned but one poor church in a neighbourhood preferred to keep it in being so that they could go on choosing a clergyman, even with a small stipend. In Exeter, where there were several poor churches, another solution was possible: appointing vicars choral of the cathedral. These men could run the city churches in tandem with their duties in the choir, and gain a small additional income for doing so.

The number of new churches and parishes formed between 1291 and 1535 was not much greater than those that disappeared. About ten chapels that had previously been under the control of a parish church and its patron and clergyman managed to achieve independence. Ashford, Haccombe, and Shillingford, which had been moving in this direction in 1291, completed the transition. They were joined by Broad Nymet, Jacobstow, and Nymet Rowland in the early fourteenth century; by Calverleigh later in that century; and by Templeton, Welcombe, and Woolfardisworthy West in the early sixteenth century. In addition, Netherexe, originally a chapel of Brampford Speke, gained virtual freedom at some unknown date.[14] Other chapels had supporters who wanted to make them into parish churches, but this process was strongly resisted by the patrons, clergy, and congregations of the mother churches to which they belonged. This explains why so few attempts to secede were successful. It was crucial to gain the consent of the authorities at the mother church, and Welcombe and Woolfardisworthy West were able to succeed because they belonged to Hartland Abbey which also owned their mother church of Hartland. The abbey lost nothing by giving them separate status. One may be sure that the other new parish churches mentioned above were the result of private negotiations and probably the payment of compensation to the patron and clergyman of the mother church.

Monasteries and Nunneries

The twelfth and thirteenth centuries had been the great era of monasteries, with new foundations, acquisitions of lands and churches, and many recruits. In contrast after 1300, the monastic sector of the Church ceased to advance and, in some respects, went into retreat. The last house of monks to be founded in Devon was Buckland Abbey in 1278 and that of nuns Canonsleigh Abbey, which changed from a male to a female community in 1285. By 1300, it was becoming too expensive to found and endow a monastery with lands and churches, and the monastic life was losing something of its reputation. Religious houses continued to be established after 1300, but they took a different form, that of collegiate churches, which we shall examine presently.

The major abbeys and priories that existed in 1300 were strong enough in their endowments and their ability to recruit novices to survive until the 1530s. They numbered four Benedictine houses (St Nicholas (Exeter), Pilton, Tavistock, and Totnes), one Cluniac (Barnstaple), five Cistercian (Buckfast, Buckland, Dunkeswell, Forde, and Newenham), three Augustinian (Frithelstock, Hartland, and Plympton), one Premonstratensian (Torre), and three nunneries (Canonsleigh, Cornworthy, and Polsloe). Along with these must be counted three lesser establishments which survived as cells or dependencies of larger houses: Cowick, which came to belong to Tavistock; Kerswell, a possession of Montacute Priory (Somt.); and St Mary Marsh, an outlier of Plympton. On the other hand, seven small houses ceased to exist between the late fourteenth and the early sixteenth centuries. Three of these were victims of the economic changes after the Black Death, which left them too poor to survive. The Order of St John closed the preceptory of Bodmiscombe and transferred the property to its house at Minchin Buckland (Somt.). The Trinitarian houses at Crediton and Warland (Totnes) were shut down by Bishops Stafford and Arundell respectively in 1410 and 1503, presumably on the grounds of their ineffectiveness. The Trinitarian Order tried to dispute the closure of Warland but it was not strong enough to obstruct the bishop.[15]

The other four houses belonged to French monasteries, and the main factor in their disappearance was the Hundred Years War. The English crown and the governing classes were more conscious of their Englishness by 1300 than they had been in the twelfth century. They now saw the French monasteries as part of a different kingdom and their English cells as 'alien priories', meaning foreign ones. Such cells were, to a large extent, still staffed by monks from France. The Hundred Years War aggravated this situation. The king and Parliament in England objected to revenues going from the alien priories to their mother houses, where the money might be taxed by the French kings and used to finance their armies. So from 1294 onwards, whenever there was war, the English kings took control of alien priories in England. The priories were not closed down, but they were allowed to keep only sufficient income to support their members and the surplus was seized by the crown. During the fourteenth century, the periods of control grew longer and the control more stringent. It grew difficult for the French mother houses to appoint monks to staff the priories, and eventually in 1378 Parliament ordered that foreign monks should leave the country unless they were priors in charge of a house. This left the priories with only one person to serve them, unless they could persuade the king to allow them to import new monks. Their revenues were now often in the hands of the crown, or those of favoured laymen to whom the crown had leased them.[16]

There was a way to escape these restraints. An alien priory could break its links with its French mother house and apply to the crown to be granted 'denizen' status. The house then became independent and its monks Englishmen. During the early years of the fifteenth century, this status was acquired by Barnstaple and Totnes, as well as by Montacute which enabled the survival of its cell at Kerswell. The rest of the alien priories fell victim to an act of Parliament in 1414 that dissolved them and gave their properties to the crown. This led to the disappearance of St James (Exeter), Ipplepen, and Otterton, although their properties remained in clerical hands, mostly passing to Henry V's foundation of Syon Abbey (Middx.) and Henry VI's of King's College (Cambridge). Cowick and Modbury limped on for much of the fifteenth century. The Cowick community did not leave until 1451, after which the priory's possessions were awarded to Eton College (Bucks.), but this award was short-lived and in 1462 they were transferred to Tavistock Abbey, which resurrected Cowick as an English daughter house.[17] Modbury lingered until about 1466 under a French prior and a single French companion, partly through the support of local people. They held their lands from the priory, were used to dealing with its monks, and did not relish a change of ownership. Only when the last prior died did Modbury cease to be a priory and pass into the hands of Eton.[18]

The reduction in the number of monasteries was paralleled by a fall in that of the clergy who staffed them. Here, for convenience, we shall consider all the religious houses in Devon, as we did in the previous chapter.[19] In the late fourteenth century after the Black Death, there may have been about 82 clergy in the cathedral and the collegiate churches (including Crediton), 53 Benedictine and Cluniac monks, 51 Cistercians, 55 regular canons, 80 friars, 34 nuns, and half a dozen Trinitarians and Hospitallers: say 360. This represented a substantial fall from the 550 of the late thirteenth century. During the fifteenth century, recruitment improved at some of the larger monasteries: Tavistock, Torre, and the Cistercian houses, but this was offset by the loss of the alien priories. By the early 1500s, the figures may have been 87 in the cathedral and collegiate churches, 47 Benedictine and Cluniac monks, 59 Cistercians, 56 regular canons, 80 friars, and 39 nuns, making a total of 368, say 380. Thus the general number of clergy did not change very much, but at a local level there were some substantial variations. Hartland and Torre each had 11 canons in the late fourteenth century, but by the early sixteenth Hartland's complement had fallen to 6 while Torre's had risen to 18.

The most vivid glimpses of English monasteries of the later Middle Ages are to be found in the records of those who visited them officially: bishops and heads of religious orders. The issues that these visitations raised are well illustrated in Devon from those relating to Tavistock, its wealthiest abbey. In 1345, Grandisson sent commissioners to Tavistock whose reports formed the basis for injunctions that he afterwards sent to the monks. He was disturbed, he said, by the charges reported to him. The monks had abandoned their monastic dress and were wearing clothes like parish clergy with sleeves, buttons, and improper shoes. Three monks were especially at fault. The abbot, contrary to the bishop's warnings, kept company with secular people by day and by night; this must cease and the abbot must choose a respectable monk to sleep in his chamber and say the services with him there. The abbot, the prior, and Brother Thomas Coffyn were keeping hunting dogs at the cost of the abbey; these must be expelled and Coffyn confined to the monastic cloister. Three servants of the abbey were suspected of embezzling large sums of money from the estates; they were to produce their accounts before two of the monks elected by their brethren. The abbey was to enforce these measures within a fortnight of receiving the bishop's commands.[20]

Brantingham delivered injunctions in 1388. He began by warning the abbey to observe the statutory round of services, silences, and fasts. Dress should avoid such secular embellishments as buttoned hoods, tapering boots, and linen shirts. Monks other than those with official duties were not to leave the monastery without permission, and when they did they were not to talk to women, especially those of dubious reputation, or go to meals or drinkings. Women employed as laundresses or for other purposes should not have access to the monastic quarters. All the monks were to eat together in the refectory, listening to the reading of the scriptures, and not in their own private rooms. The abbot should set an example by eating with them, at least on fish-eating days, and by sleeping in their dormitory. The room called the treasury was to be secured with three locks for the safety of the abbey seal and archives. All the abbey officials were to present their financial accounts before the rest of the monks.

The bishop stipulated that the novices and young monks should be given at least one tutor to teach them the services and the rules of the order. All the monks should spend their spare time reading the monastic rule and other books in the cloister. Drinking at undue times, especially after compline in the evening, was to cease unless it was sanctioned by the abbot. Repairs should be carried out to the dormitory, refectory, and cloister, and the bell-tower of the church should be completed. The

Figure 19 Confirmation. A major duty of bishops was to confirm the baptisms of all Christians, a task often deputed to suffragan bishops in the later Middle Ages. Confirmation could be done at any age, and is here being given to babies.

doors of the monastic area were to be shut and locked at due times, and surplus bread, ale, meat, and fish were not to be sold as they had been, but to be given away by the almoner. Old clothes should be given to the poor. The abbey servants were to be kept in order, and not allowed to foment discord within the community; they too should be prevented from taking food or drink out of the monastery.[21]

In 1438, it was the turn of Lacy to intervene. He or his deputies had collected a list of serious charges against the abbot, apparently based in part on rumours and information submitted by people of the neighbourhood or from the abbey itself. The abbot had squandered the abbey's goods and appropriated money that did not belong to him. He had committed fornication or adultery with five named women, including his laundress, and incest with his sister. His attendance in church and in the chapter house was irregular, and he was often so drunk that he could neither speak nor stand. In such a state, he would swear at the monks, threaten to kill them, and actually strike them. He had imprisoned the prior on a diet of bread and water for opposing him. He had refused to present the annual accounts to the community, and had granted leases of the abbey's lands to his family and other people without the consent of the monks. The bishop instituted legal proceedings against the abbot, and sent commissioners to investigate the charges. The sexual allegations seem to have lacked foundation because they were no longer mentioned. The abbot rebutted the other charges, claiming that he had acted for the good of the monastery, and was able to exonerate himself with the support of his brethren. He submitted himself to the bishop, and the bishop issued a further set of injunctions for the abbey.

These covered similar ground to Brantingham's. The daily services and other observances were to be properly carried out. The abbot was to avoid excessive eating and drinking, and to attend the services regularly. No monk should go outside the abbey precincts without permission, except for those with official duties, and the abbot was to abstain from all contact with women, especially those of poor reputation. Women were not to enter the cloister area, and its doors were to be kept locked. The business of the house must be better conducted. It should take place before all the monks in the chapter house in the late morning, before midday dinner. The seal of the abbey should be kept under lock and key, and be applied to documents only with the consent of the community and in its presence, or at least with the consent of the majority. No pensions or corrodies (permissions to retire to live in the abbey precincts) were to be granted without unanimous agreement. Records should be kept of the money that passed from the abbey's officers to the abbot, and he and they were to present detailed accounts to the rest of the brethren. The abbot and monks subsequently wrote to the bishop protesting that they had been defamed and were truly of good reputation, but assuring him that they would abide by his orders.[22]

Accusations and injunctions of this kind were not unique to Tavistock. They are found all over England from the fourteenth century to the Reformation. Accusations sometimes came from feuds within the community or enemies outside it, and not all could be substantiated. Injunctions represent a truer assessment of things. They point to the tension between a monastery's ties with the world and its attempt to withdraw from the world. The values of the world dictated that abbots and priors should live in style to demonstrate the importance of the house and defend its interests. Important people expected to stay and be entertained, and the hunting dogs may have been kept for this purpose. The abbey's business in the world required its officers to travel outside their walls. Gradual improvements in the standard of living led monks, like other people, to desire better food, clothes, warmth, and accommodation. It was often difficult to reconcile these things with the monastic Rules which had been formulated hundreds of years before. The Rules prescribed an unvarying life of prayer and study, and in practice it was hard for monks to sustain this life with enthusiasm year after year.

The very recruitment of monks was done in a different way from how a modern organisation would gather its staff, or even a modern monastery. Each house admitted a group of novices every few years, and took whoever was available at that time. Links with the monastery through land-holding or family relationships were probably important factors in choosing candidates. Even today, an appointing board cannot know how a young recruit will behave after ten or twenty years, and that was the case in the past. In 1492, when the archbishop of Canterbury sent officers to visit the houses of Devon, they were told of three unsatisfactory monks and one nun. St Nicholas Priory had received a man who had been ejected from Brecon Priory for insolence and who was now accused of damaging property, threatening the brethren, and annoying the servants. Plympton had lost a canon who was wandering on the borders of Wales and had been excommunicated. A monk of Totnes had stolen goods, robes, and even the priory seal with which he had granted himself a pension of £4 for life. He was now in the prison of the bishop of Bath and Wells. The nun, from Canonsleigh, was described as shameless and disobedient; she confessed the disobedience but said that she had done her punishment. Still, these were only four cases out of about 90 monks and nuns surveyed in the visitation. The vast majority, if not always godly or learned, were at least not criminals.[23]

A visitation of almost any organisation, even today, is likely to reveal lapses in procedures and failures to address certain problems. Visitation records need to be judged alongside other evidence of monastic life. Unfortunately the chief activity of monks, the daily services, is almost wholly unrecorded except when its details were criticised at the visitations, yet it went on every day. It also evolved, in that polyphonic music increased in popularity in the fifteenth century. Cathedrals and colleges developed choirs of boy and adult singers in their Lady chapels, and this was imitated in monasteries. Buckland, Forde, and Tavistock had such choirs by the eve of the Reformation, and probably other houses of their size.[24] From the thirteenth century onwards, monasteries often supported a number of 'almonry boys' who lived in their outer precincts and received board, lodging, and education in grammar, in return for some small duties in the church.[25] Originally the boys were chosen mainly from monks' relatives or friends of the monastery, but the popularity of polyphony led to some of them being selected for the quality of their voices. They were then used in the Lady chapel choirs, singing a morning mass in honour of the Virgin Mary and an antiphon in her praise every afternoon. No Devon monastery, however, is known to have maintained a school for the general public, as is sometimes found elsewhere in England.

The education of monks themselves improved. Originally, they had concentrated on learning the daily services and the monastic Rule. In the mid fourteenth century, the papacy laid down that all monasteries should have a lecturer in grammar, logic, and philosophy who could be a monk or an outsider. Monks who prospered in these studies should be sent to university, and university colleges for Benedictines were established at Oxford, followed somewhat later by ones for Cistercians and Augustinian canons.[26] Monks who went to university studied theology or canon law, the courses for which lasted for several years. The cost of maintaining the students was considerable, and only a few from Devon would have been sent, but the practice went on. One Cistercian, William Slade (died 1415), not only studied at Oxford but wrote tracts on ethics and theology, before becoming abbot of Buckfast.[27]

At home, the monasteries collected books. John Leland, who toured the monasteries just after their closure in 1542, noted five significant titles at Tavistock, six at Plympton, nine at Forde, and eighteen at Buckfast.[28] Administration was generally taken seriously. Charters of land were transcribed into cartularies for easy reference, and registers of business were kept.[29] Financial accounts would have been compiled by bailiffs of estates and the monastery's chief officers, feeding into a general account for the monastery itself. At least some attention would have been given to improving land, encouraging trade, and renting out property to good advantage, although the wish to please powerful local people and favour kinsmen was also a motive in these matters.

The larger houses were the most sophisticated in these respects, but attention has recently been drawn to the religious and cultural activities of small ones with as few as two to five clergy.[30] The brothers of the little preceptory of the Order of St John at Bodmiscombe raised £30 a year for crusades from well-wishers in Devon in the 1330s, and had formerly gathered more.[31] The priory of Cowick (Exeter) had two claims to fame. It was a mausoleum for the early members of the Courtenay family, earls of Devon, who were the patrons of the house and stayed there from time to time. It also boasted its own saint, Walter of Cowick, a monk of the priory in about the twelfth century who made a supernatural journey to purgatory. After Tavistock governed the house in 1462, attempts were made to draw pilgrims to his shrine.[32] The hospital of St John (Exeter) had a tiny staff of Augustinian canons, yet there are five surviving manuscripts from its book collection. Not only do they include sermons, chronicles, and a collection of medical works, but three of them have catalogue numbers which suggest that the original number of books was much larger.[33] Finally, Kerswell had a notable prior from 1514 until about 1532 in Thomas Chard, who was made bishop of Solubria by the pope and acted as suffragan bishop in the dioceses of Bath and Wells and Exeter.[34]

The three Devon nunneries continued in their restricted and largely unobtrusive way of life during the later Middle Ages. Their recruits, as far as we can tell, came not only from Devon but from Cornwall, Dorset, and Somerset, and tended to be women of some wealth and status. Heads of houses are recorded from the gentry families of Arundell, Beauchamp, Bloyou, and Dinham.[35] In January 1320, Stapledon issued injunctions to Canonsleigh and Polsloe which give a general sense of how nuns were expected to live.[36] The convent day centred on the saying of the daily services in Latin but the women were not required to have a full understanding of the language. The bishop's injunctions were written in French, and he told the nuns that when they needed to ask one another for things in church, they should use simple Latin words such as *candela, liber,* and *vinum* without regard to grammatical rules. They were required to seclude themselves from outsiders as much as possible. Two doors at Canonsleigh were to be closed, having given rise to suspicions about unlawful comings and goings, and the number of female servants at Polsloe was to be reduced. No nun might leave the house except with the permission of its head, and only in the company of a colleague, chosen by the head of the house not the nun. If a nun gained leave of absence on another occasion, a different colleague should be assigned to go with her.

Nevertheless, nuns like monks needed to have contacts with the outside world. Property had to be managed through men, and accounts of income and expenses drawn up. Nuns (escorted as above) could visit their families for a month each year, and those of Polsloe could go into Exeter (perhaps on convent business) and even stay overnight, as long as they had a priest or servant to chaperone them. Secular ladies could stay in nunneries, again for up to a month, and longer stays were allowed if the bishop gave permission. In 1333 Grandisson allowed Alice, the wife of John Damarel, to stay at Cornworthy for nine months.[37] The fact that nuns did not learn Latin to a higher level than was necessary for saying the services meant that they did not study the language like monks, but they had religious and edifying

Figure 20 Ottery St Mary parish church. The church and other property was bought by Bishop Grandisson from Rouen Cathedral and turned into a large collegiate church with impressive buildings in 1337.

books in French and English for their relaxation. Canonsleigh owned a copy of the *Ancrene Rule*, the famous English guide for anchoresses, and Polsloe was given a book of the deeds of Charlemagne, very likely in French.[38] All the nunneries may have taken in rich people's children to board and be taught to read, although the only recorded example is at Cornworthy, where two daughters of a gentleman, aged seven and ten, stayed for over five years in the 1450s or 60s. Their bills were never paid and the prioress was forced to appeal to the chancellor of England for redress.[39]

Friars

The three Devon friaries of the thirteenth century, the Dominicans and Franciscans in Exeter and the Carmelites in Plymouth, were joined by a fourth in 1383: the Franciscan house at Plymouth. As we have seen, friars provoked controversy through claiming exemption from the bishop's authority, criticising the reliance of other clergy on property, and competing for pastoral work. One such occasion was in 1301, when the Exeter Dominicans tried to hold the funeral of a knight, Sir Henry de Ralegh, who had died in their friary. The canons of the cathedral insisted on their own rights in the matter, removed the body by force for the purpose, and stirred up a quarrel that lasted for several years.[40] Another row followed the foundation of the Franciscan friary in Plymouth, which took place without consulting the bishop or the redoubtable vicar of St Andrew's, Michael Cergeaux. Cergeaux appealed to the pope. He gained an order stopping the building of the friary church, and the bishop, Brantingham, forbade the use of the church. But the friars and their Plymouth supporters ignored the judgment, and the next vicar had to take the case to the pope again. In the end, the friars prevailed, but at the cost of annoying their fellow clergy.[41]

For the most part, however, the friaries played more constructive parts in local life. They recruited members from Devon (we encounter surnames such as Barnstaple and Champernown) and also from Cornwall. Some of these recruits were boys in their early teens, and the friars were sometimes accused of stealing or hoodwinking those too young to have a religious vocation. In 1411, the pope asked the bishop of Exeter to investigate a complaint by Henry Witberi that his father had placed him with the Exeter Franciscans when he was only in his eleventh year, with the intention, so Henry claimed, of disinheriting him.[42] On the other hand, friars took seriously the education of their members. All the houses would have owned scholarly books, although only a few are recorded.[43] Youths were taught Latin if necessary, and a friar in each house acted as lecturer in philosophy and basic theology. The Franciscan house in Exeter acquired a further distinction in 1337 when it was made the study centre for friars of the order in the west of England.[44] All friars were expected to learn basic theology to a higher level than that of most monks and parish clergy, and their best recruits were sent to Oxford and Cambridge, where they lived in the friaries there.

The result was to produce a scattering of friars from the Devon houses at university and of university graduates in the Devon houses. Among the Exeter Franciscans, we find John de Whatele, 'master' (i.e. doctor) of theology in 1320, and John de Preston, an Oxford doctor of theology, licensed as a confessor in Exeter diocese in 1330. A third academic friar of this period was John Welles, who may have been born in Exeter and studied in the Franciscan houses there and at London and Oxford, taking the degree of doctor of theology in 1368.[45] In the case of the Dominicans, we may be able to count Richard de Winkley (fl. 1331–43) as a Devonian in view of his surname. He was a doctor of theology by 1331 when his superiors sent him to Italy to lecture at the friary at Bologna, and Grandisson gave him a letter of recommendation to the pope. He later became the provincial prior of his order in England and a confessor to Edward III. David Carnu from Cornwall was at the Exeter friary in 1426–8 before going on to study at Oxford, where he was awarded the degree of doctor of theology and remained for some years.[46] At the same time, friars moved into Devon from elsewhere in England and even from overseas. We hear of Irish and German recruits at the Dominican and Franciscan houses during the early fifteenth century.[47]

The emphasis on study reflected the work done by friars in preaching, hearing confessions, and offering spiritual counsel: work that needed a higher standard of learning. Their expertise in these matters led to their employment by bishops and the cathedral as preachers and confessors. The friars of Exeter were often invited to preach at the cathedral where sermons took place on the Sundays of Advent and Lent. At Michaelmas 1389, for example, the cathedral exchequer paid 17*s.* to the two local houses for preaching by their members on fourteen occasions during the previous year.[48] Friars could preach in parish churches with the permission of the clergyman, and their visits to Colyton were remembered appreciatively in 1301.[49] The nobility and gentry liked their sermons too. In 1524, the steward of Katharine Courtenay, countess of Devon, gave 6*s.* 8*d.* to the Dominican prior of Exeter for preaching before her in her private chapel at Columbjohn in Broadclyst parish.[50]

Confession was another regular activity. In 1300, following complaints from the parish clergy that it undermined their powers, bishops were authorised to license friars for the purpose, and the working of the system can be illustrated in relation to the Dominicans of Exeter. In 1330, Grandisson appointed Prior Hugh and William Bugaleys as penitentiaries with authority to hear and absolve sins normally reserved to the bishop. In 1342, he granted licences to John de Burgo and ten of his brethren to hear confessions throughout Exeter diocese in 1342, provided that they respected the rights of the parish clergy.[51] In 1377, Brantingham licensed Prior John Laurence to absolve sins in reserved cases, although in 1380, after a dispute with the Dominicans, he limited their licences to one friar for each archdeaconry.[52] People of status often employed a friar as their personal confessor. Quinil is said to have chosen Peter Kenefeld for this role in about 1290, and in 1320, Stapledon appointed a Dominican and a Franciscan to do the same for the nuns of Polsloe.[53]

Some contemporaries, such as the writer of the famous late fourteenth-century poem *Piers Plowman*, accused friars of cultivating the rich rather than the poor. This charge cannot be verified, because the written sources about the friars' relationships with the public relate almost wholly to the wealthy. Here they certainly forged strong links. In 1352, for example, the Dominicans called on the help of the Black Prince after certain men of Exeter had caused them unspecified injuries. The prince wrote to the mayor and citizens, asking them to redress any wrongs done and to let the friars enjoy their rights.[54] From at least 1305, their house included a suite of rooms for the use of the earl of Devon when he was visiting Exeter.[55] Although friars were chary of acquiring property and the Franciscans even tried to avoid handling coins, they often allowed the rich to deposit money or documents in their houses as safe places. In 1538, the Dominicans had in their friary 346 ounces of plate (precious metal) left as pledges, and over thirty documents.[56]

Another sign of the friars' links with the wealthy was the burial of such people in their churches. The Exeter Dominicans gave resting places to knights and gentry such as Sir Henry Pomeroy (died 1281), Oliver Dinham (1299) and his wife Isabel (1300), Sir William and Lady Eleanor Martyn (before 1329), Sir John Dinham (1458) and his wife Jane (1497), and Thomas and Elizabeth Calwoodleigh (before 1480). When their church was excavated in the early 2000s, it was found to be packed with graves whose occupants would have included Richard Seler, a mayor of Exeter (1344), and John Colshill, a merchant (1518), as well as Colshill's brother Peter who had died earlier. The Exeter Franciscans were not so successful in attracting the aristocracy, although their church housed the tombs of Lady Katherine Arundell (1479) and Lady Katherine Huddesfeld (1499). But they gave burial to a number of prosperous Exeter citizens and their wives including William Wynard, the founder of Wynard's Almshouse (1442), and John Taylour (*c*.1500), whose gravestone still survives with an inscription naming him as a tin merchant.[57]

Such links spread further: among the clergy, among the middling laity of Exeter, and out into countryside where friars went on pastoral and preaching tours. Wills provide a good deal of evidence on the subject. At least three bishops of Exeter gave bequests to the friaries in the diocese: Bitton, Grandisson, and Brantingham.[58] It was common for the citizens of Exeter to leave small sums of money to each of the city friaries, and cathedral canons sometimes gave the bread allowances to which they were entitled for a year after their death.[59] The geographical range of the friars' contacts can be seen in Devon by legacies to them from people such as a rector of Churchstow, a vicar of Honiton, and Sir John Speke (a landowner in mid Devon).[60] In Cornwall, there were similar gifts to the Plymouth houses by a gentleman of Calstock, a farmer of St Cleer, a merchant of St Columb Major, a justice of Callington, and the lord of a manor in Goran, among others.[61] But people did not delay supporting the friars until the end of their lives. Each friary would have had a confraternity or 'league of friends', to which living people made donations and had their names recorded in a register to be prayed for.[62]

This leaves unresolved how far the friars worked among the poor. Here, there are two intriguing references, suggesting that the Dominicans and Franciscans ministered to the criminals in Exeter gaol. Not only that; some appear to have become so close to the prisoners that they helped them to escape from custody. In 1351, King Edward III issued pardons to four Franciscans accused of aiding in the rescue of three men who were being taken for execution at Heavitree outside the city. The friars must have been involved in the affair, since they had to agree to stand trial if anyone witnessed against them, and their superiors were ordered to punish them with imprisonment. A generation later it was the turn of the

Dominicans to be implicated. In 1383, Richard II ordered a friar named John Lambreston and two other men to be sent from confinement in Exeter to the Tower of London along with a recaptured offender whom they had allegedly freed from prison in Exeter.[63]

Pastoral services and the quest for donations brought friars close to many people, both clergy and laity, and this closeness must have led to a good deal of social and cultural intercourse. Some records of this survive about the Exeter Dominicans. The sixteenth-century bibliographer John Bale mentions a copy of the romance of Guy of Warwick which Walter of Exeter, a Dominican friar, had written or copied in 1301 at the instance of Baldwin de Windesor, a citizen of Exeter.[64] The romance was probably in French and was a literary rather than a religious work, although its crusading hero ends his life as a hermit. In 1408–9, we hear of the city spending 5s. on seven gallons of wine and four loaves when the mayor 'and his fellows' visited the priory 'at the time of the play there': very likely a religious drama.[65] A third such instance relates to the visit of the historian William Worcester to Exeter in September 1478, while returning to Norwich from a pilgrimage to St Michael's Mount. He met Friar John Burges at the friary or elsewhere, and they talked about Worcester's interest in local saint cults. Burges told him about Exeter's two saints, Sidwell and Walter of Cowick, as well as Wulfric of Haselbury (Somt.) and Branwalader of Milton Abbey (Dorset).[66]

Minsters and Colleges

The outstanding religious house in Devon after 1300 continued to be the cathedral, as it had been since its origin. Indeed it reached the peak of its medieval prosperity at the end of the thirteenth and the beginning of the fourteenth centuries. So wealthy were the bishop and the cathedral clergy at this time that they set out to remodel the building on a larger and grander scale. One of their motives was to modernise what had become an antiquated Romanesque building, overtaken by the Gothic style of Salisbury. Another was to provide a greater space for services. There were now more clergy than there had been when William Warelwast started his rebuilding in the 1110s, necessitating a larger choir to accommodate them and more chapels in which to say mass.[67]

The rebuilding began in the 1270s, probably on the initiative of Bishop Bronescombe, and was completed in about the 1340s. It produced a magnificent building in the Decorated style, more up-to-date even than Salisbury. The costs were met by the bishops (Stapledon was particularly generous), by the cathedral canons who gave part of their stipends, and by lay people through individual donations. Bishops issued indulgences for anyone who contributed, and hundreds of copies of these were made by hand for sending to churches throughout the diocese. The cathedral was completed just before the onset of the Black Death: fortunately so, because the wealth of the foundation went into decline. The number of clergy fell for a time during the mid and later fourteenth century, due to the smaller population and to rising wages and prices. Clergy numbers began to recover in about the 1370s, however, and the foundation enjoyed a reasonable level of prosperity during the fifteenth century. More resources were allocated to increase its income, especially from parish tithes; new chantries were founded in the building; and a four-sided cloister was erected on the south side of the nave.

The cathedral was well enough resourced and sufficiently under the bishop's eye to maintain high standards in its worship, administration, and public roles. Crediton, the other ancient minster, was less successful in this respect. It lacked a leader, having only a precentor and treasurer to manage its music and care for its equipment, and most of its eighteen canons did not reside. Their duties were carried out by vicars choral, as at the cathedral, but the Crediton vicars were less well paid. Several bishops attempted to make reforms with little result, the most effective being two sets of statutes issued by Grandisson in 1334 and 1361. He insisted that the precentor and treasurer should always reside, and promoted one of the vicars choral to be 'dean' of the college: acting as the clergyman in charge of the parish and as rural dean of its peculiar. He improved the stipends of the dean and the other vicars, and ordered them to live in a common building. Even so, Crediton continued down to the Reformation as an old-fashioned minster, most of whose nominal clergy were never there.[68]

It was the more old-fashioned because there was a revival of interest after 1300 in churches of the minster type, staffed not by monks or regular canons but by secular clergy able to live and work in the everyday world. This revival came about for at least two reasons. First, the world was no longer regarded as so subversive of religious life as it had been in the twelfth century: a change of view partly due to the success of the friars in working among the people. Second, as has been mentioned, the cost of building and endowing a monastery had grown too high. Accordingly, wealthy benefactors who wished to found religious houses turned to a new kind of template: the college or collegiate church. 'College' originally meant a 'collection' of clergy without implying academic functions. It has acquired the latter meaning because nearly every college was suppressed at the Reformation, apart from those that were based in the universities and gave part of their time to scholarly work. The clergy of a college were similar to parish clergy and did not take monastic vows. They differed from minster clergy in being more strictly regulated. Their founders usually gave them codes of statutes defining their organisation, worship, stipends, and daily life. Stipends were measured more rationally, with clergy of each grade getting similar sums, and residence was usually essential to qualify for payment.

Figure 21 St Mary Magdalene chapel, Taddiport in Little Torrington. In the fourteenth century, the chapel served a leper hospital; later, the hospital became an almshouse and the chapel survived in use for occasional public worship.

The earliest college to be founded in Exeter diocese, and one of the earliest in England, was Glasney College at Penryn (Cornwall), created by Bronescombe in 1265.[69] The next, in a sense, was Exeter College (Oxford), established in 1312–14 by Stapledon to maintain twelve clerks and a chaplain from the diocese, studying at university.[70] Stapledon also planned to endow twelve scholarships for boys learning grammar in Exeter, although his plans were not realised till after his death,[71] and it is arguable that he conceived the first double foundation in England of a school endowment and a college, anticipating William Wykeham's creation of Winchester College and New College (Oxford) by some sixty years.[72] Admittedly, the numbers he provided for were much smaller than Wykeham's, and since the places had to be shared out across Devon and Cornwall, it would not have been easy to gain one. However, Exeter College was large enough to take in other students who could pay their own way and it owned Hart Hall, now Hertford College (Oxford), which became a hall of residence for west-country men of a similar kind.[73] Altogether, three or four dozen students could be accommodated at Oxford in places where they would find colleagues from their own part of the country.

The early fourteenth century, when Stapledon founded his college, was a time when the population was large, clergy plentiful, and clergy wages low. This enabled some patrons of parish churches to turn them into small non-academic colleges with the rector as 'archpriest' in charge of a group of four or five chaplains. In Devon, Bere Ferrers (1328), Haccombe (*c*.1341), and an abortive foundation at Whitchurch (1322) fell into this category, with Slapton (1370–3) as a similar later example.[74] Ottery St Mary, founded by Grandisson in 1337, was a more ambitious project: a smaller version of the cathedral in its constitution and layout (Figure 20, p. 84), with a staff of some forty canons, priests, and clerks.[75] The last college to be founded in Devon was that of the vicars choral of the cathedral. They had long existed as a group of individuals, but in 1382–7 Brantingham built them their own residential premises, and in 1401 they gained recognition as a legal body in their own right. A code of statutes for their government was drawn up four years later.[76]

The college of Bere Ferrers did not survive the period of the Black Death when clergy became fewer and stipends rose. Haccombe and Slapton remained small institutions of merely local importance. That left Ottery as the only significant college in Devon, with which we may group the cathedral and Crediton as having much in common in terms of their personnel and activities. The main work of minster and college clergy was the performance of the eight daily services as well as the celebration of masses for the dead, especially for the founder. The daily services were sung to plainsong, but during the fifteenth century, it became fashionable to stage polyphonic music as in the monasteries: a daily mass in honour of the Virgin Mary in the Lady chapel and an afternoon anthem in her honour. Choristers were used to extend the range of voices in the polyphony, and expert musicians were hired to organise the music and to write masses and anthems for performance.[77]

The recruitment of choristers meant that they had to be taught to read and sing in a song school, and colleges sometimes extended their involvement in education to providing a grammar school for the public. Exeter Cathedral was loosely associated with the High School in the city from early times, but Ottery had a schoolmaster from its foundation in 1337 and Crediton probably acquired one by the 1540s. The cathedral owned a large number of books which, by the early fifteenth century, were housed in the north walk of the cloisters, and Ottery came to possess a book room which is mentioned in the will of John Exeter, canon of the college, in 1445. He bequeathed 'all my books, thirty-six in number, which I have written for the most part with my own hand to be chained together in the library of Ottery.'[78] Crediton, too, acquired a collection of books.[79]

Cathedrals and colleges can therefore be regarded as centres of literary culture, which included graduate clergy, teachers, and learners, but the Devon colleges have little to show in terms of original writings. Apart from a short Latin chronicle produced at the cathedral, the chief authors worth mentioning are Grandisson and Alexander Barclay. Grandisson composed a Latin Life of Thomas Becket, and may have been responsible for the surviving Life of St Sidwell.[80] Barclay was briefly teacher of music at Ottery in 1508–9, where he translated into English Sebastian Brandt's satirical work, *The Ship of Fools*, and added to it mocking remarks about his colleagues and local people. Wisely, he left for a career elsewhere in England before it was published.[81]

Hospitals, Hermits, and Anchorites

Hospitals did not share in the prosperity of colleges during the fourteenth and fifteenth centuries.[82] Like most religious houses, they suffered from falling revenues and rising costs after the Black Death, and social changes were in progress that made them less necessary. One of these was a gradual decline in the number of lepers or at least in the fear of leprosy, which led to less need and support for leper hospitals. Another was a rise in the personal wealth of many people, enabling more of the sick to be cared for at home or by doctors, and a third was the appearance of more inns to accommodate travellers. Some of the leper communities mentioned in the previous chapter have not been located after the mid fourteenth century, such as those at *Clony*, Dartmouth, and Okehampton. The smaller non-leper hospitals fared equally badly. We have already noticed the disappearance of those at Crediton and Warland in 1410 and 1503, and they were joined in this respect by the hospital for infirm priests at Clyst Gabriel which seems to have petered out in the 1480s. In 1509, Bishop Oldham granted its site and properties to the vicars of the cathedral.[83]

The only flourishing hospital in Devon during the later Middle Ages was St John (Exeter). It had substantial endowments and was well supported by the citizens as a kind of civic church in opposition to the cathedral. Many of them were buried in its chapel.[84] Its functions as a hospital, on the other hand, are little recorded. It seems to have operated chiefly as a small priory of a master and two or three brothers who performed daily worship, as well as providing rooms and meals for a few infirm people and for Stapledon's scholars attending the city High School. Most of the other larger and more formal hospitals survived, including those at Barnstaple, Honiton, Pilton, Plympton, Taddiport (Figure 21, p. 90), and Totnes, but they gradually lost their leper connections and turned into almshouses for the poor, the disabled, or the elderly. The social needs of the later fourteenth and fifteenth centuries seem to have required almshouses rather than hospitals, and the word 'almshouse' itself dates from this period. Almshouses differed from hospitals in usually having no clergy or communal life, which made them cheaper to found and build. They simply provided accommodation and sometimes small payments of money to a few people who lived in a row of cottages. Fifteen such almshouses were founded in Devon, mostly in towns, between about 1407 and 1540. Exeter acquired seven, and the list of other places included Cullompton (1527) and Tiverton (1529), where the houses were gifts of local merchants.[85]

Beyond the organised communities of clergy, there were people who lived a life of celibacy and prayer on their own. This might be done informally by anyone, such as widows or widowers, but a formal vow to live in such a way could be made with the bishop's approval, which gave public recognition to the person concerned. There were two kinds of solitary life: that of a hermit which was confined to men and that of an anchorite which was open to both sexes. Hermits lived near a chapel where they said informal prayers. They were allowed to move about in the world, and sometimes did charitable work such as collecting money for the upkeep of a bridge. Most were probably pious men who, from temperament or education, were not suitable to become monks or priests. Anchorites were confined to a cell attached to a monastery, parish church, or chapel. The cell was a small house, where the occupant followed a reclusive life of prayer and self-discipline, although he or she was allowed to communicate with people outside the cell. Those who followed this vocation were more varied socially and intellectually than hermits. Some were widows and others clergy. Lacy received applications to live in this way from a canon of Plympton Priory and an Augustinian canoness of a monastery in Ireland. William Tredewy, who dwelt as an anchorite at Torrington in the early fifteenth century, must also have been a cleric since he was commissioned by the bishop to act as a confessor in special cases, like some of the friars.[86]

Hermits and anchorites all relied for their support on a pension of some kind from a monastery or lay lord, or on donations from members of the public. In consequence, most of them are recorded living near towns and monasteries where such support was forthcoming.[87] In Exeter, we hear of anchorites from the thirteenth to the sixteenth centuries: one of them in the hospital of St John and a second in a chapel in St Leonard's churchyard outside the city. Others are mentioned at Crediton, Pilton, and Plympton, as well as Torrington, while hermits occur at Ottery St Mary, Plymouth, and Tavistock. The most rural locations were those of Beatrice of Colyford who secluded herself in a chapel at Colyford in 1332, and Margaret Holt who did the same near Dodbrooke in 1412. Both of these were widows, however, and may have had local ties and supporters. There were probably more hermits and anchorites than we know of, but never very many and not necessarily a series in any one place. They had a local impact, and sometimes a more than local one since we find them receiving small donations in wills of people outside their districts, but as a whole, they can have made little difference to the operation of the Church in Devon.

Parish Clergy

The main task of relating the Church to the world belonged to the parish clergy: rectors and vicars, the parish chaplains who assisted or deputised for them, and the priests of chantries and guilds. As was suggested in the previous chapter, these clergy differed in social origins. Some were sons of the nobility and gentry, others of merchants and yeomen farmers, and yet others of peasants or craftsmen, although rarely below these ranks. Their education continued to vary too. A youth with a prosperous father might attend a grammar school, while one of more modest wealth might have to make his way to the priesthood through working as a parish clerk with duties that will shortly be described.[88] Young men of the nobility and gentry could afford to go from grammar school to university, and about one in five of the rectors and vicars who were instituted under Lacy (1420–55) was a graduate.[89] Some other parish clergy, who were not graduates at the time of their institution, used their benefices to enable them to study at university. They gained the bishop's licence to go there on condition of appointing a chaplain to carry out their duties. This practice of studying after gaining a post rather than before seems odd today, but it was tolerated and enabled more clergy to benefit from higher education than would otherwise have been the case.

Education was one of the qualifications for ordination: at least for what were called the 'major orders' which allowed a man to function as an adult cleric. There were in practice five grades of ordination. A boy could be tonsured as a clerk at seven and ordained as an acolyte at fourteen. Neither of these 'minor orders' involved a life-time commitment to a clerical career, and such a boy could enter a lay occupation or marry when he grew up. A definite commitment to life as a cleric, which involved a permanent vow of celibacy and abstinence from secular work, came with the major orders, of which there were three. One could be made a subdeacon at seventeen, a deacon at nineteen, and a priest at twenty-four (Figure 22, p. 95). Most of those who aimed at being adult clergy, however, delayed committing themselves until they were twenty-four and could become priests. Then they took all three of the higher degrees: one at each of the bishop's quarterly ordinations. All candidates for these grades had to be of the appropriate age, legitimate in birth, free in status (not serfs), and physically perfect, as well as able to read and sing the Latin of the services.

Up to the Black Death, large numbers of men sought ordination because it provided a career in a crowded world, albeit a poorly paid one for the humblest of them. The biggest ordination ceremony ever held in Exeter diocese took place at Crediton on 21 December 1308 when Stapledon, who had just taken office after a vacancy,

Figure 22 Ordination. Large numbers of parish clergy, monks, and friars were ordained up to the middle of the sixteenth century. Here they kneel at the ceremony before a diocesan bishop or his suffragan.

ordained 273 clerks, 473 acolytes, 161 subdeacons, 81 deacons, and 17 priests. Normally, numbers were much smaller than this, but there could be from 30 to 60 candidates for the major orders at any one ceremony even after 1349, which invites the question whether candidates were examined to ensure that they satisfied the requirements. Records of the matter are hard to find, but checks were certainly made at times. In 1319, Stapledon ordained five men as subdeacons and deacons with the proviso that they could not be further ordained until they had learnt to sing.[90] In 1374 Brantingham ordained a deacon and two priests but made them swear to study: one for one year and two for two.[91] The names of ordination examiners are recorded in the early sixteenth century; they included senior graduate clergy and the grammar master of Exeter High School, so that literary standards seem to have been upheld.[92]

Ordination qualified one to become a parish clergyman, but a post as rector or vicar could only be obtained from the patron of a benefice, subject to the bishop's approval. Patrons, as in previous centuries, included the king, bishops, cathedrals, monasteries, the nobility, and local lords (or ladies) of manors. The king also acted as patron of churches belonging to bishops while there was no bishop in office. During the fourteenth century, the popes made a determined effort to gain some of this patronage for themselves. Arguing that they were the overlords of bishops, abbeys, and cathedrals, they claimed the right to 'provide' or appoint some of the clergy of these patrons' churches, on the grounds that they would appoint more deserving candidates. Prudently, they did not extend the claim to churches in the patronage of the king, nobility, or gentry.

Papal appointments, known as 'provisions', had some support in England from clergy without much status and influence, and the universities sent lists of deserving candidates to the pope. But far more powerful interests were opposed to them. Bishops and abbeys wanted to keep their own patronage, and the king and the aristocracy took the same view because they were accustomed to request the clergy to appoint the protégés they favoured. Further annoyance arose because some of the papal provisions were 'expectations': promises of a church in the future. This meant that when a vacancy arose, the patron's choice of cleric might be challenged by one or more persons possessing an expectation. A good many papal provisions were made in Devon during the fourteenth century, especially to posts at the cathedral, but in 1351 and 1365 Parliament enacted statutes forbidding the practice. By the end of the century, it was uncommon and virtually disappeared after 1400.[93]

We have seen that Devon contained just over 400 parish churches in the fourteenth and fifteenth centuries, most of which were staffed by a rector or vicar, although not all were resident. Some had leave to study at university; others held two or more benefices. Cathedral canons could hold one parish church along with their canonries, and they and the well-connected among the parish clergy could apply to the pope for a dispensation to hold a second parish church as well as the first. When a clergyman did not reside in his parish, he was required to pay a deputy to do his duties there: the usual term was 'parish chaplain' rather than 'curate'. This requirement seems generally to have been observed, since parishioners could complain if it was not. Rich clergy sometimes employed a chaplain to help them even if they were resident. Such a man could say mass in his employer's stead, be ready to baptise the newly born, and – best of all for the employer – go out on a wet winter night to a dying person in a distant house. After the Black Death, it became more difficult to find clergy willing to serve as parish chaplains, and bishops sometimes issued 'compulsions' to chantry priests to do the work instead. Thus in 1420, Lacy ordered Roger Hunt to accept the request of Exeter Cathedral to work at Buckland-in-the-Moor, or to appear before him to show cause why he should not.[94]

A taxation list of about the year 1490 informs us that there were then 356 chaplains in Devon who were not rectors or vicars.[95] About half of these were running parishes, while the other half did tasks of other kinds, chiefly in saying mass and daily prayers.[96] The nobility and gentry maintained chapels in their castles and houses, and the wealthier among them employed chaplains to staff them, although most of the gentry probably relied on occasional visits from the parish priest for this purpose. During the thirteenth century, it became popular among wealthy people to have mass said every day for the salvation of their souls in life and after death, and a class of lowly clergy grew up to provide this service. The commonest arrangement was for a man or woman approaching death, or their relatives afterwards, to arrange for a priest to say such masses for one or more years. At first, a year's worth of masses was called an 'annual' and the priest who said them was an 'annuellar'; later on, the terms 'chantry' and 'chantry priest' came into use. A smaller number of very rich people endowed masses to be said for their souls for ever. This involved allocating money or land to produce a yearly income to pay the chantry priest, and an arrangement of this kind has come to be known as 'a perpetual chantry'. One of the earliest such foundations in Devon was endowed by Sir John Montacute in Exeter Cathedral in 1224–8.[97] By the fourteenth century, some of the wealthier guilds also employed permanent priests. The arrangement was the same, in that the guild paid the priest to say a daily mass for the souls of all its former and present members.

Some formality was required to set up a perpetual chantry. A governing body was needed to look after the endowments, appoint the priest, and pay him. This body might be a local religious house or a group of lay trustees. Sometimes the priest was presented to the bishop and instituted to the chantry like a rector or vicar, but this was true only in a small number of cases. To comply with the law, it was necessary to get royal permission to endow a chantry, but this was sometimes avoided as it involved costs. In the 1540s, when chantries were abolished, there were about 83 posts for perpetual chantry priests and guild priests in 66 churches and chapels in Devon excluding the cathedral.[98] One needs to allow for non-perpetual chantry priests as well, and in 1540 there appear to have been about 200 perpetual and non-perpetual priests in the county, the cathedral again excepted.[99] Since a few of the bigger churches, like Bampton, Cullompton, South Molton, and Tiverton, had two or more priests, it follows that the majority of parish churches had none. The modern practice of calling side-chapels in medieval churches 'chantry chapels' should therefore be avoided unless there is specific evidence for such use, as we shall see in the following chapter.

From the early thirteenth century, the Church authorities tried to fix the wages of clergy who worked for money, and they were not generous in this respect. In 1225–37, Brewer's synod laid down that parish chaplains should receive at least £2 per annum, and this sum was raised to £3 by that of Quinil in 1287.[100] Neither synod specified rates for other kinds of hired priests, and they may have received somewhat less. After the Black Death of 1348–9, labour of all kinds was in short supply, and wages and prices rose. Parliament set wage rates for labourers in 1351 and the archbishops those of the hired clergy in 1362. The maximum wages of parish chaplains were now fixed at £4 and those of chantry priests at £3 6*s*. 8*d*., but these sums proved insufficient and they were increased to £5 6*s*. 8*d*. and £4 13*s*. 4*d*. in 1368, the rates being confirmed in 1414.[101] In practice, employers need not always have paid these rates, and if they were clergymen they could board a chaplain in their house and lower his wages. The only well-paid chantry priests in Devon were those of the cathedral. Their wages ranged between £4 and £7 in the early sixteenth century, but they were able to supplement this by earning money for attending funerals and anniversary masses for the dead, and by taking on minor offices at the cathedral as financial clerks, music instructors, librarians, or porters. Some of them may have earned as much as £10 a year, like the rectors and vicars of many parishes.

Parish Clerks

Rectors, vicars, chaplains, and chantry priests were not the only clergy in parish churches. Every priest needed a clerk to assist him because most services were dialogues requiring responses, and churches had such clerks, as we have seen, from about the late tenth century.[102] Their Latin title in the Middle Ages was *aquebaiulus*, 'holy water clerk', because one of their duties was to look after and administer the holy water used in services. In English it was simply 'clerk', with the term 'parish clerk' coming into use towards 1500. The clerk was in minor orders (tonsured or an acolyte). He rang the bell, prepared the altar, read the epistle at mass, and made the responses in the services (Figure 23, p. 101). He was also likely to assist at blessings, baptisms, marriages, and funerals.[103] Each parish had one such clerk, and some may have had more if they were large or contained important chapels of ease. A will relating to Tiverton in 1427 mentions a clerk 'of the town' and others 'of the land', meaning the rural parts of the parish.[104] For most of the Middle Ages, parish clerks were adolescents or young adults who often intended to become priests when they reached the age of twenty-four. The job taught them how to lead services, and the modest income attached to it allowed them to attend a grammar school in the intervals of their duties, if there was a school nearby.

Some useful light is thrown on parish clerks in Devon in 1440 as a result of a dispute about the authority of the rector of Witheridge over the chapel of Templeton. Witnesses were called, including three former clerks of Witheridge who gave evidence on behalf of the rector.[105] James Edmund had held the office from about 1421 to 1429, Thomas Rugge from about 1429 to 1434, and Thomas Ford from about 1434 to 1439. They were all in their late teens when they were appointed and probably stayed until they were ordained priest at the age of twenty-four. Parish clerks were chosen by the rector or vicar of the parish, and were therefore likely to come, as the rector did, from a family of middling importance rather than from the very poor. Edmund, Rugge, and Ford gained posts themselves as rectors fairly soon after their ordinations, at Meshaw, Washford, and Cheldon respectively, which confirms their status as people with patrons and influence.

Originally, the earnings of the clerks may have been rather haphazard. A reference of about 1450 to three parish clerks of Exeter at the city High School includes a complaint that they earned only meagre payments for their work. 'Today we have received a notable reward for [bell] ringing: three half-pennies and a farthing's worth of thin ale!'[106] By the late fifteenth century, however, their income was more defined. The clerk of Ashburton seems to have been paid cash sums of up to £3 a year from the 1510s, while his counterpart at Morebath, a more remote and rustic parish, was entitled to 4*d*. a year from every household along with a bundle of corn-sheaves.[107] In the early fifteenth century, canon law still insisted that clerks should be tonsured and unmarried.[108] Later on, there was a tendency for them to serve for longer periods and to become more like laymen than ecclesiastics. The clerk of Morebath in the 1550s was both the vicar's nephew and a married man with a child, and this change produced the typical parish clerk of the seventeenth and eighteenth centuries: a local layman, doing his duty in church alongside his secular work.[109]

The Parish Clergy: Daily Life

Quinil's synod of 1287 prescribed in detail how the clergy should live. They ought to be good, honest, and holy, teaching others by example as well as by words. Their heads should be tonsured, their clothes plain and unornamented. They must not keep concubines (since marriage had long been forbidden) or have sex with other women, on pain of the strictest penalties. They should take pains to avoid drunkenness, shunning parties unless invited by lords and then with care to be temperate, and never entering taverns unless on a pilgrimage. They should not keep birds or dogs for hunting, but give their time assiduously to prayer and reading. They should not engage in trade, secular administration, or money-lending, or give or write a legal judgment that involved the death penalty. Of course, laws and their observance are not the same, and such prohibitions were sometimes modified by general consent or broken by individual clergy. Still, these were the standards required, and they remained a potent force throughout the later Middle Ages.[110]

The parish clergy's day was framed with prayer. All were required to say the eight daily services or 'hours' like clergy in religious houses. Quinil's synod, which laid this duty down, exonerated the parish clergy from doing so at the regular times observed in cathedrals and monasteries, beginning with matins at midnight. Instead, they were ordered to say the first three hours of matins, lauds, and prime when they got up in the morning. Mass would be said in the mid morning, certainly on every Sunday, and be followed by the short hours of terce, sext, and none, ending at about 10.00 or 11.00am. There followed a long break for midday dinner and other occupations, after which the priest would say vespers and compline at about 3.00pm. The services of prayers for the dead, 'placebo' and 'dirige', had also to be said at some time.

On Sundays and festivals, all the services were sung with plainsong in church. The synod of 1287 implies that the daily offices should also be performed in church on weekdays, with the concession that they could be said not sung.[111] Some clergy certainly followed this practice. In 1342, for example, the vicar and ministers of Tavistock claimed that they could not do so each day, because of the leaky state of their chancel.[112] But it is not impossible that clergy sometimes said the weekday services at home, especially if they were unwell. This is suggested by the fact that the book used for the offices, the breviary, was also known as the 'portuous', meaning that it could be 'carried out of doors' and used wherever a cleric should happen to be.

The celebration of mass every Sunday and festival morning was a definite requirement, since this was the major parish service of the week. The synod was less clear about the duty to celebrate mass on weekdays, but it is likely that many clergy did so, if not all. In town churches, leisured people were likely to wish to attend daily masses, and in all churches there was a demand for masses on behalf of the dead through which fees could be earned. In 1301, the people of Colebrooke complained that their vicar did not celebrate mass on every weekday, but only on every other day.[113] The mass was one of the five sacraments that parish clergy were

Figure 23 A priest and clerk at the altar. The parish clerk was an important figure in parish life from the eleventh to the nineteenth centuries. He assisted the priest at services and, in the Middle Ages, often studied to become a priest himself.

authorised to celebrate. Two of the other four were planned and happened by arrangement: confession (mainly confined to the first weeks of Lent) and marriage. The remaining two could be asked for at any time: baptism, since babies were christened on the very day of birth, and the administration of unction to the seriously ill. When sick people died, the priest was required to say prayers of commendation at their homes, lead the bringing of their bodies to church, and conduct a funeral on the following morning, including the celebration of mass. The framework of the day was therefore both prescribed and unpredictable.

There were secular tasks to consider as well. The rectory or vicarage house would possess a hall or principal room for daytime use, a chamber for more privacy and sleeping, a kitchen, and outbuildings such as a brewery and stable.[114] One or two men would need to be employed to act as manservant and cook. The glebe of land belonging to the church would be cultivated with other servants unless the clergyman preferred to rent it for money. Thomas Dunham (died 1425), rector of Little Torrington, who worked his own glebe, grew corn and rye and kept animals: oxen, cows, and sheep of either sex. His will mentions his two carts, one with iron-bound wheels and one without, and his timber and ladders.[115] At particular times of the year, tithes had to be identified and gathered, and vicars in appropriated parishes sometimes acted as agents to collect the tithes that went to the appropriator. There was an ethic that parish clergy should provide hospitality to travellers and alms to those in need, and the synod of 1287 was scathing about clergy who gave to their concubines what ought to have gone to the poor.[116] An exemplary cleric in this respect was Henry Newton, the rector of Newton Ferrers in 1342, who rebuilt his rectory and provided a good and suitable chamber for guests.[117] But as yet the clergy had no public secular functions, which still largely belonged to lords of manors in the countryside. It was not until the mid sixteenth century that the Tudor monarchs made the parish into a unit of local government, with the clergyman as a pivotal figure in the administration of secular matters such as the poor law.

The mental and social life of the parish clergy is hard to reconstruct. Those of Devon have left us no financial accounts or letters of significance. The most personal records that we possess are their wills, and wills have two deficiencies. They were conventional documents which nudged a will-maker into doing what was expected, and Devon lacks the inventories of goods that were drawn up after death, so that the goods we know about are merely those named in the will. Nevertheless, wills are better than nothing, and their value can be illustrated by taking seven that were made by rectors and vicars between 1424 and 1445, proved before the officers of Lacy, and transcribed into his register. They are those of the incumbents of Churchstow, Colyton, St Laurence and St Mary Major (Exeter), Haccombe, Little Torrington, and South Brent.[118] In terms of wealth and status, their makers were in the middle of the clergy hierarchy: below the cathedral canons and those with more than one benefice, but above the poorer parish incumbents and chaplains whose wills did not come into the scope of the bishop's jurisdiction.

The wills throw light on lifestyles and possessions. A cleric dressed like other men in shirt, breeches, stockings, and shoes. Over these, he wore a tunic or a long gown which the synod, following canon law, required to be of sober black or grey. In practice, some clerics' clothes were more colourful. The will-makers had tunics of blue or green and robes of brown, blue, or motley (mixed hues), with linings of white or otter fur. Around their waists they buckled belts of green, black, or blue, decorated with silver trimmings and in one case with an image of St Christopher. The belt, as well as gathering in the tunic, carried a dagger or knife for eating. At night, the clergyman retired to sleep on a wooden bedstead cushioned with a mattress and provided with pillows, sheets, blankets, and a quilt or coverlet. The bed might have a canopy or hangings, with a design such as fleurs-de-lys. Elsewhere in the house, his kitchen was supplied with spits, tin dishes, brass pots and bowls, and doubtless plenty of pottery. Outside, the stable would house a horse or two for travelling to distant parts of the parish or to the market town, with the necessary equipment for riding: bridles, saddles, and saddle-bags.

His other chief possessions were his silver plate and books. The plate included ewers and basins for washing hands, silver spoons, silver bowls, and silver drinking cups with covers. Drink was also taken from a mazer (a wooden bowl of beech) or a 'nut' (a coconut) made into a cup and mounted with silver. Cups of silver or coconut might be highly decorated: 'a cup of silver standing on three lions', 'a nut cup standing on three feet of silver gilt, with a silver cover bearing a griffin on the top.' They might be inscribed with a man's initials or those of friends who had bequeathed them, and contain mottoes in Latin or English. Some of these were religious: 'In God is all my trust', 'Jesu have mercy on me', and 'IHS' for 'Jesus' at the bottom of a mazer. The number and nature of a cleric's books are hard to estimate, because they are only casually mentioned, but they probably centred on works in Latin relevant to his calling (Figure 24, p. 106). These included church service books (such as the breviary, psalter, and antiphonal), books of sermons, the *Pupilla Oculi* (a guide to the duties of parish clergy), and the occasional work of academic theology or canon law. That does not rule out clergy owning works of literature in English, such as mystical works or poetry, which occur in some clerical wills from other parts of the kingdom.

One learns a little from the wills about the clergy's contacts and horizons. Their careers often involved a migration from their birthplace to their benefice, and the birthplace might be remembered in the will. Nicholas Collecott of St Laurence (Exeter) seems to have come from Winkleigh, to whose church he bequeathed a chalice, and John Hylle of Colyton from west Dorset, perhaps Long Bredy to whose poor he gave 6*s.* 8*d.* A cleric's family and lay friends usually appear in his will, receiving bequests of clothes and equipment or modest sums of money. It was considered inappropriate to give one's family too much of the wealth one got from one's parishioners, but of course such giving could be done before the will was made. Beyond the family, the wills show a geographical horizon a few miles away, within which the makers were likely to make bequests to other churches and fellow parish clergy. The latter were often asked to say prayers for the deceased will-maker, and frequently chosen as executors or supervisors of wills. Such bonding, of course, reflected a common profession and the practice of meeting for worship or Church business. A few clergy had travelled beyond Devon, chiefly to Oxford to study but occasionally to London on business or through family contacts, and these places feature in wills. Those who had belonged to an Oxford college often felt moved to give a book or money in return.

The wills also demonstrate clergy links with local religious houses, and most of them remember the friaries of Exeter or Plymouth. This no doubt reflects the fact that friars travelled in their work and met the rural clergy as they did so. Small gifts to friaries were a convention in wills, but their presence in those of the parish clergy show that there could be good relationships alongside the ill feeling that sometimes existed. The same is true of monks, and our group of seven wills includes one cleric who wished to be buried in Buckfast Abbey and bequests by others to Frithelstock Priory, Polsloe Priory, St John Hospital (Exeter), Milton Abbey (Dorset), and the Order of St John. Money was sometimes left for the upkeep of bridges, which depended on charity for their support and would have been crucial in enabling clergy to travel. One will-maker gave to seven of them. Finally, there were the poor, who were sometimes asked to attend the will-maker's funeral with a promise of food or small sums of money in return for their prayers.

Wills are biased in showing clerical life at its most successful in terms of possessions and relationships. Such life must also have been stressful at times. It could be lonely because of physical isolation in the countryside, lack of neighbours with similar knowledge and interests, and the distancing from lay people that a religious vocation produces. Society was not continuously or uniformly devout. As we shall see in the following chapter, the parish clergy had to cope with failure to attend church, uncouth behaviour in church, opposition to the payment of tithes, and non-conformity to the Church's rules, especially on sexual behaviour. A clergyman might earn relief by tolerating these things at the cost of his conscience and reputation, or try to confront them at the risk of becoming unpopular. Although in theory he could call on the Church courts to enforce the law, this would provoke animosity unless the parish leaders took his side. Occasionally, ill feeling led to violent attacks on clergy, either as individuals or as representatives of some unpopular church like the cathedral or a monastery. Four clergy of the cathedral were attacked in the building itself in 1379, two others by a group of laymen in 1397, and two more – a canon and his vicar choral – in 1426.[119] Worse still, Robert Gyffarde, a chaplain of Plymouth, was seized and castrated there in 1388,[120] and John Hay, vicar of South Brent, was abducted in 1436 after saying vespers in his church, dragged out of the building and through the churchyard, and finally murdered.[121]

The effectiveness of the parish clergy is difficult to summarise. The range of their personalities and capabilities must have been as great as the evidence about them is small, but the visitation records of the parishes belonging to the cathedral in 1301 and the following years throw a little light on the subject. Opinions about ten vicars were expressed by their parishioners.[122] In five places, the vicar was said to behave honestly and to exercise his office properly. In a sixth, Dawlish, where the vicar did not reside, the chaplain who took his place was similarly commended. There were four exceptions. The incumbent of Clyst Honiton was elderly and infirm and not capable of parish duty; the church building was in a bad state and the parishioners had evidently lost interest in parish life. His counterpart at Colebrooke expounded the gospels on Sundays as well as he knew how, but did not teach the creed, the commandments, or the seven deadly sins. More seriously, he was reputed to be having an affair with a woman. The vicar of Colyton was also a poor preacher, yet he refused to allow friars to give supplementary instruction, unlike his predecessors.

The most unsatisfactory situation was at St Marychurch. Its vicar was accused of appropriating gifts for the upkeep of the church, having his malt prepared in the building, storing his grain there, and pasturing his beasts in the churchyard. He preached and did his duties well when he was resident, but often withdrew for a week or a fortnight to Moretonhampstead. No services were then provided unless a local chaplain happened to be present. It is likely that a similar range of judgments could have been collected at any point during the fourteenth and fifteenth centuries.

Old Age and Death

The Church insisted that its clergy should be fully able to function, hence the need for a candidate for ordination to show that he was sound and whole in body. Critics of the clergy tended to assume that they were all healthy and should be active. In practice, of course, the clergy fell ill and grew old like everyone else. It was difficult for them to work if they became blind and could not read their service books, or infirm and unable to ride round their parishes. What happened to them then depended, as usual, on wealth.[123] The rector or vicar of a well-endowed benefice could continue to occupy it until he died by employing a chaplain to do his duties. If he did not do so, the bishop might appoint a priest as coadjutor for the same purpose.[124] Alternatively a clergyman could resign from his benefice and reserve a pension from the income, which meant that until he died there was less for his

Figure 24 The Hailes Psalter, commissioned by Christopher Urswick (died 1522), chancellor of Exeter Cathedral and chaplain of Henry VII. The book, which shows him kneeling beside King David, illustrates the liking of wealthy clergy for beautiful artefacts.

successor. Pensions needed the bishop's permission and were often fixed at one third of the income. One sometimes encounters parish clergy becoming chantry priests, and this may have been prompted by a need for a sedentary post because of ill health.

Many benefices, however, were too poor to allow a sick incumbent to appoint a curate or receive a pension. This caused problems like those of Clyst Honiton in 1301, where the vicar could not serve the parish properly yet there were no resources with which he could retire or pay an assistant.[125] Hired chaplains on low wages were also vulnerable. They stood to lose their posts if they grew ill or old, and had no means of saving for such a contingency. The only help available to them was a place at Stapledon's hospital at Clyst Gabriel, but that was limited to twelve infirm priests from the whole of the diocese, and after the Black Death its resources were only sufficient for seven. In the 1480s, as we have seen, the hospital ceased functioning altogether. We do not know what happened to the poor disabled clergy for whom it did not cater, but their lot cannot have been an easy one.

Rectors and vicars often asked in their wills to be buried in the chancel of their church. Most commonly, their graves would have been covered by a simple floor slab or 'ledger stone', carved with their name, their date of death, and a request that God have mercy upon their soul. A priest with more money and ambition might pay for a brass image to be set in the stone, like John de Northwode (1349), formerly at Ottery St Mary, and William Langton (1413), still in the cathedral, but few of these have survived in Devon.[126] Large table tombs or full-sized effigies were also unusual for clergy in the county, except for bishops in the cathedral. Even the deans and canons did not receive such tombs, with the exception of Canon William Sylke who got his effigy (a cadaver) inserted into the screen of the chapel of the Holy Cross, which he probably paid for. As for the poor chaplains, they may well have been laid to rest in churchyards in the open air. There they would have shared with the laity the lowliness they had endured in their lives.

Chapter 4

The Later Middle Ages: the Laity

The Parish Church: a Description

To the lay people of the Middle Ages, the Church meant first of all their parish church. By 1300, it had existed (on average) for three or four hundred years, but hardly anywhere was it still the original building. The Anglo-Saxon churches were rebuilt in the twelfth or thirteenth centuries, and most of the new structures were remodelled again by the Reformation. Sometimes this was done in the fourteenth century, notably at Bere Ferrers, Ottery St Mary (Figure 20, p. 84), and Tawstock, but the process appears to have quickened between about 1400 and 1530. Most of the ancient churches that we see around us bear the stamp of that period. Fabric of earlier times may often be present, especially in the walls, but most of the prominent features – towers, porches, aisles, windows, and chapels – come from the end of the Middle Ages rather than from their heartlands. In part, this process of rebuilding reflected a more affluent society after it recovered from the first effects of the Black Death. In the countryside, a smaller population enjoyed greater shares of the produce of the land. In the towns and ports, industries like cloth-making and trade in cloth and wine brought further prosperity.

The medieval churches of today are in good condition, by and large, thanks to Victorian restorations and modern repairs. This was not always the case in the past. The visitation of the archdeaconry of Totnes in 1342 makes numerous mentions of buildings in a poor state, with leaking roofs, broken glass, and dark interiors that came perhaps from boarding up windows.[1] Sometimes this was the fault of an appropriator. The cathedral was to blame at Widecombe-in-the-Moor, and the abbey at Tavistock.[2] Sometimes clergy were responsible. Rectors were bound to maintain their chancels and if they did not, they or their executors were liable to pay dilapidation costs to their successors. But it was often hard to extract this money. In the case of Mary Tavy, the executors were in Cornwall and were said to have no conscience about their duty.[3] Other churches were better cared for, and there was probably a wider range in this respect than we experience today.

Rebuilding churches was expensive. The visitation of 1342 estimated sums of £10–£20 as needed for the repair of chancels alone, and this was before the inflation of the later fourteenth century.[4] Conscientious appropriators and clergy maintained and rebuilt chancels with their own money, like the nunnery at Cornworthy and the rector at Newton Ferrers.[5] Lay people faced with renewing a nave had to engage in strenuous fund-raising, and might struggle to succeed. Church patrons and lords of manors were often helpful here. Sir William Hankford (died 1423) paid for half of the rebuilding costs at Monkleigh and was willing to pay for the rest if the parishioners could not afford to do so. He also left money to repair the roof and walls of Bulkworthy.[6] An inscription in the chancel of Spreyton records that it was rebuilt in 1451 with the help of the patron (the prior of Cowick), the lord of the manor (Richard Talbot), and the vicar (a Frenchman, Henry le Maygne). Merchants in some towns gave generous assistance. Thomas Yogge of Plymouth (mid fifteenth century) paid for the tower of St Andrew's church and for one of its chapels.[7] John Greenway of Tiverton provided the south porch and south chapel of St Peter's church in 1517 (Figure 35, p. 161), and John Lane (died 1529) the outer south aisle of the nave at Cullompton, the 'Lane aisle'. Both latter projects were embellished with symbols and inscriptions in honour of their donors.

It is not the purpose of this book to provide an architectural history of the parish churches of Devon. Instead, it aims to explore how they were used and what they can tell us about religion and society. Ashburton is a good surviving example (Figure 25, p. 112). By 1500, and often long before, one entered a church like this through a porch placed usually outside the south door of the nave. The porch was not only a shelter but an anteroom to the church, and included a basin for holy water built into the wall by the door, unless it was placed inside the church itself. Incomers sprinkled some water on themselves as an act of purification. The porch provided a space for rituals that involved the symbolic bringing of a person from the world into the church: the first part of the baptism service, the churching of women after childbirth, and the exchange of vows in marriage. From the porch, one passed into the nave, still the part of the church designed for the use of the laity. Near the nave door was the font with the locked wooden cover prescribed by Quinil's synod, its site announcing the fact that baptism gave entry to the Church.[8]

Naves differed from place to place as to whether they were simple halls or had appendages. As in previous centuries, aisles and transepts might be present on the north side, the south side, or both. When churches were rebuilt after the thirteenth century, aisles were made wider than before to give space for seating, which was a feature of every nave by the later Middle Ages.[9] The seating usually took the form of uniform pews in blocks, with gangways between them for access and for processions of clergy. Most pews had wooden backs and side pieces (bench-ends) towards the gangways, the latter decorated with tracery, initials, the symbols of Christ's Passion, or scenes from everyday life. There are good collections of bench-ends at East Budleigh and High Bickington. The walls of the nave might be beautified with geometrical designs or images, and the glass of the windows display figures of Christ or the saints. St Christopher was often depicted on the wall opposite the south door – there was a notion that seeing his picture kept you from sudden death that day – and a painting of Christ surrounded by tools and equipment for games was sometimes to be found. Morebath formerly had one. This painting, incorrectly described as 'Christ of the trades', was known as 'St Sunday' and warned the onlooker against working or playing sports on that day, at least at service times.[10]

The seats in the nave faced eastwards and the worshippers' horizon was defined by the screen placed in front of or beneath the archway that separated the nave and the chancel: the screen now known as the 'roodscreen' from the 'rood' or crucifix that stood above it. Roodscreens were universal by about 1300, if not earlier, and can still be seen in many Devon churches especially Ashton (Figure 26, p. 117), Atherington, Cullompton, and other places.[11] Some were of stone, as at Colyton and Ottery, but the majority were probably of wood like most of those that survive. The typical roodscreen was about twelve feet tall, with panels at the bottom and open arches above them, permitting a view of the chancel. Above the arches was a coving supporting the roodloft: a gallery containing the crucifix flanked by the Virgin Mary and St John. These images were sometimes backed by a tympanum of boarding which filled the upper part of the archway and might depict Christ presiding over the Last Judgment. Alternatively, such a scene might be painted on the stonework above the archway. The screen had a central door giving access for the clergy, but this was not used by ordinary lay people during services and would be locked at other times. The woodwork was often adorned with carvings of a high standard, and the panels decorated with prophets or saints. Screens and lofts were objects of prestige and some parishes spent large sums of money upon them. William Sellack gave £36 towards the roodloft of Tiverton in 1523, and that of Ashburton cost at least £43 at about the same date.[12]

One of the Latin words for 'screen' is *pulpitum*, from which 'pulpit' is derived. Originally, announcements and preaching may have been made from the rood-screen by the clergyman standing in front of it or even upon it, but by about the fourteenth century, separate pulpits were coming into use. They were usually placed away from the screen, either beside it if there was room or by the north-east or south-east pier of the nave, a bay to the west of the screen. Pulpits could be of stone or wood, and survive at Dartington, Harberton, Torbryan, and elsewhere. We associate them with preaching, but the extent to which this took place is uncertain.

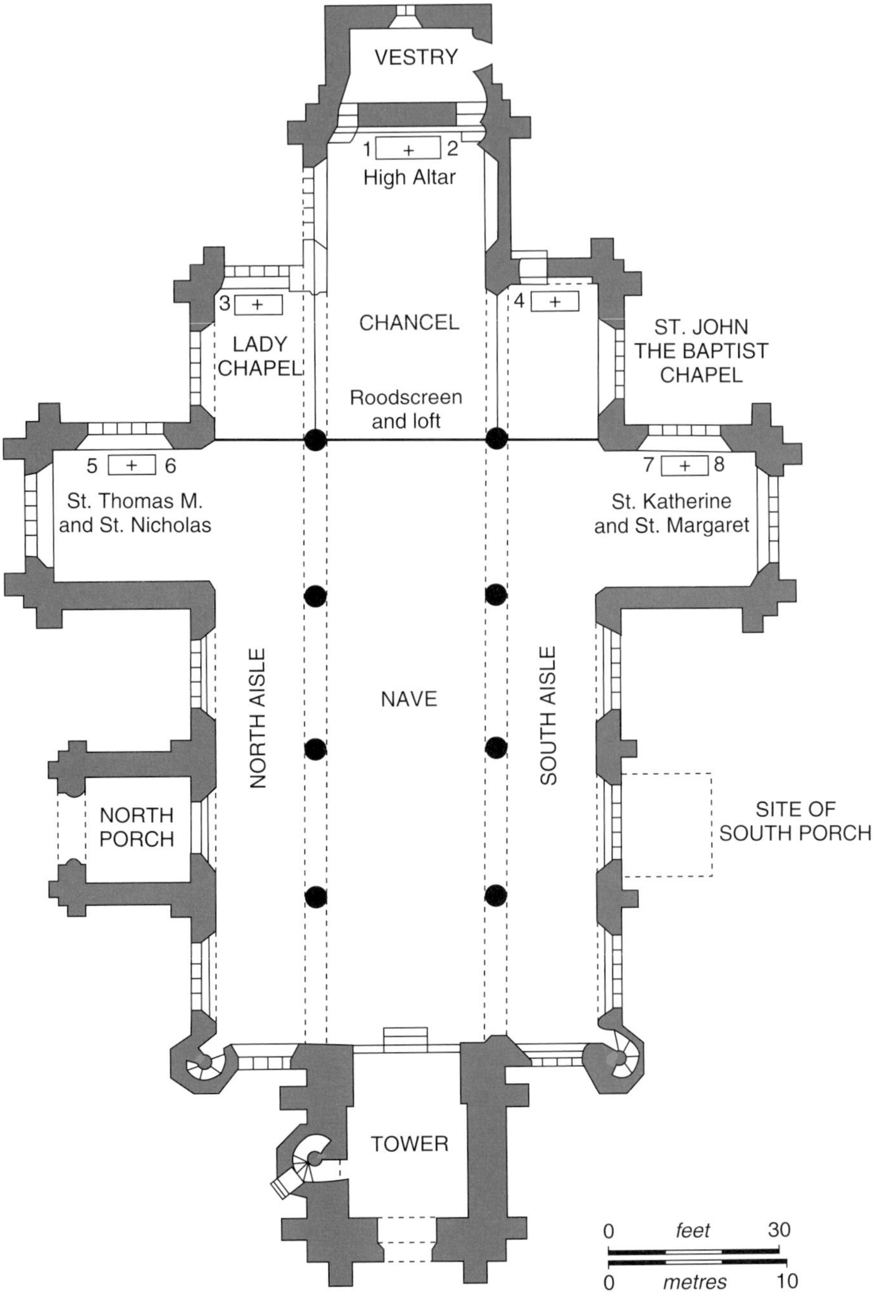

Figure 25 Ashburton parish church before the Reformation. The plan indicates the sites of some of the altars and images in a complex building made up of a series of rooms. Images: 1 Andrew; 2 and 3 Virgin Mary; 4 John the Baptist; 5 Thomas Becket; 6 Nicholas; 7 Katherine; 8 Margaret.

The visitation records of 1281 and 1301 mention the expectation of parishioners that they would get some instruction from their clergy, but this may have been limited (as Quinil required in his synod) to explaining the basic prayers, the Ten Commandments, and so on.[13] As late as 1561, a survey of Devon clergy found that very few of them preached, even in their own churches.[14] The chief use of the pulpit was for the reading of the bede-roll by the clergyman during mass on Sundays. This was a written list of parishioners, chiefly the dead, for whom the congregation was asked to pray: a list not of everyone but those who had paid, or whose families had paid, for the privilege of inclusion. Thomas Reymound, for example, left money in 1418 for the names of himself and his family to be mentioned in the bede-roll of Holsworthy church on every Sunday of the year.[15]

Many churches retained transepts from the thirteenth and fourteenth centuries when their construction was in vogue. It has already been suggested that these were instituted by wealthy people or guilds as private chapels, since some have piscinas that point to the presence of altars. Transepts may often have been screened from the rest of the church, or even usually so. The traces of such screening have generally disappeared since the Reformation, although part of the nave wall of the south transept at Brampford Speke survived until the nineteenth century.[16] More frequently, indications of the privacy of transepts survive in the form of 'squints' or holes cut through from the inner eastern corner of the transept into the chancel. The holes suggest that the transepts were in use during mass, and that their users (a fairly small number of privileged people, such as a family) gathered at the squint to watch the priest at the altar. The rebuilding of churches in the later Middle Ages often led to the provision of other chapels, especially to the north and south of the chancel. These were separated from the nave by the roodscreen and from the chancel by 'parclose' screens, with doors for access.

Chapels within churches are frequently described as 'chantry chapels', but the term is a misleading one. Only a minority of churches had chapels served by a chantry priest or guild priest, either on a temporary or permanent basis, and very few of these had more than one priest at a time.[17] The chapel on the north side of the chancel was often designated as a Lady chapel in honour of the Virgin Mary. The others must usually have been chapels of gentry families or groups of parishioners of the kinds shortly to be discussed. None of these was normally served by a full-time priest. The Lady chapel may have been used by the parish clergyman to say the hours of the Virgin Mary or to sing an antiphon in her honour. The rest would have been chiefly places for private prayer and occupancy during Sunday services, as well as for family burials. Masses at their altars would have been celebrated only infrequently by the parish clergyman, or a priest hired with his permission, on the feast of the chapel saint or some similar occasion. We need to be alert to the variety of ways in which space was used in parish churches, and avoid simplifying this variety with the concept of chantry chapels.[18]

The chancels of the later Middle Ages followed their predecessors in being smaller than naves and containing the 'high' or chief altar of the church against the eastern wall. The clergyman celebrated mass facing the altar with his back to the rest of the church. As we have seen, the Quinil synod required a canopy to hang above the altar, along with the pyx containing the consecrated wafer. From at least the thirteenth century, the more ambitious church builders provided sedilia, stone seats for the clergy at mass, in the church wall to the south of the altar. Wooden stalls were usually fitted at the west end of the chancel, near the roodscreen, for the use of the clergyman and clerk in saying the other daily services. The furnishings of the chancel also included statues of the patron saint and the Virgin Mary, with an Easter sepulchre for use on Good Friday which was either portable or built into the north wall.

The chancel is generally understood to have been a place for the clergy alone: rector or vicar, parish clerk, and any curates or chaplains attached to the church. This is largely but not wholly true. Ordinary lay people came into the chancel chiefly on their wedding day, when they were led to the high altar by the priest for a blessing. When they died, their bodies may have rested in the chancel during the funeral although it is equally possible that those of ordinary folk reposed in the nave. However, medieval society was deferential to the nobility and gentry, and if the patron of the church or the lord of the manor lived in the parish, he or she and their family probably expected to sit in the chancel where, in addition, their tombs were often placed. Some English churches contain a range of stalls on either side of the chancel: eight, twelve, or more in number. In a cathedral or collegiate church, these would be occupied by clergy, but that cannot have been true of ordinary parish churches. A few churches indeed maintained small choirs by the end of the Middle Ages. Ashburton had one by 1480, but the chief business of a choir was to sing polyphonic music in the Lady chapel, and it is not clear that its members would have occupied stalls in the chancel.[19] Such stalls may therefore have been used by the gentry; if not, they would have required different seating in the vicinity.

It was a mark of the status of the parish church to have a tower, since this distinguished it from most chapels which were denied one. The surviving towers of Devon churches date largely from the later Middle Ages and are of moderate height with battlements. Some in north Devon are taller, like Chittlehampton, Hartland, and South Molton, and resemble the great towers of Somerset. Spires on towers were not so common, but Exeter Cathedral once possessed them and they have survived at a number of parish churches such as Barnstaple and Bishop's Tawton in the north as well as Diptford, Modbury, and elsewhere in the south where the spires are of stone. Towers held bells, important for ringing to announce services, mark festival days, and ward away evil in times of storm. Bells were major expenses for a parish, and were often marked with religious inscriptions and called after saints or benefactors. The cathedral had bells named Mary and Peter, while Crediton's Jesus bell inspired a Latin poem praising its loudness in proclaiming the faith.[20] Bells were rung simultaneously, not in a changing sequence as became normal after the Reformation, and the importance of a particular festival was marked by the number of bells and by their depth of sound.

Some towers came to have clocks: at first marking time with a bell rather than hands on a dial. There was one at the cathedral by the end of the thirteenth century, and they slowly spread first to monasteries and later to parish churches. Ottery may have had a clock from the fourteenth century, and Ashburton did so by 1513.[21] But long before the latter date, by about 1400, clocks were common enough for people to reckon the day by the hours, as we do today, rather than by the sun or church services as was the case before. This was a major cultural change from a flexible day, whose length changed with the seasons, to a day that was observed in a regular way.

The Parish Church: an Assessment

Parish churches were designed and furnished for reasons that were spiritual and social, and therefore instruct us both about people and about their religion. The medieval Church emphasised the difference between the sacred and the secular, particularly in its insistence that worship should be led by ordained clergy committed to celibacy and should take place in surroundings removed from the laity – except, of course, for pastoral services like christenings and marriages. This explains the screening of the chancel and the other chapels, so that a medieval church was not a single space with an open plan like most of its modern successors. Rather, it was a house of several rooms and areas: porch, tower, nave, font (Figure 27, p. 121), chancel, transepts, and chapels. One was not meant to see a vista from one end to the other.

To this extent, how a church was laid out and what went on inside it was dictated by the clergy. Yet equally, churches were works of the laity. Their tithes maintained the chancel and their contributions the nave. Some of the saints whose images stood in the church were their choices. Most significantly, the seats were due to them. No order survives from any pope or bishop that seating should be provided. It was the people's preference: a creation from the grass roots and not primarily with a religious purpose. Seats were wanted because they were more comfortable than standing or sitting on the floor. Not all of a service was spent sitting, of course, but even if you were kneeling, it was easier to do so with something to lean on, and the woodwork of the seat kept off the draughts. So benches were introduced for comfort, but they also affected how people behaved in church. Once there was seating, all were obliged to do the same. They could not stand up or sit down unless their neighbours did so, and had to moderate their speech and gestures to avoid annoying others. Long before the Church leaders of the Reformation insisted on uniformity of belief and behaviour, the parishioners of England were becoming uniform in their worship because of their fondness for seats.

Seating was also popular because it embodied the social hierarchy so dear to many people. Parishioners were not free to sit where they pleased, despite Quinil's pronouncement of 'first come, first served'. We do not know where people placed themselves in Devon's churches during the later Middle Ages, and the rules may have varied from place to place as they did in later times. By the seventeenth century, seating in country parishes was often based on one's place of residence, so that a man sat with his spouse and family in the seat assigned to his dwelling. Some churches segregated men and women: perhaps more commonly churches in towns. Whichever custom was used, we may be sure that the sittings reflected the social structure of the parish. The gentry would be in privileged places such as the chancel, transepts, or chapels. The leading families beneath the gentry would occupy the seats at the front of the nave, while artisans, cottagers, servants, the poor, and sometimes children would sit at the back.

Burials were ranked in a similar way. The gentry would be allocated spaces in the chancel, transepts, chapels, or a prominent part of the nave. They might, if they so chose, have table tombs or tombs with effigies. Wealthy people who were not gentry could be buried inside the church, most likely the nave, in return for a payment to the churchwardens. At Ashburton, the fee was 3*s.* 4*d.*[22] Such burials would be topped by a ledger stone flush with the floor and marked with an inscription. The majority of the population would lie in the churchyard beneath the shallow mounds of earth piled on their graves.

Sunday Worship

The greater survival of church buildings after about 1300 makes it easier than before to envisage what happened inside them on Sundays and festival days. We also possess the service books of the Use of Sarum, the later versions of which contain instructions for how worship should be done.[23] The pattern of services has already been outlined. On a Sunday morning, the clergyman and parish clerk sang matins (encompassing the first three 'hours' of matins, lauds, and prime) in the chancel at about 7.00am, followed by mass at about 9.00, and evensong (vespers and compline) at about 3.00pm. Matins consisted of Bible readings, psalms, hymns, and prayers. No ceremonies were involved, and the service could well have lasted for an hour

Figure 26 Ashton parish church, the roodscreen. A typical wooden screen of the later Middle Ages, it extends right across the church. Until the Reformation, it would have been surmounted by a gallery containing statues of Christ on the cross flanked by the Virgin Mary and St John.

and a half. Lay people were encouraged to attend, but had no part to play and could only have said their own prayers. Evensong was like matins but shorter, and occupied about an hour or so.

The principal Sunday service was mass, attendance at which was an obligation on adults, although one cannot say how many came. Adults were expected to go to at least one service on the Lord's Day, but that was difficult to enforce and there were plenty of complaints that people stayed away. However, mass was probably the best attended service because it was more colourful and was thought to be more beneficial spiritually. The most likely to be present, apart from the very devout, were the wealthy of the parish who had more leisure, more interest in religion, and more to gain socially by being seen at church. The most probable absconders were the poor, the disaffected, and servants. Servants were needed to look after farm animals and get the dinner ready for those who had been to church. They may not even have come on Easter morning. It is recorded soon after 1500 that some parishioners in the Cornish church of Lanteglos-by-Fowey received their Easter communion on the evening before Easter Day: very likely those who had tasks at home on the day itself.[24]

Mass took about an hour. The service began with a procession of priest, clerk, and any other clergy or assistants through the nave and the screen into the choir. The material included a confession, collect (prayer of the day), the epistle read by the clerk, the gospel by the priest, and the Nicene Creed. After the creed, there might be a sermon but more commonly the reading of the bede-roll. Next came the prayers known as *Sursum corda*, 'Lift up your hearts', followed by the 'canon' of the mass or 'prayer of consecration'. At this point, the priest, who had previously spoken audibly, dropped his voice to indicate the holy nature of what he was doing: the consecration of a wafer of bread and a small chalice of wine and water. In order that the congregation knew when the consecration took place and Christ, in the Church's teaching, became bodily present in the form of bread and wine, small bells were rung by the clerk while the priest held the wafer above his head, and again while he held up the chalice (Figures 23, p. 101 and 28, p. 126). The priest alone consumed the bread and wine. He then reverted to his normal voice and said the Paternoster followed by other prayers, concluding the service with words of dismissal *Ite, missa est* ('Go, the mass is completed').

The congregation had little formal involvement. The priest addressed them directly in the sermon if there was one, and asked them to pray for the people named in the bede-roll. They may have joined in saying the last line of the Paternoster, *Sed libera nos a malo* ('but deliver us from evil'), since this line was usually said as a response. Apart from this, they were acknowledged only twice. After the priest had consecrated the bread and wine but before he consumed them, he passed the kiss of peace around the church by kissing the 'pax' or 'paxbrede': a little tablet of metal or ivory containing a picture of Christ, on the end of a rod. The clerk then took it to the congregation, and offered it to everyone to kiss in order of precedence. After mass, there was the ceremony of the holy loaf. This was provided by every household of the parish in turn, and blessed by the priest who distributed small pieces of it among the adults present. This again was done with regard to their rank.

The mass therefore required little active engagement from the laity. What then did people do? They were meant to participate quietly and devoutly, but they were left to achieve this in their own ways. If they were prosperous and literate, they might take a prayer-book and read it. The prayer-book was usually the simplified Book of Hours in Latin or English, which was not what the priest was using but which the reader would murmur aloud as a private devotion. A very few of the best educated might have their own missal, in which case they could follow the exact words of the service; missals are occasionally mentioned in wills. The majority of people, who did not have books, would have said the three basic Latin prayers: Paternoster, Ave Maria, and Credo, over and over again, often with the use of a rosary. They were free, of course, to offer their own prayers or engage in meditation.

Such a service was not concerned with instruction. The Bible readings at matins and mass were in Latin, as was the material of every service except for the exchange of vows at a wedding. There might be little or nothing in terms of a sermon, unless you lived in a church with a graduate priest or in a town where there was more demand for preaching. Instead, a service in a medieval church can be likened to a visit to a concert or a medical appointment. At a concert, you do not understand the music unless you are a literate musician, but you receive it emotionally. That is still a valuable experience, and going to church was emotional in that way or, rather, devotional. The other reward for going was medicinal. You confessed your sins. Jesus appeared in the bread and wine of the mass, and gave you blessing. You came out of church cleaner and holier than when you had gone in. And that too was satisfying, or at least was so to many people.

Chapels

Churches were not the only places where services and prayers went on. As the parish system crystallised in the tenth and eleventh centuries, there came to be places of worship that did not qualify to be parish churches with a fully independent status. The term that described them, 'chapel', was originally the name of the cloak of St Martin which gave its name to the oratory in France where the cloak was kept, thence to royal chapels in England, and by the mid twelfth century to small places of worship in general. Here the word will be used of free-standing chapels, not those within parish churches that we have discussed.[25] The earliest such chapels recorded in Devon are St Michael, East Teignmouth, in 1044 (which was then termed a church, 'chapel' not being in use) and the chapel of Exeter Castle, built probably soon after 1068 but possibly continuing an earlier Anglo-Saxon foundation.[26]

There were a great many chapels in medieval Devon (Figure 14, p. 54). Mrs Jeanne James, who has made a detailed study of them, found documentary references to about 1,300: some three times the number of parish churches, and it is possible that more may be discovered.[27] The abundance of the references reflects the fact that chapels were licensed by bishops and that the bishops of Exeter were more careful than their colleagues in other dioceses about recording the licences they issued. Or rather, some of the bishops displayed this care. Stapledon's register records 27 licences, Grandisson's 82, Brantingham's 452, Stafford's 326, and Lacy's 383, a total of about 1,270 over a period of about 150 years. These figures do not equal numbers of chapels, because some licences were issued for more than one building and some chapels received more than one licence. After Lacy's death in 1455, the licences largely disappear from the bishops' registers, making it appear that chapel foundations dwindled in number, which may not be true. No one should be surprised at finding evidence of a chapel for which there is no surviving licence, even within the great period of licence recording.[28]

Medieval chapels fell into three principal groups, although some can be placed in more than one of these. First, there were private chapels intended for a noble household or a privileged group of people. These included castle chapels at Okehampton and Torrington; chapels on the bishop's manors at Bishop's Clyst, Chudleigh, Paignton, and elsewhere; and numerous chapels in the houses of the gentry, such as the Courtenays of Tiverton and Powderham, the Dinhams of Hartland and Nutwell, and the Speccotes of Merton. Rectories and vicarages often contained a chapel, of which there are records at Challacombe, Charleton, Heanton Punchardon, Newton Ferrers, and other places. In the course of time, some private groups of people came to own chapels. The city council of Exeter created one in their guildhall and the Exeter guild of weavers and tuckers another in theirs, while the guild of shoemakers took over the older chapel of Christchurch off the High Street. In Ashburton, there was a guild chapel of St Laurence distinct from the parish church, and some chapels in other places were probably run by guilds, as we shall see, and may have been founded chiefly for the use of their members.

The other two kinds of chapel were chapels of ease and cult chapels. A chapel of ease existed to serve a larger body of people, those of a neighbourhood, but was still limited in its ministry to a particular area. In Devon, where some parishes were large and many roads were difficult to pass because of mud and streams, chapels came to be built in outlying places so that their inhabitants would be 'eased' of frequent travel to the parish church and have a local place of worship. In the wide parish of Crediton, this role was fulfilled by chapels at Kennerleigh, Sandford, Yeoton, and other places, while Hartland had similar buildings at Cheristow, Meddon, Philham, and Welcombe. When new settlements were created by lords of manors in the thirteenth century with the hope of developing trade and income, these too were provided with chapels in such places as Bow, Newport (Bishop's Tawton), Newton Poppleford, and South Zeal. Cult chapels were built to honour Christ or a saint, and their builders wished not to restrict their operation but to attract as many people and from as far away as possible. Chapels of this kind included St Anne and St Clair outside Exeter, St Michael at Brentor and St Michael on Burgh Island in Bigbury parish, and St Nicholas, patron of sailors, on Drake's Island in Plymouth harbour.

Chapels were built in a wide range of locations, extending the imprint of Christianity upon the landscape that had begun with minsters and parish churches. They were present in nearly all the towns especially Barnstaple, Exeter, and Plymouth. Exeter had at least seven within its walls and eight in its suburbs, as well as those in canons' houses. One, St Bartholomew, stood near the city's east gate. Elsewhere, chapels were placed alongside roads like St Anne (Exeter) and South Zeal, and frequently on or at the approach to bridges. Barnstaple, Bideford, Exeter, Ottery St Mary, and Totnes all had pontine chapels. They were built in churchyards alongside but

Figure 27 Baptism. Everyone was baptised in England by the Norman Conquest, usually on the day of birth. Here a priest christens a baby boy in a font along with a clerk to hold his book, two godfathers, and a godmother.

separate from parish churches: at Barnstaple (Figure 29, p. 130), Moretonhampstead, Nymet Tracey, Pilton, and Tiverton, for example. Some were sited near parish boundaries, such as Billingsmore (Bradninch) and Nomanschapel (Thorverton). Others were placed at spots of environmental significance. They lay in or near woodland at Frithelstock, St Giles in the Wood (Torrington), and St James in the Wood (Lewdown). They stood on hills at Brentor, Firebeacon (Hartland), and South Brent, and looked out to the sea from promontories at St Anchorite (Holbeton), St Nicholas (Ilfracombe), and St Katherine (Plymouth Hoe). The chapels of Burgh Island and Drake's Island formed part of a chain of similar buildings on islands round the coasts of England and Wales.

The founders of chapels were the gentry in their houses and groups of local people in the case of chapels of ease, perhaps with the backing of a lord of a manor. Cult chapels were probably the work of one or more enthusiasts. St Anne (Exeter) was built in 1418 by John Wygwar, a chantry priest of the cathedral, with the help of the earl of Devon and other important people.[29] Baselake chapel (Bere Ferrers), according to a tradition in the founder's family, was created by Henry Ley, a gentleman soldier of Henry VII. He dreamt while on campaign abroad that he should found a chapel there in honour of the Virgin Mary, and did so when he returned.[30] If public, a chapel would be maintained by its lord or by a guild like that of St Anne (South Molton), with the help of contributions from its worshippers and visitors.[31] Some chapels obtained indulgences from the bishop to encourage donations, but the indulgences were small in value and so were the donations, it seems, except at the larger chapels of ease. Three small chapels near Exeter recorded profits of a few shillings in the fifteenth century; when their costs are taken into account, their earnings can rarely have exceeded about one pound per annum.[32]

All chapels were subject to the church and clergyman of the parish in which they lay, but the extent of subjection differed from case to case. Some chapels of ease came close to being parish churches in that they had a recognised 'sub-parish', a chaplain paid by the parish clergyman, and Sunday services. Such chapels often had substantial buildings approaching the size of a church, but they were frequently denied a font and a burial ground, and their congregations had to behave as members of the parish church in terms of paying tithes, going for confession, and attending the church on major festivals. Other chapels of ease, and all private and cult chapels, were lower in status and their buildings were usually smaller. They had no allocated priest and had to purchase the services of the parish incumbent as necessary or someone approved by him. Mass could be celebrated in such chapels only on a weekday so as not to compete with the parish church. The clergyman and the church congregation took no responsibility for maintaining the chapel, but the chapel's supporters had to sustain not only its costs but pay any profits to the clergyman and still bear their full share in the upkeep of the church.

The typical small chapel was a building the size of a one-storey house made of stone or even cob. Ayshford (Burlescombe) and Fardel (Cornwood) are good surviving examples.[33] Such a chapel would be divided with a screen, as in a church, so that worshippers would occupy the outer section or antechapel while the priest led the service from the inner part at an altar flanked by the statue of the patron saint. Such services might be infrequent. Lacy licensed mass in the chapel of St Bridget (Wembworthy) only once a year on her feast-day, and in the chapels of St James, St Margaret, and St Michael (East Budleigh) only on theirs.[34] There are numerous other such licences. The typical chapel at a manor house may have been chiefly used by the owners for their private daily prayers, and public chapels by local people or travellers to say the Paternoster and Ave Maria and to light a candle in honour of the saint. Such worship, largely led by lay people in chapels often sited in remote locations, anticipated the non-Anglican meeting houses that were to take their place after the middle of the seventeenth century.

Medieval chapel worship was Catholic, of course, and imitated what went on in a parish church. Yet even so there could be a tendency to non-conformity or at least eccentricity, because chapels were relatively free from scrutiny and control. Several examples of unusual activities in chapels came to the notice of the Church authorities.[35] In Devon, Grandisson was shocked to hear in 1351 of a dubious cult that had sprung up at a chapel by a wood at Waddycleave, close to Frithelstock Priory. The chapel had been built by a canon of the priory without the bishop's permission, apparently in honour of the Virgin Mary, and had become a popular place of resort for what Grandisson called 'fortune telling'. Presumably people asked the Virgin to predict the future or to find lost objects. The bishop ordered the building to be destroyed, calling it fitter for 'proud and disobedient Eve or lewd Diana' than for Mary, and he was not pleased to hear from his agents that they had merely removed the altar and the candles offered by pilgrims. He insisted that the walls should be demolished and was reassured on this point, although there is some doubt as to whether his demands were fully obeyed. There were still traces of the building on the site in the eighteenth century.[36]

The foundation of a chapel inevitably led its supporters to lessen their involvement with the parish church, and this sometimes prompted disputes. The larger chapels of ease were prone to develop ambitions to secede from the mother parish and turn themselves into independent churches. Such ambitions were usually resisted by the patron of the parish church, its clergyman, and its core parishioners, all of whom stood to lose financially from such a departure, and the bishop invariably gave them his backing. The people of Sandford in Crediton parish tried to develop their chapel into a parish church. In 1432, Lacy allowed them to have Sunday services but revoked his permission when they began to withdraw from Crediton church. Sandford renewed its attempt in 1524 and Bishop Veysey sanctioned the holding of services and funerals, but in all other respects the people were told to fulfil their obligations to Crediton.[37] In 1439, a determined attempt was made to remove the chapel of Templeton from Witheridge parish by the Order of St John, which owned the surrounding manor of Templeton, and by the local inhabitants. The bishop ordered an enquiry which found that a friar had been brought in to consecrate the chapel as a church. Following this, a chaplain was hired, baptisms were administered, and a graveyard was created, allegedly with false graves to suggest antiquity. The bishop's judgment is not recorded but he would certainly have upheld the rights of Witheridge.[38]

As we have seen, only about ten chapels of ease succeeded in breaking away from their mother churches during the fourteenth and fifteenth centuries, probably through negotiation.[39] Others, like Sandford and Templeton, gained freedom during the changes of the Reformation. By the 1540s, there were also a few buildings known as 'free chapels'. These included the chapels of the bridge (Barnstaple), Blackborough (Kentisbeare), Colcombe (Colyton), Fremington (Instow), Taddiport (Little Torrington, Figure 21, p. 90), and Washbourne (Harberton).[40] They were free of some control by the parish church, but not necessarily in all respects. Blackborough was a former parish church which had dwindled into a chapel, while Taddiport had been the chapel of a leper hospital, so that they inherited their independence. All held endowments of land and had a paid chaplain, who held services and was presumably appointed by the patron of the chapel. Whether they all had rights of baptism, marriage, and burial is less certain.

Wells and Crosses

Other holy sites were based at wells. This is a difficult subject in Devon and elsewhere, because so many attributions of 'holy wells' come from the eighteenth and nineteenth centuries when folklore and antiquarianism may have given them a sanctity that they did not possess in earlier times.[41] Nevertheless, there were certainly many such wells in medieval Devon. We have already noted the words in the place-names Halwell in Brixton, Halwell near Totnes, and Halwill in north Devon, all found before 1100.[42] Similar place-names occur in later times at Manaton (1333), Morebath (1249), Parracombe (1330), Shebbear (1322), South Milton (1309), South Pool (1333), Tawstock (1390), Walkhampton (1333), and Whitchurch (1353).[43] Other sites are mentioned in legends of local saints. Sidwell of Exeter was linked with a well close to her church; Nectan of Hartland was said to have carried his head to a well near the parish church; and Urith of Chittlehampton allegedly caused a spring to appear at the place of her execution.[44] Some medieval chapels were built near wells. They include St Mary at Ladywell (Chulmleigh) mentioned in 1379, St Clair at Parker's Well in Matford Lane (Exeter) in 1430, and St Mary and St Michael at Holywell (Dittisham) in 1452.[45] The water of Parker's Well was reckoned good for sore eyes in later times, and since Clair was a patron saint of eye disorders, the chapel was probably built in his honour for that reason.

At least thirty-six wells in Devon with religious associations are certainly or probably recorded before the Reformation, the collection of data being greatly frustrated by problems of evidence.[46] As in Cornwall where numerous wells are known, they existed by late Saxon times in widely scattered places. In terms of structures, the Devon wells were generally provided with small stone hutches or well-houses to protect the water, and there is no known example of the elaborate pavilions that survive in Cornwall at St Cleer and Dupath, although both counties had chapels near wells. On either side of the Tamar, wells might lie close to churches as at Halwell near Totnes, where the well gave its name to the church, and St Sidwell's. Equally, they might be sited far away, like those in Devon that gave rise to minor place-names. In both counties, wells were often linked with the saints of the local parish church, most of whom in Cornwall were Brittonic and many unique to one place, although wells of Jesus and Our Lady are also recorded. In Devon, these features were reversed. A few of the wells were associated with Brittonic saints, but more were apparently named after national and international figures like Mary and Peter. There is no reason to suppose that wells were used for baptism in either county, since that rite had to take place in church, but it is possible that their water was used for filling fonts. A more certain function was to heal disorders: in Devon's case eye-strain, fevers, and respiratory problems are mentioned in modern times. In Cornwall after the Reformation, they were also used for divining the future, and that may have been so in medieval Devon although the practice is not yet attested.

Both counties were widely embellished with standing stone crosses.[47] These had begun to appear in Anglo-Saxon times: sometimes with intricately carved shafts like those that survive in Devon at Colyton, Copplestone, and St Nicholas Priory (Exeter). Copplestone's, as we have seen, stood at the intersection of three estates or parishes. By the later Middle Ages, it was usual for churchyards to contain a stone cross on a stepped plinth, examples of which may be seen at Clyst St Lawrence, Langtree, Pancrasweek, and elsewhere. Similar crosses were often built in the streets of towns and villages such as Northlew and Plympton, while smaller ones without plinths were placed alongside roads and tracks, sometimes to mark the boundaries of estates or parishes. Four crosses in South Brent parish, denoting the borders of Brent Moor, are recorded in 1557.[48] Others were put along the routes to the parish church, and were points where processions halted while carrying the dead to their funerals.[49] It was common to pray at crosses of all kinds by saying the Paternoster, especially for the souls of those who had died.[50]

The larger crosses in churchyards and elsewhere are often known as 'preaching crosses'. That can hardly have been their normal function since any preaching by the parish clergyman (and even perhaps by visiting friars) would be done in the

Figure 28
The eucharist. A priest holds up a consecrated wafer at an altar with a gold chalice upon it. The parish clerk and a group of privileged lay people kneel behind him.

church. Rather, they were visible symbols of Christianity in churchyards, with a special role on Palm Sunday when the clergy and parishioners went round the church in procession and stopped at the cross for the reading of the gospel and the singing of Latin texts.[51] The records of Ashburton, Morebath, and other churches call such crosses 'palm crosses' because they were decorated on this occasion.[52] In the sixteenth century, Reformers came to dislike crosses as they disliked images, for their association with Catholic worship and prayers for the dead. Some bishops ordered the removal of churchyard crosses and in other cases they were unofficially damaged or destroyed by Protestant activists.[53] Sir John Chichester pulled down Barnstaple's as early as 1552–3.[54] That probably explains why so few remain in Devon, although a good many of their shafts and socket stones survive near their sites, perhaps through fear of using them for other purposes.

The Religion of the Community

Christianity emphasises the community as well as the individual, and much of medieval religion took a communal form. First of all, there was the obligation of the parishioners to maintain the parish church and its furnishings: usually (but not always) excluding the fabric of the chancel. By the late thirteenth century, officers existed to raise money or find materials for the purpose, and Quinil's synod required them to account for their work each year to the clergy of the church and a select group of parishioners.[55] By the fourteenth century, these officers were known as 'church reeves' and by the fifteenth, as 'wardens' or 'churchwardens'. There were generally two of them, but sometimes four, and they might have assistants: Ashburton had four wardens and an oligarchy of eight men who helped to run parish affairs. Wardens served for a year, and it was often expected that the head of each household, or at least the respectable ones, would hold the office in turn. That meant that a widow might be a warden from time to time.

By at least the end of the fourteenth century, some wardens in England were keeping written accounts of the moneys they handled. Accounts of this kind survive from about twenty-five parishes in Devon for periods up to the mid sixteenth century: a large number by national standards.[56] A church's income came from church ales (convivial parties for which ale was brewed and sold), the sale of candles, the hiring of the church cross and large wax 'torches' for funerals, small donations, and occasional fees for burials in church. Some churches owned fields or cottages, and rented them out. Guilds and stores (which are discussed below) contributed money as well. This income was spent on maintaining the nave and its furnishings; the repair or renewal of service books, ornaments, and vestments; and the provision of wafers, wine, incense, and charcoal for services. The church bells had to be thought of (bell ropes were often replaced), along with the maintenance of an organ and a clock if the church had them. In the case of a large project, such as the installation of a new roodscreen or new seating, the wardens would need to engage in additional fund raising, perhaps for several years.

As well as supporting the running of the church, the community was involved with its chief religious activities. Here the calendar was a strong influence, since most communal religion was linked with the Church's festivals and the seasons of the year. Christmas Day and the following week were a time of some relaxation from work, celebration, and the observance of a series of holy days that ended with Epiphany on 6 January. More important was Lent in February or March, depending on the date of Easter. This was a time of penitence and fasting. It began on Ash Wednesday with a service at which lay people were smeared with ashes on their foreheads, after which all men and women over the age of puberty were required to abstain from eating meat or dairy foods until Easter Day and to confine themselves to fish or vegetarian fare. No marriages were permitted and it was a requirement of the Church that all adults should come to confession: the one occasion in the year when this was demanded.

The way in which confession worked in Devon can be reconstructed from a fifteenth-century copy of Quinil's synodal statutes preserved in Exeter Cathedral Library.[57] In the copy, someone towards the end of the century added a Latin note to the effect that 'This is the order of the parishioners of Bere Ferrers for confessing sins'. There follows a list of places within the parish: farmsteads and hamlets, grouped under days of the week beginning with the Monday after Ash Wednesday. The places are arranged in a topographical order, going round the parish clockwise. It was the invariable practice that confession took place in the parish church, not in people's homes, and the list of places and weekdays provided a timetable for people to attend church for the purpose. The Thursday and Friday after Ash Wednesday are not mentioned in the list, perhaps because this was when the rector heard the confessions of the lord of the manor and his household.

On the following Monday, the dwellers at Stone, Ley, and Tuckham came to the church, followed by those of Liphill, Clamoak, and Peche on Tuesday, and so on. The system ensured that the rector of the parish did not wait in church for his flock to arrive, and that those who came were not kept too long for their turns. It was also equitable in that, apart from the lord, it avoided placing people in order of rank. In church, the clergyman sat in his stall in the chancel or in a special confessional stall, and drew his hood over his head (Figure 30, p. 135). The adults knelt beside him in turn and made their confession, but how long this took and what advice and penances were given are matters that we can only surmise. Serious sins could only be handled by experienced clergy known as penitentiaries, like the friars whom we encountered in the previous chapter. These men were appointed by the bishop, one for each rural deanery, but again we know nothing about their work.

The climax of Lent came with Holy Week, the week before Easter. Palm Sunday was a festival day on which clergy and parishioners went in procession around the church and returned to be greeted by the hymn *Gloria laus et honor*, 'All glory, laud, and honour', sung in the case of the cathedral by the choir on the exterior gallery above the west front. The rest of the week was penitential. The ceremonies of Maundy Thursday included the washing of feet by the priest and the giving of alms to the poor. The altars were stripped of their coverings. On Good Friday, the Passion narrative was read (in Latin) and the congregation venerated a portable cross held by the priest's assistants, 'creeping to the cross' with bare feet across the church floor. After that, a consecrated wafer was put into the Easter sepulchre, to represent the burial of Christ. A watch was then kept on the sepulchre until Easter morning by members of the clergy or congregation.

On Saturday afternoon, the altars were dressed again, a baby was baptised in the font if one had been born in the previous week, and new fire was kindled and used to light the Easter candle. On Easter Day itself, all adults were expected to receive communion: a rare event for which they had been prepared by their Lenten confession and fasting. Given the social hierarchy, it is likely that communion was given in order of rank while kneeling in front of the roodscreen. Each person received a consecrated wafer, placed into the mouth, while a towel was held below the recipient's chin lest crumbs of Christ's body should fall. This was followed by a sip of unconsecrated wine from a cup. Consecrated wine was not used, again because of the fear that spilling such wine would be spilling the blood of Christ.

Spring and early summer were the season of the great church processions. There were six of these apart from Palm Sunday: St Mark's Day (25 April), the Rogation days (the Monday, Tuesday, and Wednesday of the sixth week after Easter), Ascension Day (the Thursday of the same week), and Corpus Christi (the second Thursday after Pentecost or Whitsunday). Their significance differed from one to another. Palm Sunday, Ascension Day, and Corpus Christi were days of celebration of Christ's coming as king, his ascension to heaven, and his presence in the communion bread and wine. In Exeter, Corpus Christi was a day for plays: probably a cycle of plays in English like those of York on the history of the world from Adam to Jesus and the Last Judgment.[58] The other days were penitential, when people were expected to use a restricted diet or even to fast for part of the day, and the purpose was to offer 'litanies' or prayers of supplication to God to protect the world from evil and to bless the growing crops.

All adults were expected to join the processions which went on journeys of varying lengths: the shortest being that of Palm Sunday. The Corpus Christi procession

Figure 29 The chapel of St Anne, Barnstaple. Built in the parish churchyard above a charnel where bones from the churchyard were stored, it was one of the hundreds of chapels that characterised the South-West of England in the later Middle Ages.

went further, bringing the sacrament in a portable shrine round the streets, and the Rogation processions were the longest of all, taking the participants into the fields and as far as the parish boundary or beyond.[59] At Exeter Cathedral, these processions left at about 10.00am and went to another church in the city or the suburbs: probably to a different church each day. Country churches appear to have done the same, utilising the chapels that stood in most of their parishes. At Lifton, the Monday procession was made to the chapel at Ashleigh, about a mile and half from the church.[60] At Chulmleigh, processions were made, no doubt on different days, to the chapel at Ladywell and to another named after St Nectan.[61] The beating of the parish bounds, which came to be associated with the Rogation processions after the Reformation, is not emphasised in medieval records and probably reflects the growth of the parish as a unit of local government during the Tudor period. Indeed, it is possible that some parish processions met one another at a convenient spot for a joint service. This practice is recorded in Cornwall, and may account for a few of the remoter chapels found in Devon. Nomanschapel (Thorverton) stood near the boundaries of four parishes, and could well have been used for a joint celebration of mass.

The Rogation processions had a character all of their own. The walkers were led by a dragon held up on a pole, its long tail stiffened with straw. Next came three banners marked with red crosses, a banner displaying a lion, other banners, clergy and clerks with candles, incense, and a casket of relics, and finally the laity, doubtless in order of rank. On Monday, everyone fasted until the procession arrived at its destination and mass was celebrated, after which there was apparently picnicking. On Tuesday, the fast was less severe, but the procession followed a similar form. On Wednesday, a change took place (Figure 8, p. 28). The lion banner now took precedence and the dragon was demoted to follow the other banners; furthermore, the straw was removed from its tail, so that the latter hung 'drooping and depressed'. This symbolised the history of the world. Monday and Tuesday represented the first two ages: before the Law of Moses and the period under the Law, when the Devil (represented by the dragon) was in power. Wednesday signified the age of grace, when Christ overthrew the Devil, hence the leadership of the procession by the banner with the lion, Christ being termed the 'Lion of Judah' in the Book of Revelation.

The rest of the year, from June to December, saw further communal events. Midsummer Day, 24 June, was both a religious festival, St John the Baptist's Day, and a day (or rather an evening) for making midsummer bonfires. Lammas Day, 1 August, the feast of St Peter in Chains, was the day to present the first loaf of the harvest in church. Otherwise, harvest celebrations were secular rather than religious. The custom of holding the church's dedication feast at harvest time (celebrating the day on which the building had been dedicated) began at the Reformation; previously, dedication feasts might be held at any time of the year. Harvest coexisted uneasily with the Church, because it was the time when farmers had to pay their grain tithes to the rector or appropriator. Later in the year, Michaelmas Day (29 September) was a festival with social accompaniments such as the eating of a Michaelmas goose fattened in the grain stubble, and as the season darkened, the time arrived for dressing up by children. On the feasts of St Clement and St Katherine (23 and 25 November), boys attired as priests, bishops, and women went singing from house to house, gathering food or money. On St Nicholas Day, 6 December, and Holy Innocents' Day, 28 December, this practice entered the church itself, with the selection of a boy bishop to lead the services, accompanied by other boys dressed as clergy. On these days too, the bishop and his companions roamed the parish, asking for contributions.[62]

By about 1500, most church communities had acquired premises in which to hold social events. The assumption is often made that parish churches themselves were used for feasting and drinking. While this may have happened occasionally, it was not encouraged by the Church authorities. Bishop Brewer's synod barred clergy from even announcing in church that ale-feasts were to be held, and the bishop of Winchester in *c.*1247 forbade drinkings in church, especially in Lent when clergy baked the eucharist bread there and people apparently gathered to speed the process in a convivial way.[63] It is likely therefore that the authorities drove the holding of social events from the church to other places at an early date, and by the fifteenth century, the 'church house' was a familiar feature of most parishes and their social life. It was typically built on the edge of the churchyard in the form of a long narrow building facing the street. At first this may have comprised a simple hall with a raftered roof, traces of which survive at Throwleigh, but by the sixteenth century, it had become a more elaborate structure of two storeys like those that survive at South Tawton and Widecombe. The lower storey contained a fireplace and oven where ale could be brewed or food cooked, while the upper provided the space for eating, drinking, or merriment.[64] The building was used by the whole community for its gatherings, or was rented out to individuals for parties.

The Religion of Groups

Parish activities brought people together, but not all religious practice was communal. Ever since guilds are first recorded in the tenth century, groups formed within the community to interact and worship. Much more is known about such groups in the later Middle Ages, thanks to wills and churchwardens' accounts that often mention them. They were based on three institutions: stores, companies, and guilds. A store was a fund. The church itself had a store named after the patron saint, which was the income administered by the churchwardens. Other stores belonged to the images in the church, and consisted of the offerings made to them by devotees in the form of money or livestock such as cattle, sheep, or bees. One or two wardens would administer the store and use the profits to burn a light in front of the image, to refurbish it, or to support the costs of running the church. A store made a common bond between those who supported it but did not necessarily generate group activities, although its supporters may have met in church for mass on the day of the saint and even have shared a meal afterwards.

The other two institutions had a stronger social structure. A company, to use a modern term, was a group of parishioners of a particular age and gender. In the parishes where such companies existed, there were generally three of them: the young men, the maidens, and the wives. One became a full member of the church at puberty: twelve for girls and fourteen for youths. The young men were those aged from fourteen until the mid twenties, when people married, and the maidens were the equivalent group of girls. The wives were the married women and possibly also the widows. The married men did not have a company, perhaps because they usually ran the church as churchwardens and dominated any parish guilds. The three companies therefore represented those of lower status in the church community. They each formed a kind of guild (although the word was not applied to them) which raised money for the church through brewing and selling ale or other activities, and probably held convivial events for themselves from time to time. In church, they might venerate a particular saint's image: the wives most likely the Virgin Mary. Ashburton had two groups of young men: those undifferentiated, who probably lived in the town, and those described as 'rural' or 'on land' who came from the countryside.[65]

The last kind of institution was the guild or fraternity, which we have met in previous centuries. This was more formally constituted than a store or company. In the larger towns, the ruling body itself was a kind of guild: the city council in Exeter and probably the guild of St Nicholas in Barnstaple.[66] Where there were large groups of craftsmen, they formed guilds to establish working practices and to protect their members, like the guilds of the weavers and tuckers, shoemakers, and skinners in Exeter. All such guilds had a spiritual dimension, and worshipped at least occasionally in a particular church or chapel. Smaller towns and prosperous rural parishes were more likely to have one or two guilds with a stronger religious focus, often named after a saint and also based in the church or a local chapel. The wealthiest guilds accumulated lands through members' donations, enabling them to employ a priest for part or all of the time. In the 1540s, there were guilds employing clergy in the parish churches of Bradninch, Buckland Brewer, Cullompton (two), Halberton, Hatherleigh, Silverton, Totnes (two), and Winkleigh, as well as the chapel of St Laurence (Ashburton).[67] In view of what we know of social structure, it is likely that parish guilds were controlled by men, although their wives and widows might also be members, and by the upper orders of society. Members may have worn a distinctive livery on special occasions to show their importance. Gentry might be invited to join, but the main power would have lain with yeoman farmers in the countryside and merchants and substantial tradesmen in the towns. Such guilds were influential local bodies.

We do not know how many guilds were based in parish churches, because one of the main sources – churchwardens' accounts – is concerned with money and therefore refers to 'stores' which may have been simple stores or stores belonging to guilds. At Ashburton, it is not certain if any of the stores was also a guild. However, there can be no doubt that organisations of one kind or another – stores, companies, and guilds – abounded in churches by the end of the Middle Ages. In the early sixteenth century, the modest parish of Iddesleigh had at least four stores, and its counterpart Morebath, on the borders of Exmoor, six stores and two companies: young men and maidens.[68] There were at least six stores at Honiton and at least seven at South Molton, while Ashburton boasted about sixteen as well as four companies.[69] When these figures are multiplied by the number of churches in Devon, there must have been two or three thousand of them in the county, supported by anything from a handful of people to a substantial body of powerful men.

Guilds, companies, and stores all had a spiritual patron: the Trinity, Christ, Corpus Christi, an angel (usually Michael), or a saint. The most popular male saints were Andrew, George, James, John the Baptist, John the Evangelist, Peter, and Thomas Becket, and the female ones the Virgin Mary, Katherine, Margaret, and Mary Magdalene. Only two of Devon's own saints enjoyed support beyond a single locality: Nectan of Hartland, who had a chapel at Chulmleigh and a statue in the cathedral, and Sidwell of Exeter who acquired an altar at Morebath; both of them were also honoured in Cornwall.[70] During the later fourteenth and fifteenth centuries, a few other saints – hitherto almost unknown – came into fashion from the Continent. The most popular of these was Anne, allegedly mother of the Virgin, whose cult spread widely over Devon from Kentisbury to Bigbury.[71] Others were John of Bridlington (died 1379), an Augustinian canon, venerated at South Molton and elsewhere, and Syth (died 1272), an Italian girl, patron of servants, keys, and lost objects.[72] Roche (died *c*.1380), a Provencal hermit and plague-victim, was invoked by those in the grip or the fear of plague. He was commemorated by a hospital in Exeter, and both he and Syth appear on roodscreens in Devon.[73]

The Religion of the Individual

Not all religion was based on the whole community or on groups. The Church consisted of millions of individual people, whose piety differed according to status,

Figure 30
Confession. Every adult parishioner was obliged to attend confession during Lent. Here a parishioner kneels to confess before a hooded priest, while others await their turn.

interest, or commitment. Piety was most often expressed in prayer, but little is recorded of how people prayed. Since Anglo-Saxon times, Christians had been expected to know by heart in Latin the Paternoster (Lord's Prayer) and the Apostles' Creed, to which the Ave Maria (Hail Mary) was added in the twelfth century.[74] Not everyone knew them, however, since there are literary references to people's deficiencies in this respect. When the prayers were known, they were often said over and over again with the use of a 'paternoster' or rosary. The beads guided the user to say the Paternoster, followed by ten repetitions of the Ave Maria, and finally *Gloria patri* ('Glory be to the Father'). This sequence was repeated up to fifteen times, the whole recitation being described as 'Our Lady's psalter'. The basic prayers could be said in their own right as prayers to God and the Virgin Mary, or offered for a good cause. They were appropriate to use as an intercession for someone who had died, the merit of doing so devoutly being transferable to help that person's soul.[75] Lay people must often have prayed for the dead, because many epitaphs on tombs request the onlooker to 'Pray for the soul of . . .'. Reports of miracles indicate that it was also common to call on saints for help in times of trouble.

From at least the thirteenth century onwards, richer and literate people had prayer-books for use at home or in church. One such was the 'primer' which contained the three basic prayers, the Ten Commandments, the Confession, and some of the psalms. Most primers were in Latin up to the 1530s, but versions in English sometimes survive. In either language, they often begin with an alphabet, which seems intended to help the possessor learn to read or to teach a child to do so. At a higher level, there was the 'Book of Hours' (confusingly, also known as the primer) which included simplified versions of the daily Latin services with particular devotion to the Virgin Mary. Much prayer was said aloud while using the rosary or the Book of Hours. An Italian visitor to England in about 1500 noticed people reciting the book in church with a friend, 'verse by verse, in a low voice, after the manner of the clergy'.[76]

Two manuscript prayer-books have survived which belonged to private owners in north Devon during the fifteenth and early sixteenth centuries.[77] One is connected with Tawstock, but does not reveal if it was used by a cleric or a lay person. The other was owned by one of the Rayny family of gentry from Eggesford and later passed to the Harewode family of South Molton. Each is a standard copy of the Book of Hours, such as one would buy from a bookseller, beginning with a calendar listing the festivals of the year and the major saints' days. The owners of both books then made them personal by adding the feast days of two local saints (Nectan and Urith), the dedication festivals of the owners' churches (South Molton and Tawstock), and (in the Rayny book) the dates of deaths of members of the family. This enabled the user to mark the passing of the Church year both as it was kept throughout Europe and as he or she wished to observe it in north Devon.

Each volume contains extra devotions that shed light on popular religion at the end of the Middle Ages. The Tawstock book recommends fasting on bread and water on the twelve Good Fridays of the year, explaining when these occur. God will protect those who do so from an evil death or a death without confession; the Devil will not know of their passing and will therefore fail to intercept their souls as they leave the mouth and seek to fly to heaven. The South Molton book includes a Latin prayer with a similarly reassuring outcome: a prayer allegedly composed by St Peter. Those who say or write it will be treated well by important people, able to calm storms at sea, invulnerable in battle, cured of haemorrhages, and safely delivered in childbirth. To a modern observer, these pieces of advice look like superstitious practices that claim to save the soul and body through mechanical rituals rather than through prayer of a normal kind. That is true, but they also remind us of something that is timeless. The people who used these books had the same fears that we have of disease, disaster, and sudden death, and the same wish to find a trustworthy way of avoiding them.

People were urged to practise their Christianity in deeds of charity. Household accounts of gentry elsewhere in England record the alms that a gentleman or his wife might dispense to those in need: pennies or twopences to prisoners, poor infirm people, poor scholars, or friars.[78] In Devon, the chief evidence on this subject comes from wills, which have limitations in what they tell us. Those that survive were chiefly made by wealthy men and follow predictable lines, in which charity is more formalised and given on a larger scale than it would have been on a day-to-day basis. About twenty wills of lay people are recorded in the registers of Stafford and Lacy, between 1405 and 1450.[79] They begin with directions for where the will-maker wishes to be buried, the management of the funeral, and the masses to be said when their makers were dead. Bequests are made to the makers' parish churches and to guilds and stores within the churches. Sometimes a church elsewhere is remembered, where the will-maker was born. Small bequests to friaries are common and sometimes the list of gifts is extended to monasteries, nunneries, and hospitals.

Many wills make gestures of help to the poor. A frequent practice is to provide small sums of money to those who come to the funeral, no doubt with the expectation that they would offer their prayers in return. Sometimes the poor are made a part of the funeral: given mourning clothes to wear and provided with candles to carry. Less often, other bequests are made to them of money or livestock, and Thomas Reymound remembered the prisoners in the king's and bishop's gaols in Exeter. Another outlet of charity was public works. One citizen of Exeter, Simon Grendon (died 1411), bequeathed £40 to improve his city's water supply, while another, William Wilford (died 1413), left £10 and a tenement for the same purpose. More often, people gave money for the repair of bridges in the districts where they lived, as we have seen was done by some of the clergy.

The Church encouraged men and women to pray and do works of charity by means of indulgences, or 'pardons' as they were more often known.[80] Pardons forgave sinners some or all of the penance that they were required to do to expiate their sins. The device originated with the popes at the time of the Crusades. They offered warriors who went to the Holy Land a complete or 'plenary' remission of all the penances they had incurred. Later on, wealthy people could purchase plenary remissions from the papacy for use at the time of their death. Partial remissions of penance also became widely available. Bishops could grant forty days of pardon for any good cause and popes an unlimited amount of time.[81] People in Devon had plenty of opportunities to benefit from pardons. Two nearby pilgrimage shrines, Compostella and St Michael's Mount, each professed to remit a third of one's penances on each visit. The cathedral asserted by the early sixteenth century that visitors and contributors could earn fifty-four years and forty days of remission: the aggregation of all the grants that the building had allegedly received.[82] Crediton church, as has been mentioned, claimed forty-one years on rather shakier grounds.[83] Grants of forty days by bishops of Exeter were made to parish churches, chapels, roads, bridges, harbours, hospitals, almshouses, individuals in need (such as the victim of a house fire, a wounded soldier, or prisoners in need of ransom), and even for prayers for dead people (usually gentry whose families had the means to ask the bishop to grant them). Institutions elsewhere in England had grants of pardons which they were anxious to advertise in Devon, and this led to the emergence of agents known as questors or pardoners who travelled the country advertising them and collecting donations. They were required to have the bishop's permission to carry out their work.

Pardoners came to have dubious reputations, as they do in Chaucer's *The Canterbury Tales*. Pardons certainly lent themselves to frauds and some pardoners were probably not blameless in that respect, but when efficient they must have been remarkably like modern charity collectors. One, Hugh Lauson, operated from Exeter in 1486.[84] The grants themselves deserve to be considered dispassionately. They arose from a rational belief that God's justice worked like earthly justice. A sin required a penalty to purge it as a crime did, but the penalty could be reduced by reparation. Pardons were meant to work as part of the confessional system, the sinner needing to be contrite and absolved by a priest at which point the indulgence could be used to offset the penance that the priest prescribed. Many indulgences did not involve money at all, but prayer, pilgrimage, or manual work on a bridge or chapel, and when money was involved, no sum was ever specified. It was left to the confessor to decide whether the given amount was suitable. Most of the forty-day pardons would have raised totals valued in shillings rather than pounds. Thomas More remarked in the 1530s, 'I never yet perceived the people to make so great offerings at a pardon that we should either pity greatly their cost or envy the priests that profit'.[85]

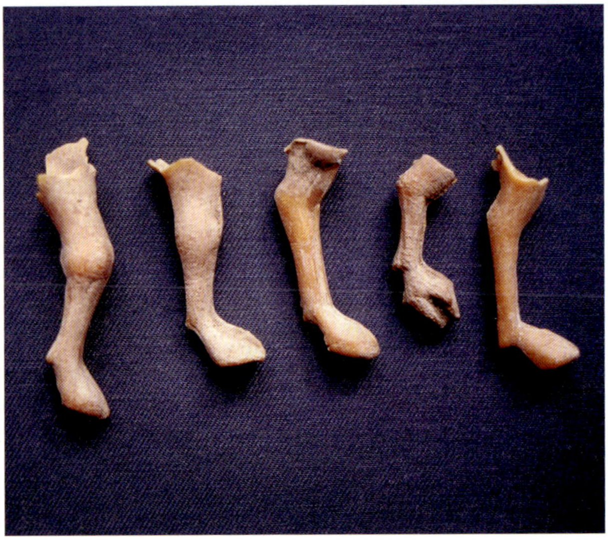

Figure 31 Wax images discovered in 1942 near the tomb of Bishop Lacy in Exeter Cathedral. They were probably offered in the hope of receiving cures to bodies, limbs, or animals, or as thanksgivings for cures received.

Pilgrimage

Pilgrimage was another personal choice. In modern imagination, it was a lengthy journey to a far-off shrine. In fact, most of those who travelled for this purpose went to places near their homes, which involved little expense of time and money. Any religious site might attract pilgrims, be it cathedral, monastery, parish church, chapel, or holy well. Such places had at least one festival a year on the day of the saint or some other significant day, when local people were likely to come to a mass or sermon and take part in secular festivities. Certain places in Devon attracted visitors more widely, but nearly all came from within the county; there was no shrine or image famous enough to draw pilgrims from elsewhere in England.

The cathedral was probably the most popular destination because it lay in the local centre of government and trade, so that many who visited Exeter for secular reasons were likely to enter its doors. It had King Æthelstan's collection of relics, and these were regularly displayed to the public during the Middle Ages.[86] The cathedral lacked an officially recognised saint like Canterbury, Durham, and many other great churches, but it contained the tombs of two bishops who were acclaimed as such by popular opinion. The first was James Berkeley, who died in 1327 after a reign of only three months. Pilgrims soon flocked to his tomb, presumably because miracles were reported there, but the Church authorities did not encourage the cult and it gradually faded away.[87] A similar burst of enthusiasm followed the death of Edmund Lacy in 1455 (Figure 31, p. 139), and this continued until the Reformation with the approval of the cathedral clergy.[88]

Two other places of pilgrimage stood just outside the walls of Exeter. On the north-east side, the shrine of St Sidwell lay in the parish church of that name, with its own keeper, a light burning constantly before it, and the holy well nearby. Devotion to Sidwell seems to have been widespread in Devon, since girls were named after her and her image appeared in other churches, notably at Morebath with its altar in her honour.[89] Across the river at Cowick Priory, there was the shrine of Walter of Cowick whom we encountered in the previous chapter. Devon's other local saints are likely to have had their devotees, although little is known about them: Brannoc of Braunton, Urith of Chittlehampton, Nectan of Hartland, Rumon of Tavistock, and others.[90]

There was more interest in venerating holy things, however, than could be satisfied by bodies and relics. During the later Middle Ages, statues of saints became popular objects of devotion. These included the image of the crucified Christ on the roodscreen and that of the Virgin Mary, especially in her act of holding the crucified body of Christ: an image that came to be known as 'Our Lady of Pity'. Every church had images of Christ and the Virgin, and these were likely to attract visitors from outside the vicinity if they were believed to confer benefits, especially in granting prayers or healing. In 1534, a Somerset rector arranged in his will for someone to visit the tomb of Edmund Lacy on his behalf as well as Our Lady of Pity at Sidbury. We know no more of the latter image than the will informs us, yet it (and probably others of its kind) was evidently famous beyond its neighbourhood.[91]

Although most pilgrimage was made within the county, some people continued to go on longer journeys as we saw in the twelfth century. Six Devonians are mentioned travelling to Whitstone (Cornwall) in 1361 in search of healing at the tomb of a clergyman there, reputed to be a saint.[92] It is likely that others went to the chief shrine in Cornwall, St Michael's Mount, as well as to the principal ones in England: of Thomas Becket at Canterbury, the Holy Blood at Hailes (Gloucs.), and the Virgin Mary at Walsingham (Norfolk). In the late fifteenth century, a cult of the murdered King Henry VI grew up at St George's Chapel (Windsor) where his body was finally buried. Miracles were ascribed to his intercession, and three of them took place in Devon. A Honiton man was relieved of a bean that had lodged in his ear since childhood, a boy from Cheriton Bishop was healed after being gored by his father's ox, and a dumb boy from an unrecorded place was enabled to speak at the age of ten. The Honiton patient was so grateful that he went to Windsor and offered a silver ear at Henry's tomb in thanks for his deliverance.[93]

Of the great shrines overseas, Compostella in Spain was closest to Devon since one could travel there by ship in about four days. The crown issued licences in the late fourteenth and fifteenth centuries for ship-owners to carry pilgrims on the *Andrew* of Plymouth, the *James* of Barnstaple, the *Margaret* of Topsham, and many other vessels. The principal points of departure were Dartmouth and Plymouth, but occasional ships set out from most of the northern and southern ports.[94] For the more venturesome, there was Rome which required a tiresome journey by land but gave people lavish spiritual rewards in the form of the pardons offered. These were increased in the years of jubilee, first held in 1300 and thereafter at intervals that were eventually fixed at every twenty-five years. Names in the visitors' book of the English hospice at Rome in 1505 included John Tregonwell, a vicar of Exeter Cathedral; Henry Peyne, a poor scholar of Exeter diocese; and Andrew Hosborne, a poor man of Ilfracombe.[95] More distant still, requiring further voyages by sea, were Rhodes, to which the knights of the Order of John went to defend Christendom against the Turks, and Jerusalem which was reached by a few intrepid English men and women, like Bishop Brewer in 1227–9.

Dissent

The evidence that we have just considered shows people at their most devout and obedient to the Church's doctrines and institutions. This may easily give a false impression, leading to the claim which is sometimes made that all or most of the population were good Catholics. It is inconceivable, given human nature, that everyone accepted all the Church's doctrines and obeyed all its rules at any time, and in the 1380s a dissenting movement emerged in England based on the teachings of John Wycliffe of Oxford (died 1384), whose members came to be known as Lollards. Lollards expressed opposition to papal authority, indulgences, Church property, transubstantiation, image worship, pilgrimages, and compulsory tithe-giving among other things. When these opinions first became public in 1382, one of Wycliffe's Oxford disciples, Laurence Steven or Bedeman, who was a Cornishman, made a tour of the diocese of Exeter teaching his master's beliefs. He did not have much time to do so. The bishop, Brantingham, at once forbade him to preach and Steven returned to Oxford. There he made his peace with the authorities, and a benefice was found for him in Devon: the rectory of Lifton. He became a conforming cleric of the diocese and Bishop Stafford used him as a penitentiary.[96]

The teachings of Wycliffe were condemned as heresies and errors in 1382, and in 1401 the death penalty was introduced for those who refused to recant them or, having done so, returned to embrace them again. Devon is not regarded as containing people of Lollard beliefs or activities, but there are two exceptions. Thomas Broke, a gentleman of Holditch in Thorncombe parish, then part of the county, was implicated in the Lollard rebellion of 1414 and spent some time in the Tower of London.[97] Seventeen years later, there was a second attempt at a Lollard rising in Wiltshire, which seems to have been the context for something that happened in Exeter. A medieval psalter belonging to the cathedral contains a calendar in which some of the clergy recorded unusual events. The earliest entry states that on 7 August 1431, Drew Steyner (some words have been rubbed out at this point) 'was deservedly burnt at Livery Dole' in Heavitree parish.[98] Burning was the punishment for heresy, and it looks as though the words erased once read 'impenitent heretic' and were removed at the Reformation. No record of the event has yet been found in any other source, so that we cannot tell whether Steyner was a Devonian or someone from elsewhere who had taken refuge in the county.

Two swallows do not make a summer, and there is no other report of heretical opinions in Devon until the early sixteenth century. Nevertheless, it would be unwise to conclude that such opinions did not exist. Lollardy must have been known about in the county, and sympathisers with it may well have escaped detection if they were discreet about their beliefs and fulfilled most of what was expected by the local clergyman and parish leaders. Moreover, the definition of heresy was made by the Church. It classified Wycliffe's opinions as heretical and persecuted those who were found to hold them. But it did not define other kinds of unorthodoxy in this way. People were forbidden to engage in extramarital sex, bury an unbaptised baby in a churchyard, withhold tithes and offerings, fail to attend church, rob a church, or assault a priest but these were not heresies. Historians have followed the Church in this respect, so that such activities are not considered part of the history of dissent, yet an activity is impossible without a thought and these activities indicate that the people concerned did not have total respect for the Church, its laws, its holy places, or its ministers.

The Church court records of offences by lay people against the Church's rules do not survive in Devon before the mid sixteenth century. However, when those accused declined to accept the courts' judgments and remained impenitent, the Church excommunicated them. After forty days had elapsed without their submission, the bishop sent a letter to the king requesting their arrest and imprisonment until they made their peace. These 'significations of excommunication' survive in the National Archives, providing the names of obstinate offenders and sometimes details of their offences. The latter were of the kinds mentioned above: refusal of tithes, fornication, arranging a clandestine marriage, violence against clergy or their property, perjury, and oath breaking.[99]

Sometimes, offenders attacked church buildings and their contents directly. One spectacular case concerned John Knyght, a 'husbandman' or peasant who went into the chapel of St John the Baptist at Newport (Bishop's Tawton) in 1441. He took a lighted candle and held it under the chin and nose of the Virgin Mary's statue until they were blackened with smoke. As he did so, he jeered, 'Mabbe [a pet-name for Mary], ware [beware] thy beard!'[100] Churches were sometimes burgled. In 1342, a chalice and missal were taken at night from North Bovey, while raiders at Morebath in 1535 broke open a chest, removed a chalice, and stole a silver shoe from St Sidwell's statue.[101] There was even an attack on Christ himself. One of the holiest objects in a church was the pyx that hung above the high altar and contained a consecrated wafer: the very body of Christ. Yet the pyx in the cathedral, the greatest church of the diocese, was stolen from its place during Grandisson's reign.[102]

This evidence survives by chance. It is hard to know how common such actions were, but there must have been others. They were grave offences against Church law, but they were not classified as heresy. Nevertheless, in a crude way, they were expressions of unbelief or hostility to the Church and, like slackness in attending worship, in fasting, or in sexual morality, they need to be included in the history of dissent.

Education, Music, and Literature

It is often assumed that the Church provided or controlled education in medieval times. This was true only to a limited extent. The Church, as this book should have shown, was not one organisation but many. Each religious house was responsible for training its own recruits. The cathedral, Crediton, Ottery St Mary, and Slapton

Figure 32 St Anne teaching the Virgin Mary to read. This scene was a popular motif in religious art from the thirteenth century onwards, reflecting the fact that wealthy girls were taught in such a way, often by their mothers.

also maintained choristers and adolescent clerks who were taught reading, plainsong, and sometimes Latin grammar. The larger monasteries had comparable youths in the persons of their almonry boys, and educated them in similar ways.[103] Boys of these kinds were not required to become adult members of religious houses, and when they left they could take up careers as parish clergy or laymen.

During the fifteenth century, polyphony – the singing of music in four or five parts – became popular in English churches. We have already noticed this development in monasteries which employed singing boys and taught them, but the monasteries only followed what was practised in royal chapels, cathedrals, and collegiate churches. Most of the polyphony took place not in the choir of the church but in the Lady chapel, where a special mass was sung in honour of the Virgin during the morning and an anthem devoted to her in the afternoon. Churches that maintained boys started to choose them more carefully with regard to their voices, and to appoint a special master to teach them polyphony, a man usually entitled 'the clerk of the [Lady] chapel'. This happened at the cathedral, Crediton, and Ottery as well as the larger abbeys and some ambitious parish churches, such as Ashburton, which had a choir of four men and four boys by 1481.[104]

The enthusiasm for polyphony became intense. Churches acquired organs or improved those that they had to enhance the singing. The cathedral spent the huge sum of £164 on installing a large new instrument in 1513–14.[105] Musicians were recruited to be clerks of the chapel, not only from within but outside the region. Two of the cathedral's clerks were local men, John Derke and James Northbroke, while others were incomers: Thomas Pack and Nicholas Toker. Works by Derke, Northbroke, and Pack survive in manuscripts, as do others by John Trouluffe who worked in the bishop's chapel and by Philip Alcock who was based at Crediton.[106] One of the most important collections of late-medieval music, the 'Ritson Manuscript', belonged to a cleric from Devon.[107] The most powerful and prestigious centre of polyphony was the chapel royal of the king, whose agents toured the kingdom looking for boys to recruit. One of these men, Robert Phillips, visited the cathedral in 1530 and 1534, receiving payments on these occasions that look suspiciously like bribes not to remove the finest choristers.[108]

The vast majority of those who had schooling in England were not taught like these boys in church institutions, or even in educational surroundings. Most learnt only to read, which was done in Latin. One began with the Latin alphabet and progressed to reading Latin words at sight. The texts used for the purpose were those contained in the primer: the Paternoster, Ave Maria, Credo, and other prayers and psalms. The meaning of the Latin was not taught at this stage and most children never learnt much of it, preferring to use their literary skills to read English which did not involve an unfamiliar grammar and vocabulary. Literate parents in the middle and upper orders of society often taught their children to read, and a common image of the time showed St Anne doing so to her daughter, the Virgin Mary (Figure 32, p. 144). Those who had no time or ability to teach their children could place a boy or girl in a private reading school, kept by a schoolmistress in her home or a parish clerk or chaplain in a corner of a parish church. Such people charged small fees for their work, but these were affordable by many in society. Nunneries often gave similar instruction to boys up to the age of seven and girls until they reached puberty, but since there were only three such houses in Devon, their impact was confined to children of wealthy families.[109]

The schooling of girls and most boys stopped at this level. They learnt to read a Latin text such as a prayer-book to the extent that they could pronounce it with devotion but not with complete understanding, and they acquired a more effective skill to read English. Large numbers of manuscripts in English containing stories and religious literature circulated among the rich, and by about 1500 the development of printing extended this to people of middling wealth through the production of cheap texts of a similar kind. To learn Latin fully, one went to a grammar school, grammar meaning Latin. Only boys did this, and only boys of fairly affluent families for several reasons. Grammar-school fees were higher than those of reading schools, writing materials and books were required, and it took at least three or four years to make progress in what was a strange foreign language. Moreover, grammar schools were mostly based in towns, so that a child who lived more than a few miles away from such a school needed to board overnight with the schoolmaster or in a private house. Then as now, the cost of boarding added hugely to the expenses of schooling.

Grammar schools catered for boys between the ages of about ten and eighteen, and taught them how to read, write, and speak Latin, including the skill of good handwriting. The teachers of these schools were laymen or priests who made their living by charging fees for their work (Figure 33, p. 148). Their schools are better recorded than reading schools, but still imperfectly so, because nobody supervised education or kept records of it. We have seen that Exeter probably had a public grammar school by the early twelfth century, and this school, later known as the High School, was the principal school of Devon.[110] The reference to Plympton school in 1263 is followed by others to Ottery St Mary in 1338 and Crediton in 1377. Tiverton may have had a school by the 1390s, and Dartmouth did so by 1490, Plymouth by 1507 (but doubtless much earlier), Totnes by 1509, and Barnstaple and Tavistock by about 1530.[111]

Little was done to create institutions of education, as opposed to private venture schools. The chief contributor in this respect was Stapledon, who has been mentioned for his foundation of Exeter College (Oxford) in 1314.[112] He intended to complement the college with an endowment for boys learning grammar in Exeter, but his murder in 1326 frustrated the project and it was left for Grandisson to complete in 1332, with the result that twelve (later nine) scholarships enabled boys to live at the hospital of St John (Exeter) while they attended the city High School.[113] In the 1380s, benefactors elsewhere in England began to found free grammar schools: free in the sense of not charging school fees, and about a hundred such schools were endowed across the kingdom up to 1530. But such initiatives were slow to reach Devon, and no free school is known in the county until the 1540s when we hear of two: at Ashburton and Barnstaple.[114] Paradoxically, this may mean that plenty of people could afford to buy education, so that charitable donors did not feel a need to help in the matter. In any case, free schooling in grammar was of little use to poor families. To send a boy to receive it, a father or mother needed to have the means to do without his earnings, the courage to send him into a higher social environment, the vision that he would profit from his learning, and (preferably) a connection with someone who would promote his career later on. The poor were better off picking up elementary education at a reading school, which would at least allow them to access material in English.

Two teenage students from Exeter in about 1450 have left us their notebooks: rare survivals of such books from medieval England.[115] Although at school at much the same time, they were as different as modern pupils might be in their talents and ambitions. William Berdon came from south Devon and was a competent Latinist. He copied grammatical texts into his notebook along with Latin exercises written or dictated in the classroom. The latter contain a number of local references like these, in translation:

> My parents, who live in the country in great penury, are put under a great strain by sending me to school to learn grammar in Exeter, and with a large family at home, acquiring food and clothes takes immense efforts.
>
> When I am at home, I live in the pleasant town of Totnes near the seaside and next to the great River Dart in which good fish abound – the best trout in the whole kingdom, they say. If only we might have three or four of them tomorrow for dinner so that we could test the popular boast about them!

William aimed at becoming a priest and was ordained as a subdeacon in 1456, but he then disappears from records. It is likely that he died young and that his book, being full of useful material, passed to another pupil.

Walter Pollard was a Plymouth lad whose father was probably mayor. He had more difficulty with his Latin and his exercises are often hard to translate; he also wrote in English, sometimes with wild spellings. After leaving school, he became a merchant dealing in wool among other things. Nonetheless, Walter was fond of

Figure 33 An English grammar school in the 1490s. The simplified scene shows a master in a chair with a birch, a boy being examined, and other boys seated nearby with their schoolbooks.

Latin and kept his notebook throughout his life, sometimes adding memoranda to it. He collected Latin and English proverbs: 'when the steed is stolen, it is time to shut the stable door'; 'when the game is best, it is time to rest'. He was fascinated by riddles. 'A crow [*cornix*] is white [*nix*] if the heart [*cor*] is taken from it.' 'If you have a bull [*taurum*], cut off the head [*t*] and it will become gold [*aurum*].' The Latin that Berdon and Pollard learnt was closely related to everyday life. Their school, like its counterparts elsewhere, trained boys to use the language for writing letters and documents, making inventories, or keeping accounts. These were practical skills that would enable them to function as gentlemen or merchants, or become clergy, lawyers, or secretarial clerks. The methods of teaching Latin and the standards reached by pupils in Devon were similar to those of schools elsewhere, showing that there was already a 'national curriculum' despite the lack of a mechanism for enforcing it.

Boys like these belonged to a literate society. Not everyone could read, but everyone's life was dependent upon written materials in one way or another. During the thirteenth century, an educational revolution took place, which has been described as the change 'from memory to written record'.[116] In about 1100, if there was a lawsuit about a piece of land, witnesses would be summoned to say what they remembered about the ownership. By the 1200s, the owner of the land would produce a written document, a charter, showing who owned the property and providing a more reliable piece of evidence. Not only property rights but much everyday business came to be written down. Royal commands, court proceedings, manorial records, financial accounts, letters, and wills all multiplied in quantity, along with prayer-books, treatises, works of fiction, and musical scores. By 1400, paper was widely available as a cheap means of recording all these matters.

Most of what was read and written in Devon during the later Middle Ages was probably practical in nature. We still possess the letters that John Shillingford, mayor of Exeter, wrote to his fellow city councillors during a protracted law-suit in London in 1447–8, as well as those that passed between the Stonor family of Oxfordshire and the managers of their property at Ermington.[117] But the wealthy of both sexes also read recreational literature, although the evidence for this remains to be fully collected. Texts of three romances in English (*Amis and Amiloun, Sir Ferumbras*, and *The Seege or Batayle of Troye*) have been linked with Devon on linguistic grounds, as well as three copies of Sir John Mandeville's popular but fictitious *Travels* through Asia.[118] Devon produced one great and original writer in this period: the lawyer Sir John Fortescue (died 1479). His studies of *The Governance of England* in English and *In Praise of the Laws of England* in Latin are pioneering works of political thought and legal history, but, as with Henry of Bracton, they grew out of a life passed in national government and politics, away from his native county.[119]

CHAPTER 5

The Reformation

The Church in the Early Sixteenth Century

In outward appearance, the Church in Devon between 1500 and 1530 was still what it had been in the fourteenth and fifteenth centuries. The bishop remained the richest man in the South-West of England. In the royal survey of Church wealth in 1535, the *Valor Ecclesiasticus*, his income was estimated at just over £1,566 per annum.[1] Those who held the office continued to be men with close links to the king. John Arundell (1502–4) had been a chaplain to Edward IV and the chancellor of Henry VII's eldest son, Prince Arthur. Hugh Oldham (1504–19) had been a chaplain to Henry's mother, Lady Margaret Beaufort, and to Henry himself (Figure 34, p. 155).

The bishop during much of the Reformation was John Veysey, who ruled from 1519 to 1551 and had a second term from 1553 to 1554.[2] He had been dean of the Chapel Royal and a forceful spokesman for Henry VIII in a dispute with the Church about criminal clergy in 1515. Veysey followed in the footsteps of Stapledon, Brantingham, and Stafford in holding a major royal office while he was bishop: in his case the presidency of the Council of the Marches of Wales. He had a tenderness for his birthplace, Sutton Coldfield (Warws.), where he built a grand house, improved the church, and endowed a grammar school. Nevertheless, he spent time in Devon and restored the manor house at Bishop's Tawton, presumably intending future visits.[3] All three bishops ran the diocese in the accustomed ways with vicars general, suffragan bishops, and archdeacons. The traditional structure of parishes, deaneries, peculiars, and monasteries existed as before.

The cathedral also prospered during the early sixteenth century. Its annual revenue was calculated at £1,180 in 1535, but that figure excludes the endowments of its dignitaries and chantry priests. If these are added, the total rises to around £1,925: even more than that of the bishop. The dean himself earned £158 and the precentor £99: sums equal to the income of a small monastery.[4] By 1500, they and the other dignitaries had their own coats of arms to show that they were members of the gentry. There were fewer resident canons than there had been before, usually about nine or ten, whose shares of the cathedral's revenues were consequently larger, and since they were allowed to hold additional benefices, they were all wealthy men. Each dignitary and resident canon lived in a spacious residence, some of which were dignified with gatehouses, and a taxation list of 1522 shows them attended by households of four to nine servants.[5]

Even the minor clergy, who bore the burden of the daily services, were in a more thriving condition than ever before. The vicars choral had their college buildings: a street with two rows of houses in Kalendarhay south-west of the cathedral, including a gatehouse, dining hall, and library. Oldham gave them the properties of the former hospitals of Clyst Gabriel, Crediton, and Warland to pay for daily meals in their hall.[6] Two new chantries were founded in the 1510s and a third in about 1530, prompting the first extensions to the cathedral building since Grandisson's time. The two pretty chapels that were added may still be seen at the east ends of the north and south choir aisles. In 1528, the cathedral treasurer, John Ryse, built dwellings and a dining hall for the chantry priests (of whom there were now eighteen) next to St Martin's church. This was known as New Kalendarhay and took the form of a quadrangle like that of a small university college.[7]

All the religious houses were still in existence, apart from the little ones that had gone in the fifteenth century. Here wealth diverged, because the houses included a range of greater and lesser foundations. In the *Valor* of 1535, the richest were Plympton with £912 per annum and Tavistock with £902. These were far ahead of their nearest rivals: Buckfast with £466, Torre with £396, Forde with £373, Crediton with £331, Hartland with £306, and Ottery St Mary with £303. Three other houses had incomes of more than £200: Dunkeswell with £294, Buckland with £241, and Newenham with £227, and five of more than £100: Canonsleigh (£197), St Nicholas (Exeter) (£147), Frithelstock (£127), Totnes (£124), and Barnstaple (£123). The poorest monasteries were St John (Exeter) with £72, Pilton with £66, Cornworthy with £63, and the cells of Kerswell and St Mary Marsh, each with £28. Poorer still were the four friaries. They had tiny endowments of a few pounds, and continued to draw most of their funding from donations.

The wealth of the greater houses enabled them to increase their privileges, buildings, and amenities. In 1517, Tavistock gained exemption from the bishop's authority and a seat for the abbot in the House of Lords.[8] A few years afterwards, it acquired a printing press, of which more will be said below. Thomas Chard, the last abbot of Forde (*c*.1501–39), was an ambitious builder who reconstructed the abbot's lodgings and began a new cloister. He built in a sumptuous manner, far removed from the sober style of the early Cistercian Order, leaving work that was good enough to be kept by the Tudor gentry who took over the monastery. The larger houses cultivated polyphony, as we have seen, and provided education for at least a few children. Monks and friars continued to study at Oxford. During the early sixteenth century, we know of five from the Exeter Dominicans, two from the Exeter Franciscans, two each from Buckfast and Tavistock, and one each from Forde, Plympton, Torre, and Totnes. There were doubtless more, because the records tend to embrace only those who graduated, not the others who came up for a year or two of study. One or two followed the arts course, but the majority addressed themselves to the scriptures and the commonest degree to be taken was that of bachelor of theology.[9]

We hear less of internal problems: ill discipline, disputes within communities, poor management of buildings and estates, and friction with local people. This is not because such things did not exist but through lack of evidence about monastic life in this period. The bishops' registers of the early sixteenth century contain fewer records of visitations than those of Grandisson, Brantingham, and Lacy. Tavistock and Cowick were now out of the bishop's control, while the Cistercian houses and Torre had never been in it. In 1535, the crown instituted visitations of every English monastery but their findings have not survived from Devon. It is unlikely that every house was always well conducted or exempt from problems. The rule of Thomas Whyte, abbot of Buckland, appears to have come under criticism in the 1520s because of his age, and he was pressed to resign by the marquess of Exeter, Henry Courtenay. The marquess described the monk who succeeded him, John Toker, as badly behaved and extravagant.[10] We shall shortly encounter an abbot of Hartland, John Prust, who was portrayed in 1534 as having 'no learning sufficient to rule', and a prior of Plympton, John Howe, who was accused of gross negligence in the provision of pastoral care for the priory's parish of Wembury.

Turning to the parishes, we may remind ourselves that they numbered about 410 by the 1530s: only a little more than the figure of 1291.[11] Statistics about their clergy can be gleaned from three different sources. The *Valor Ecclesiasticus* lists 381 benefices that were held by rectors and vicars, the other parishes being mostly run by religious houses through their brethren or through chaplains.[12] The number of rectors and vicars was actually smaller, because some clergy held more than one benefice within the county, and fewer still of these lived in their benefices. As well as the clergy with two or more churches, there were others who were absent from their parishes with permission because they were canons of the cathedral, servants of the king and the bishop, or university scholars. It may be sufficient to put the number of resident rectors and vicars at about 250–300 on the eve of the Reformation.

Alongside the beneficed clergy were the unbeneficed, whose names and employers appear in a survey of 1540.[13] The survey contains 404 names: more than the 356 of about 1490 and probably increased by ex-monks and ex-friars who moved into parish work after their houses were closed in the two preceding years. About half of these, 195, were curates or parish chaplains. Some of them were running the parishes close to former religious houses, which did not have rectors or vicars. Others were assisting resident clergy with parish duties, deputising for absent clergy, or serving important chapels of ease. The remaining 209 clergy were chantry priests, guild priests, or private chaplains to members of the gentry. Finally, from 1534, we possess the names of 588 Devon clergy of all kinds (excluding the cathedral and the collegiate churches) who signed their repudiation of the pope's headship of the Church in England.[14] This is a smaller total than those of 1535 and 1490 added together, but no doubt reflects the fact that some rectors and vicars held more than one benefice or were living or staying outside the county. It may be a guide to the number of parish clergy to be found in Devon on any particular day.

Most clergy, whether beneficed or not, can be traced in the bishops' registers where their ordinations throw light on their ages and sometimes on the districts from which they came. Even in the sixteenth century, little is yet known of their families and education. The majority probably still prepared themselves for ordination by attending a grammar school or serving as a parish clerk. A smaller number had wider experiences. Some Devon clergy began their careers as teenage 'secondaries' or adult vicars choral and chantry priests at the cathedral. If they found favour there, the dean and chapter might present them to one of the fifty-four rectories or vicarages in their gift. A man arriving in such a post from the cathedral would have had a good training in the performance of services, which may have influenced what he did in his own church, although we cannot be sure.[15] Widest of all was the experience gained from a university. About one in five of the beneficed clergy had a degree, and some others had spent time at Oxford without graduating, but such men had wealth or connections because higher education was expensive, and they were less likely to take posts in the poorer and more rural parishes or to be resident even in the richer ones.[16]

The beneficed clergy included dutiful and hard working men. One of the best known, Christopher Trychay, served as vicar of Morebath for over half a century, from 1519 until his death in 1574.[17] Born at Culmstock in the early 1490s, he came from a middling farming family with enough money to give him a grammar-school education, possibly at Exeter. He was ordained priest in 1515, and spent a few years as a chaplain before he was presented to Morebath by a neighbouring gentleman. Soon after coming there, he made an inventory of the church's possessions and began to compile the churchwardens' annual accounts: strictly speaking as clerk to the wardens but in practice with a strong influence over their work. He expounded the accounts to the parishioners at the annual audit, and sometimes wrote them up in the first person: 'this church had a sack of lime of me, Sir Christopher, vicar.'[18]

Figure 34 The effigy of Bishop Hugh Oldham (died 1518) in Exeter Cathedral. Oldham was a moderate reformer who closed two redundant Devon hospitals, improved the lot of the lesser cathedral clergy, and assisted with the foundation of Corpus Christi College (Oxford).

The accounts reveal him making the kinds of small changes that clergy like to bring to their churches. Morebath had a side altar in its north aisle, apparently dedicated to Jesus. Trychay was a devotee of St Sidwell, and on his arrival he presented the church with an image of her. This was placed by the side altar, which came to be known by her name. He was ambitious for the parish to possess a set of black vestments for requiem masses, and gave his wool tithes every year to a fund for buying them. It took twenty years to raise the money, and when they were bought in 1547 they had only a few years of use before the Reformation made them redundant. The church was not always easy to run. There was the burglary mentioned in the previous chapter, and two disputes with parishioners about funding the parish clerk. The parish was a relatively poor one. The vicar's income was only £8, and the laity had little to give for church projects. Nevertheless, Trychay appears to have served his parish conscientiously, trying to ensure that the church's worship was carried out correctly and its furnishings kept in good order.

Even when a parish had a non-resident incumbent, it could still function in an acceptable way. The vicars of Ashburton from 1517 to 1556 were canons of the cathedral. They spent their lives elsewhere and paid curates to do their duties. We do not know what the curates earned, perhaps £5 or £6 per annum with the right to live in the vicar's house, but the terms were attractive enough to keep them for long stretches. William Austen served from at least 1497 to 1524 and Nicholas Laneman from at least 1529 to 1557. Our knowledge of their work comes only from passing allusions in the churchwardens' accounts, but it appears that the yearly calendar of religious observances was duly carried out, and funerals are regularly mentioned. As well as the statutory services which the incumbent had to provide, the parishioners paid for extra ones: masses in honour of the Virgin Mary, masses of Jesus, and anniversary masses commemorating the dead. The curates were sometimes employed for these purposes. Austen received sums varying from 3*s*. 4*d*. to 29*s*. 8*d*. for 'wages', doubtless for presiding at these masses.[19]

Equally, there were parishes where matters were less satisfactory, although it is hard now to identify them. Discontent in Wembury was such that some of its parishioners were prompted to write a petition about its affairs in 1534. The parish (they alleged) had a population of 500 of whom about 420 were adults. Yet there was no resident cleric and the appropriator of the church, the prior of Plympton, sent chaplains or canons from the priory which was four miles away. Services were provided only on Sunday mornings, when the visiting cleric hurried through matins, mass, and evensong before departing for his midday dinner. If a baby needed baptising or a dying person required the last rites, a messenger had to go to the priory for help that was slow in coming if it came at all. Nine adults were alleged to have died without a priest at hand. A sickly new-born child expired before it could be christened, another child's corpse waited all day for a priest to hold its funeral, and no clergy came on the festivals of Easter Monday (when three women wished to be 'churched') or St Thomas's Day. The petitioners claimed that the parishes of Brixton, Plymstock, and Shaugh Prior, which had similar relationships with the priory, were just as badly served.[20]

The rebuilding of parish churches, which we encountered in the previous chapter, continued during the early sixteenth century and even into the period of the Reformation. It is often difficult to distinguish what was done before and after 1500, but enough dates are recorded to show that much activity took place under Henry VIII. As well as the additions at Cullompton and Tiverton (Figure 35, p. 161), which we have noted, a substantial south chapel was built at Colyton at the expense of the vicar. Honiton acquired a new east end through the generosity of John and Joan Takell, and Ottery the beautiful 'Dorset aisle' given in part by the countess of Wiltshire (Figure 36, p. 166). Axminster gained a new north aisle and porch, and Broadclyst and Cullompton new towers. Church fittings were also improved. The screens at Hartland, Holbeton, and Northlew can probably be dated to the 1530s, and that of East Allington was erected as late as 1547. Other churches installed new benches: those of Coldridge carry the date of 1511 and those of Dowland 1546. Some of the designers of screens and bench-ends were already turning their back on the art of the later Middle Ages in favour of the Italian Renaissance, with swirls, swags, medallions, and putti instead of the instruments of the Passion or scenes of everyday life.[21]

Inside and outside churches, people went on taking part in religious activities of the kinds that we have examined: privately, in groups, and as communities. Churchwardens' accounts record the continuing round of the ancient Church year with its seasons: Lent, Holy Week, Easter, and Rogationtide. Stores devoted to saints remained in being as well as guilds and companies of wives, young men, and maidens. Bishops continued to grant small indulgences: to Teign Bridge in Kingsteignton (1520), a wounded soldier (1521), St Nicholas chapel at Ilfracombe (1522), and Thornbury church (1524). People still went on pilgrimages, although it is impossible to gauge whether they did so more or less than in earlier times. The cache of wax images discovered above Bishop Lacy's tomb in 1942 suggests that those with cramp and arthritis went on resorting there until the practice was forbidden in 1538 (Figure 31, p. 139).[22] In the north of the county, devotees appear to have visited the shrine of St Urith at Chittlehampton and the newer chapel of Our Lady of Loretto at Pilton: the latter possibly built in the form of the Virgin Mary's house, as at Walsingham.[23] Further away, there was Walsingham itself to which Edward Gurgoyne, a vicar choral of Exeter Cathedral, gained permission to go in 1528, and Compostella to which his colleague James Tremyllyon was allowed to travel in the following year.[24] As late as the 1530s, an observer noted groups of pilgrims from Devon and Cornwall arriving at the shrine of King Henry VI in Windsor Chapel, 'with candles and images of wax in their hands'.[25]

Towards the Reformation

Alongside these apparent continuities, inconspicuous changes were in train that would help to bring about the Reformation. That event was in part a break with the past, but it also grew out of the past. One of the changes was a greater respect for monarchy than had been so before. There are signs of this in churches. The Speke and Oldham chapels in the cathedral, built in the 1510s, display royal coats of arms and emblems. The roses of Henry VIII and the pomegranates of Katherine of Aragon adorn the pillars of Thorverton church. People had not felt the need to be so deferential in previous centuries. The deference reflected the greater ambitions and effectiveness of the monarchy, and these began to press more heavily on the institutional Church. Benefit of clergy – the privilege of clerics (including literate layfolk) to be tried for crimes in Church courts – was reduced by a series of statutes after 1489. Sanctuary – the right of criminals to take refuge in churches and sometimes in their precincts – was also diminished.[26]

Cultural changes were in progress as well. Literacy was common, and the written word was more conspicuous in churches. It appeared not only in the books used by the clergy but in primers used by lay people and by texts displayed on walls, windows, and tombs. Exeter Cathedral displayed a Latin chronicle of its history and Tavistock church a Latin poem.[27] Tombs carried inscriptions: at first in Latin, but increasingly in English. Grammar schools were altering what they taught. From about 1480, boys began to learn 'humanist' or classical Latin rather than the Latin of the Middle Ages. Most of the Christian works that had been read in school, including the hymns and sequences of the Church services, were abandoned in favour of classical authors. Schools remained Christian in ethos, of course, but their culture was less close to that of the Church.

Meanwhile, Caxton began to print at Westminster in 1476 and printed books were imported from the Continent. Manuscripts were already common and we have seen that the cathedral circulated hundreds of indulgences as far back as the fourteenth century, but the new technology increased the supply and cheapness of books. Most such books in England were produced in London or distributed from there, but in about 1505, Martin Coeffin, a French stationer and bookbinder living in Exeter, commissioned two Latin schoolbooks from a printer in Rouen, presumably to sell them locally.[28] Later, Tavistock Abbey ran its own printing press and printed at least two books: a translation of *The Consolation of Philosophy* by Boethius (1525) and *The Statutes of the Devonshire Stannary* (1534).[29] At first, there was no sign that printing would threaten the Church, but in the 1520s, when the Reformation began in Germany, it was much easier for unorthodox literature to spread into England through this means. And the Reformation of the Church in England was in part an outcome of printing, involving the acquisition of a Bible in English by every parish church and later a series of English Prayer-Books.

Two cases of suspected heresy came to the bishop's attention in the early 1500s, the first recorded in Devon for over seventy years. In 1506, John Atwill, a man of substance from Walkhampton, was accused of a mixture of anticlerical and unorthodox views. He claimed that the prayers in the parish bede-roll benefited the priest rather than those who were prayed for, and that a recent papal indulgence was chiefly promoted for money. He said that his servants could hear his confession as well as any priest, and that Christ suffered only for the impious and sinners, not for those who lived well, and that the latter would be saved without His atonement.[30] Ten years later, Otto Corbin, a freeman of Exeter, was charged with making mock of religion in both Exeter and Dartmouth. He admitted saying 'I will never worship the five wounds of Christ until I have my fifth wife', and 'I care not for my soul, so I may have an honest living in this world, and when ye see my soul hang on the hedge, cast ye stones thereto!' He expressed remorse and was assigned a public penance in the cathedral, including prayers in honour of the Wounds.[31]

It is hard to judge the significance of these cases. They were evidently regarded as serious because they were recorded in the bishop's register. However, for Atwill we have only the allegations, not the defence or the judgment, and it is not clear how far the bishop was involved. Even if the charges against him and Corbin were correct, they hardly indicate a Church that pounced on those who challenged its doctrines and practices. Atwill had been under scrutiny for some time. He had been cited before the archdeacon's court at Tavistock in the previous March, and appeared again at Paignton in August after making further statements. Corbin had vented his views for at least nine months, and he was probably brought before the bishop himself because he was an affront to Church authority at its heartland. There may have been others like Atwill who were dealt with locally by the archdeacons or their officials, whose records have not survived. But one probably had to be provoking, persistent, and unpopular to get into serious trouble.

Matters would start to change in the 1520s. In 1517, Luther began his attack on papal indulgences, and during the next few years he published the treatises in which he formulated some of the major ideas of the Reformation: notably 'justification by faith alone'. His ideas spread through Germany, and a Reformation began in practical terms. Papal authority was repudiated, religious houses were closed, and services were translated into the German language. The reading of the Bible was emphasised, also in the language that people knew, and clergy began to marry. At first, the English crown and Church authorities did their utmost to resist such innovations. Henry VIII himself wrote against Luther and received the title 'Defender of the Faith' from a grateful pope. Unorthodox books from abroad were seized, and those who adopted the new ideas were persecuted. But the genii could not be put back into the bottle. Even for the English authorities, the German Reformation opened new horizons and suggested the formulation of policies that would not have been conceivable before it began.

The Early Reformation, 1529–1538

The English Reformation is conventionally said to begin in 1529. In that year, a new parliament met which, over the next seven years, enacted a series of statutes that remodelled the English Church. The earliest statutes centred on the clergy and increased the restrictions that had previously been made to their privileges. In 1529, their rights and powers were restricted with regard to mortuaries (the gifts they claimed from dead parishioners), fees for administering wills, pluralities (the holding of more than one benefice at once), and involvement in business activities. In 1530, they agreed to pay a huge fine to the king for having allegedly infringed his laws, and in 1532, they undertook not to make new canon law without his authority.

These changes may have emboldened one man in Devon to try to hasten the process. Thomas Benet was a Cambridge graduate who married and came to the county in the 1520s, where he worked as a schoolmaster: first in Torrington and later in Exeter. In October 1531, he secretly caused papers to be fixed to one of the cathedral doors, proclaiming the pope to be Antichrist and attacking the worship of saints. After a second attempt, he was discovered, arrested, and tried for heresy before Bishop Veysey and other learned clergy. He admitted his support for Luther's teaching and resisted the urgings of his judges to recant. They duly reported him to the king's officers as an impenitent heretic, and he was burnt at the stake by order of the sheriff of Devon at Livery Dole in Heavitree on 10 January 1532. Much later, the sheriff's son and grandson founded the almshouse that still stands at Livery Dole: perhaps as a work of expiation.[32]

Benet ought to have waited. Within about two years, his beliefs began to be endorsed by the crown. In 1534, Parliament passed the Act of Supremacy declaring Henry VIII to be the earthly head of the Church of England instead of the pope. Thomas Cromwell became the king's 'vicar general' with the responsibility for making his authority effective. Royal commissioners were sent round the country to secure the consent of the clergy to the new order of things: the first of a series of such visitations during the next thirty years. The members of each religious house were required to acknowledge the king's new status and powers. In a somewhat different approach, the parish clergy were made to renounce the powers of the pope at meetings in their rural deaneries. Some of the acknowledgements and all of the renunciations from Devon survive in the National Archives, where the names of those who made them may be read.[33]

The next objective of the king and his minister was the wealth of the Church. In 1534, a parliamentary Act of First Fruits and Tenths gave the crown new powers

Figure 35 The Greenway chapel, St Peter's parish church, Tiverton, a lavish addition to the church financed by a local merchant in 1517. It features battlements and exterior carvings including sailing ships.

to tax the clergy. As in 1291, every religious house and all the beneficed clergy became bound to pay the crown one tenth of their income each year. But far more stringently, anyone who obtained a new benefice, whether as a bishop, canon, rector, or vicar, had to forfeit the whole of the first year's income to the king – ten tenths, as it were, for that year – and all such people had to provide guarantors to undertake that the sum would be paid.[34] The new valuation of Church incomes, the *Valor Ecclesiasticus* of 1535, set out to ensure that the incomes were properly calculated. It probably fell somewhat short of the truth, but it was far more accurate and up-to-date than the Taxation of 1291 and produced more tax for the king from the clergy than had ever been taken before.[35]

A third aspect of the royal supremacy over the Church was a determination to reform it, and this remained an objective throughout the Reformation although it was much harder to achieve than the extraction of the Church's wealth. Cromwell and Thomas Cranmer, the archbishop of Canterbury, with the partial but never quite certain support of Henry VIII, wished to turn the emphasis of the Church away from what they considered superstitious practices to godly and useful ones. Most people in the South-West of England, like other parts of the country, were accustomed to the old ways of thought and habit, however little they actually followed them. The Exeter historian John Hooker, writing after the Reformation, believed that when Benet was burnt, ordinary people sought eagerly for sticks or bits of furze to throw on the fire.[36]

To counteract these views, the crown sent the Reformist cleric Hugh Latimer on a preaching tour in June 1534 to promote the Reformation. He delivered three sermons in Exeter to very large crowds, provoking (according to Hooker) both praise and hostility.[37] Most of the cathedral canons, the most influential clergy locally, were fervent opponents of change. A young Dominican friar, who was asked to preach in the cathedral in the winter of 1534–5, commented that the canons 'were not inclined to the fashion of the world that goeth now' and wished instead that 'we should do as we have done in times past and live after the old fashion'. The friar accordingly delivered a sermon criticising the king's assumption of the headship of the Church, to the horror of his superiors who put him in prison.[38] From now on, fear was an effective weapon in changing how people spoke and behaved.

Next, the crown pressed ahead with laws to change people's religious habits. Indulgences were early casualties. An act of Parliament in 1536 made it illegal to teach or maintain any aspect of the pope's authority,[39] and Bishop Veysey granted the last known indulgence in Devon on Christmas Eve of that year for Cowley Bridge near Exeter, which was currently being rebuilt.[40] Meanwhile, in the autumn of 1536, Cromwell published commands or 'injunctions' to the clergy in the king's name. These ordered them to preach regularly against the authority of the pope and in favour of that of the king. They were warned not to promote the undue worship of saints, images, or pilgrimages, but to encourage the laity to please God through their work, by giving charity to the poor, and by saying the basic prayers in English not Latin: a major change of practice.[41] At the same time, a royal decree directed that there should be a drastic reduction in the number of holy days. Feasts commemorating the days when churches had been dedicated were to be held only on 1 October. Feasts in honour of the patron saint of the church were not to be kept as holidays unless the saint was a major figure whose day was generally observed. This was less of a threat to Devon than it was to Cornwall, where so many saints were unique and local, but it would have affected churches with Brittonic saints such as Brannoc and Nectan or minor ones from Europe.[42]

In May 1538, Veysey issued injunctions of his own for the diocese.[43] Never one to lead the field in change, he followed the spirit of the 1536 injunctions, only for these to be overtaken by a second and more radical set published by Cromwell in the following October. This set had a greater impact on lay people, contradicting the assumption that is sometimes made that Henry VIII's Reformation was directed only at the clergy. Positively, the movement in favour of the English language continued. For the first time ever, the reading of the Bible in English received official blessing, and each church was obliged to acquire a Bible of this kind. A new translation was published for the purpose in 1539 (Figure 37, p. 172). The injunctions also ordered that parishioners coming for confession in Lent should be tested on their ability to say the Lord's Prayer and Creed in English. They were warned that they might be denied communion at Easter if they did not learn them.[44]

In another innovation, the second injunctions required the clergy to record every baptism, marriage, and burial in a register. This measure was claimed as helping to authenticate births for legal purposes, but it probably also aimed at ensuring that everyone was baptised, married, and buried according to law. The 1520s and 1530s had seen the emergence of Anabaptists in Germany who practised adult baptism, and registration made certain that parents in England would have their children christened as infants. Equally important in the second injunctions were the prohibitions. No images or relics were to be venerated by worship, lighting of candles, or pilgrimage. Any that had been venerated were to be taken away. Soon afterwards, a royal proclamation of November 1538 forbade the cult of Thomas Becket altogether, because he had championed the clergy against an earlier King Henry. His images were to be removed, his festivals abolished, and his very name expunged from service books.[45] No directions were made about the churches dedicated to him, but it seems that they transferred their allegiance to Thomas the apostle.

In the summer of 1538, the crown removed another symbol of the past: the dean of the cathedral, Cardinal Reginald Pole. Pole had never visited Exeter and was now on the Continent, having refused to join the Church of England. In his place, the crown appointed Simon Heynes, a Cambridge scholar and a strong supporter of the Reformation.[46] Heynes arrived in August and soon made his presence felt. One of his early acts was to enforce the attack on images. He defaced the tomb of Bishop Lacy in the cathedral and removed a figure of Christ attached to the nearby church of St Mary Major.[47] The wax images hung by Lacy's tomb were probably hidden at this time in a nearby crevice.[48] In the parish churches, the veneration of images and shrines must also have declined or wholly ceased. The vicar of Chittlehampton later complained that his income had dropped through the loss of the offerings to St Urith, and a similar assertion was made at Pilton with respect to the images of Our Lady and Our Lady of Loretto.[49]

With Heynes's arrival, divisions among the local clergy became more apparent. He himself was strongly Reformist, and two other canons, Peter Carslegh and Robert Tregonwell, leaned towards the new ways.[50] Tregonwell, we are told, expounded some of the doctrines of Luther in theological lectures at the cathedral. The former warden of the Franciscan friary, John Cardmaker, was converted to the Reformation. In 1537, he renounced his orders, was briefly vicar of Branscombe, and later became a radical figure in London where he was burnt for heresy under Mary Tudor.[51] On the traditional side stood most of the senior cathedral clergy together with Gregory Bassett, Cardmaker's successor at the friary. Bassett had toyed with Luther's ideas in the 1520s, but had been punished and recanted. After the friary closed in 1538, he became vicar of Aylesbeare and other churches, and remained an opponent of the Reformation into the reign of Elizabeth I.[52]

The Dissolution of the Monasteries

The king's headship of the Church brought the crown into closer contact with the monasteries. The requirement that their members should acknowledge the royal headship in 1534 was followed in the spring of 1535 by the valuation of their incomes in the *Valor Ecclesiasticus*. At about the same time, John Prust, the abbot of Hartland, was deposed for alleged inadequacy, and Cromwell lobbied Bishop Veysey for the appointment of Thomas Pope, successfully so. Some of the canons petitioned the crown on behalf of the ousted abbot, and Prust boldly returned and barred the abbey against the king's representatives.[53] It was a rare piece of defiance and did not succeed. In the summer of the same year, the abbacy of Buckfast fell vacant, and Cromwell secured the election of Gabriel Dunne, a Cistercian from London whose family he may have known. Dunne used to be regarded as Cromwell's agent in the arrest and execution of William Tyndale in the Netherlands. In fact, he can be cleared of this slur, and it is more likely that Cromwell regarded Dunne, a university graduate, as a well-qualified man to take over a major Devon monastery.[54]

The year 1535 also saw the dispatch of royal commissioners to visit abbeys and priories throughout England. Devon and Cornwall were allocated to John Tregonwell, brother of Canon Robert: a Cornishman, lawyer, and diplomat, aged in his forties. He visited the houses of north Devon in November 1535, and then went into Cornwall, probably returning through south Devon early in 1536.[55] His task was to enquire into the state of the houses and bring them a special set of royal injunctions.[56] As with the parish clergy and laity, these were meant to reform the lives of the monks but they also imposed restrictions. No novice was to be professed as a monk until the age of twenty-four. No monks, even heads of houses, were to leave their precincts. This was a traditional rule, much modified in practice (often for good reasons), but now to be strictly enforced. Every monastery was to include a lecture on Holy Scripture in its daily timetable, lasting one hour, and all the brethren were required to attend.

The visitations were soon followed by a decision to start culling houses whose conduct or income was regarded as inadequate for sustaining their work. Such houses were to be closed and their endowments confiscated. In April 1536, an act of Parliament authorised the dissolution of small monasteries. It declared that houses of less than thirteen clergy were unsatisfactory in their religious life, unlike larger communities which kept it well. However, it ordered the closure of such houses not on the basis of their numbers of clergy but on whether they had an income of £200 or less.[57] Eleven houses in Devon fell into this category, of which three were exempted: Canonsleigh, Polsloe, and St John (Exeter). The first was worth only slightly less than £200, the second paid a fine to escape, and the third may have been spared because it was a hospital. Kerswell and St Mary Marsh were regarded as parts of their mother houses and were not affected. The other six were visited by royal commissioners, probably during the summer of 1536, who ordered their closure. These were the priories of Barnstaple, St Nicholas (Exeter), Frithelstock, Pilton, and Totnes, and the nunnery of Cornworthy. Their heads (except perhaps at Cornworthy) were granted modest pensions ranging from £8 to £20, and their members were allowed to move to another house or (in the case of the men) to become parish clergy.

In Exeter, the closures caused a riot. The commissioners, having suppressed St Nicholas Priory, went off to dinner and left a man in the church with orders to pull down the roodloft. A group of local women, who were accustomed to worship there, heard the news and went angrily to the priory. They broke into the church and threw stones at the workman. Alderman John Blackaller arrived to pacify them, but Elizabeth Glandfield 'gave him a blow and sent him packing'. The women barricaded themselves in the building, and the mayor, embarrassed by the affront to the king's representatives, was obliged to come down with his officers. They forced open the church door, seized the offenders, and took them off to prison. Meanwhile, the

Figure 36 The Dorset aisle in Ottery St Mary parish church, another example of expensive church building in the early sixteenth century. It includes the fan-vaulting fashionable in that period.

commissioners finished their dinner and thanked the mayor for his efforts. Before they left, they asked him to free the women.[58]

There were more serious disturbances in other regions of England, notably in the 'Pilgrimage of Grace' of the autumn of 1536, which was in part a demonstration of opposition to the suppression of monasteries in the north of England. That movement ended in defeat, however, and left the crown free to continue the process of closures. This time, the object was achieved by 'voluntary' means through which each house was persuaded to surrender itself and its property into the king's hands. The first to fall in Devon were the four friaries in September 1538.[59] Their buildings and their rather meagre possessions were seized, but the friars themselves received no compensation on the grounds that they had chosen a life of poverty. They were allowed, however, to function as parish clergy if they could find employment.

The Devon monasteries fell early in the following year. On about 12 February 1539, 'a gloomy season for a tragic tale', John Tregonwell returned to close them down. This time he came with William Paget, another trusted royal servant and diplomat. On entering the county, they separated. Tregonwell went first to Dunkeswell on about the 14th and secured a document of surrender subscribed by the abbot and all the monks. He then proceeded via Canonsleigh and Hartland into Cornwall. Paget handled the houses of south Devon. He took the surrenders of Polsloe, St John (Exeter), Torre, Buckfast, Buckland, and Plympton. Tregonwell, having dissolved the Cornish monasteries, crossed the Tamar to deal with Tavistock, and he and Paget then retraced their way eastwards. On 8 March, Paget arrived at Forde and Tregonwell at Newenham, each of which signed away its existence. These were the last two houses to fall, since St Mary Marsh came to an end with Plympton while Kerswell seems to have been closed by its mother house, Montacute, before the latter came to an end on 20 March.[60] The process had taken just over three weeks.[61] In May 1539, an act of Parliament gave legal sanction to all the closures that had taken place,[62] and in the summer of the following year, 1540, a further statute abolished the Order of St John and confiscated its property, including its Devon estates.[63]

The clergy who complied with the commissioners – and all of them did so in Devon – were awarded pensions. Heads of houses were treated generously and with regard to the wealth of their houses. The abbess of Polsloe got £30 per annum and her colleague at Canonsleigh £40. The abbots did even better: Newenham with £44, Dunkeswell with £50, Buckland and Hartland with £60, Torre with £66, Forde with £80, and Tavistock with £100. The prior of Plympton came off best with £120. Their brethren and sisters were rewarded more modestly with pensions of anything from £10 down to £2 in the case of the youngest recruits. The men were allowed, like the friars, to become parish clergy. Some found employment as chaplains and a few later rose to be rectors and vicars. Nuns, however, were required to go on living celibately, and there were no posts in the world suitable for them. They had either to return to their families or to live together in a small group, which some of them did.

As soon as the houses were closed, the crown proceeded to dispose of their assets: sites and buildings, landed estates, tithes, and advowsons of churches. A generous grant of the possessions of Tavistock was made to Sir John Russell, one of the king's chief servants, who was also given a peerage and, a few years later, created earl of Bedford. The grant, worth about £1,000 a year, aimed at making one of Henry's loyal followers a major power in Devon; even so, Russell had to pay an annual rent of £284 to the crown in return. Most other property was sold without much favour in terms of price because the king needed money, and a sum of twenty times the annual income was usually charged, which was the accepted rate of the day. Favour counted to the extent that courtiers and royal officials were in a good position to buy property, and a good many purchases were made by those who came from Devon, such as the families of Arscot, Dennis, Grenville, and Rolle. Other members of the gentry in the county also bought land, often in partnership with friends or relations: such as the Champernowns, Edgcumbes, Fulfords, and Stucleys.[64]

Alongside these temporal changes, there were others in the sphere of what contemporaries called 'spiritualities'. The religious houses had owned the patronage of many parish churches with the right to appoint their clergy, and most of these churches had been appropriated so that the house received the tithes of grain and sometimes other revenues. The crown disposed of these possessions as it did the monastic lands, leading to new patterns in the parochial system. Before the Reformation, a majority of churches were in the patronage of clergy of one kind or another: bishop, cathedral, or monasteries. Taking the parishes around Crediton as an example, fourteen out of twenty-one came into that category as against seven in the gift of lay gentry. After the Reformation, the numbers were four against seventeen respectively. It was the same with tithes. Ten churches of the twenty-one had been appropriated. In all of these, the grain tithes now passed to the gentry: the first time since the twelfth century that lay people had been allowed to receive these revenues. Lay influence over parish religion was greatly increased.

The buildings of the monasteries had various fates. Their churches were usually unsuitable for conversion to other uses, and may have inspired disquiet among their purchasers. However, Sir Richard Grenville remodelled the church at Buckland in the 1570s into one range of a grand new house, and the church of St John (Exeter) was made into two dwellings.[65] More often, churches were unroofed and their materials used or sold for other purposes. Morebath church acquired a window (glass and stone) from Barlinch Priory in Somerset.[66] Pilton's church survived because it was also a parish church, but elsewhere the demolition was so complete that only at Frithelstock do parts of a monastic church still stand, and there only in a fragmentary state (Figure 41, p. 193). Domestic buildings and abbots' lodgings were easier to adapt into the houses of the gentry who bought them. At Forde, the north cloister, chapter house, and abbot's house were all preserved as part of a new mansion, and at Torre, the gatehouse, abbot's tower, refectory, and guest hall. In Exeter, the Dominican friary became the residence of John Lord Russell, while parts of St Nicholas Priory were turned into a merchant's house (Figure 42, p. 195). In the second half of the sixteenth century, the ruins of the monasteries must have been familiar sights in their localities. To some, they signalled the triumph of the Reformation, to others its tragedy: 'bare ruined choirs, where late the sweet birds sang.'[67]

The Reformation from 1540 to 1549

The last English monastery was closed in March 1540. Hardly had this happened than Cromwell fell from power: he was executed on 28 July. The remaining six and a half years of Henry's reign were largely free of religious changes. Indeed, in 1539 Parliament passed the optimistically named 'Act for Abolishing Diversity of Opinions', now known as the 'Act of Six Articles', which reaffirmed the Catholic doctrine of transubstantiation and the practices of giving lay people communion 'in one kind' (the consecrated bread alone), the celibacy of the clergy, private masses, and confession to a priest.[68] However, the Reformation persisted in one respect: with further assaults on religious houses. All that remained were the cathedrals, ancient minsters, and newer collegiate churches, as well as the chantries in some parish churches and chapels. Henry VIII favoured cathedrals – indeed in 1540–2 he created new ones out of former monasteries – and he even looked kindly for a while on collegiate churches. But in the latter case, royal needs for money and perhaps continuing distrust of the religious life soon led to a series of closures. These began in 1541 and went on in a ragged way for the next few years. The process was not complete when the king died in January 1547.

The collegiate churches of Devon were Crediton, Ottery, and Slapton. The first two were obliged to surrender to royal commissioners in May 1545, and Slapton in the following November.[69] As usual, the clergy got pensions and most of the churches' possessions were confiscated. In December of the same year, the crown established a body of four lay governors at Ottery and granted them endowments with which to pay a vicar of the parish and the master of a free grammar school.[70] At Crediton, reform was delayed until April 1547, when a body of twelve governors was created along with a vicar, two curates, a chaplain of Sandford, and a similar schoolmaster.[71] Meanwhile in 1545, Henry considered taking control of chantries as well. A Chantry

Act allowing their dissolution along with free chapels and the remaining collegiate churches was approved by Parliament at the end of the year.[72] Royal commissioners toured the country in the spring of 1546, collecting evidence about these institutions and their functions, but Henry died before any action took place.[73]

He was succeeded in name by his nine-year-old son Edward VI and in fact by a government led by the young king's uncle, the duke of Somerset. This government soon made plain its intention of continuing the Reformation to establish a fully Protestant Church. In the autumn of 1547, teams of royal visitors toured England with fresh injunctions. These restated most of those of 1538 with some further requirements. The epistle and gospel at mass were now to be read in English, and English lessons from the Bible were introduced at matins and evensong. As in 1538, the parish clergy were told to recommend the good new practices in church once every three months, and to discourage people from the old superstitious ones. They were also to read, each Sunday, one of the *Homilies* published by Cranmer in 1547: a set of sermons in English expounding the official doctrines of salvation, obedience, almsgiving, and so on.[74]

Other changes of detail were made to worship, anticipating the larger alterations that were to follow in the next two years. Most of the processions, which had been such a large part of religious life, were forbidden. The priest was no longer allowed to lead the bodies of the dead to the church from their homes, but only to receive the dead at the churchyard. The warnings about shrines and images were repeated, and any images likely to be venerated were ordered to be removed, even from window glass. Instead, the regime strove to turn people's devotion to Bible reading, Sunday observance, and works of charity. Each church was told to acquire a chest to receive donations for the needy and to place the resources of the church guilds and stores in the chest for that purpose.

More radical reforms came with the enactment of a second Chantry Act by Parliament in December 1547. Unlike the previous act, which did not commit itself about the future of the chantries, this one began by condemning prayers for the dead. It sanctioned the dissolution of a wide range of institutions and the conveyance of their property to the crown. The institutions included the remaining collegiate churches, the endowed chantries, religious (but not craft) guilds, obits (masses on the anniversaries of people's deaths), and funds for lights in front of church images. Collegiate churches and chantries were to cease their activities on Easter Day, 1 April, 1548. The act undertook in return that chantry property would be applied 'to good and godly uses' such as founding grammar schools, augmenting the universities, and giving relief to the poor.[75]

In the spring of 1548, commissioners again toured Devon taking evidence about the chantries and their possessions. Their searches were more effective than those of 1546 and identified ninety-three endowed chantries, religious guilds, and free chapels: twenty more than on the previous occasion, as well as small assets maintaining church lights.[76] Nearly all were suppressed, their possessions confiscated, and their clergy awarded pensions. Many of these clergy, like the ex-monks and friars, took posts as parish curates and some became rectors or vicars.[77] A few institutions escaped the Chantry Act. The cathedral managed to keep its chantry endowments in the long run, although they were not formally returned to it until 1585 in return for an annual payment of £145.[78] The prebends of Chulmleigh and Exeter Castle together with the portions of Tiverton were left alone because they were not regarded as parts of religious houses. In the two places where chantry priests were keeping grammar schools in 1548, Ashburton and Barnstaple, the priests were allowed to remain in post simply as schoolmasters. This exception did not extend to the endowments of their chantries. These were still seized and the crown took responsibility for paying the masters at the rates they had received.[79] Nothing was done in Devon to provide more schools, as the act had promised.

Chapels were other casualties of the Reformation. No laws specifically ordered their closure or destruction, but the spirit of the age was hostile to them. The disuse of indulgences and the royal injunctions of 1538, with their ban on the veneration of shrines and images, hit the cult chapels which had been built to honour Mary, Michael, or some other saint, and depended on people coming to worship and make offerings. When John Leland travelled through Devon in 1542, he noticed three chapels already 'neglected' or 'profaned' on the bridges of Barnstaple, Torrington, and Fenny Bridges (Ottery St Mary).[80] The second Chantry Act removed the endowments that had maintained and staffed priests in some of the public chapels, and new rules about the celebration of holy communion made it difficult for chapels in private houses to be used for more than personal prayers. The only public chapels to survive were the larger chapels of ease, which still had some value in the community and where the parish clergyman was obliged to provide a chaplain to say Sunday services.

The first three years of Edward VI's reign saw a succession of further reforms to the Church. In 1547 Parliament abolished Henry's 'Act of Six Articles' and the medieval heresy laws, opening the way for Protestant doctrines to become lawful. When two cathedral canons, Richard Crispin and John Moreman, preached against the new doctrines, they were arrested and put in the Tower of London.[81] A series of royal orders in 1548 forbade the customs of lighting candles at Candlemas, receiving ashes on Ash Wednesday, carrying palms on Palm Sunday, and creeping to the cross on Good Friday. In February, all images were ordered to be removed from churches. On 1 April, Easter Day, a new *Order of Communion* was introduced, bringing some English prayers into the Latin mass alongside the English epistle and gospel, and requiring communion to be given 'in both kinds': the bread and

Figure 37 Frontispiece of The Byble in Englyshe. This authorised Bible of 1539 depicts Henry VIII as head of the Church distributing copies to clergy on the left and noblemen on the right. The book reaches the common people in spoken form, while they exclaim 'Long live the king!'

the consecrated wine. In the spring of 1549, royal commissioners told parishes to declare what they had in terms of church silver, and lists were made of the objects, a procedure only too likely to confirm the fear that the government wanted to seize them.[82]

The Prayer-Book Rebellion and Afterwards, 1549–1553

The culmination of these changes was a new Prayer-Book, Archbishop Cranmer's *Book of Common Prayer*, which was ordered to be used in all churches from Pentecost (9 June) 1549. The Prayer-Book contained three kinds of worship, all in English. The eight daily services hitherto said by the clergy were reduced to two: morning prayer and evening prayer, which were shorter versions of the old matins and vespers or evensong. The clergy remained obliged to say both every day. The mass became the service of holy communion. Finally, the book contained the pastoral services of baptism, confirmation, marriage, churching of women, visiting the sick, and funerals. Like the communion, they retained a traditional shape and continued to use substances that were regarded as holy – water, oil, bread, and wine – but their ceremonies were simplified and their material made more instructive. Baptism and marriage both began with explanations of what they involved, and funerals became occasions for teaching the living as well as dispatching the dead.[83]

Cranmer's decision to introduce the new Prayer-Book at Pentecost, the day that commemorates the foundation of the Church by the Holy Spirit, was admirable in principle but maladroit in practice. The monasteries had been dissolved in February, when winter kept people at home. Pentecost fell in the holiday period when they had time to spare from work and the roads allowed easy passage. This was an ancient season of unrest. The Peasants' Revolt of 1381 had taken place in May and June, and so had the Cornish rising of 1497 against Henry VII. For all Cranmer's skill and moderation in producing the Prayer-Book, the use of English would have jarred with congregations used to Latin. The new book followed a long series of unpopular changes affecting parish life, including the abolition of saints' days, guilds, and images.

While Henry VIII was king, his personality was enough to keep most people silent, but a government ruling for a child king was weaker and people were less inclined to obey it. The result was what contemporaries called the 'Commotion': a good word that encompassed what the participants saw as a protest, the crown as a rebellion, and no doubt many ordinary people as an unwelcome disorder.[84] In Cornwall, a rising broke out at Bodmin on Thursday 6 June, three days before the introduction of the Prayer-Book: perhaps when copies of the volume arrived. In Devon, reaction began at Sampford Courtenay on Monday 10 June, the day after Pentecost when the parishioners had experienced the new service for the first time (Figure 38,

p. 177). They may have heard of the events in Cornwall. The Cornish organised themselves into a mobile force and moved eastwards, first to Plymouth, then northwards to Tavistock and Launceston, and finally eastwards again where they joined up with the protestors from Devon. They reached Crediton on 21 June and Exeter on 2 July (Figure 39, p. 183).

Little is still known about the participants. Few are recorded by name and their numbers are incalculable, but population figures make it unlikely that there were more than about ten thousand. Those who can be traced from Devon came chiefly from the west and middle of the county as well as the Exeter area.[85] Socially, a few of the gentry were involved, notably John Bury of Silverton and Sir Thomas Pomeroy of Berry Pomeroy, and a handful of clergy especially Robert Welsh, the vicar of St Thomas (Exeter), who was a Cornishman by origin. Two men of Sampford, William Segar and Thomas Underhill, played prominent roles, as did the mayor of Torrington, Henry Lee. The most effective opposition to the rising came from the citizens of Exeter, probably from their fear of the crown and of looting if the rebels took the city (Figure 40, p. 188). The city closed its gates and the protesters organised themselves outside in four camps, each with a captain. The resulting siege lasted for five weeks (2 July to 6 August).

During this period, the rebel leaders drew up demands and sent them to the crown. The demands were prefixed by the robust words 'we will have . . .', although the protesters also professed to be the king's subjects, 'both body and soul'. In the main, they called for a return to the religious conditions of the end of Henry VIII's reign. The Act of Six Articles should be re-established, and all church services and ceremonies restored to what they had been before 1547. Crispin and Moreman should be released from the Tower. But some of the demands went further in asking for the modification even of Henry's reforms. The English Bible should be withdrawn. Two places of prayer should be established in each county where the chief abbeys had been, endowed with half of the lands of the abbeys and chantries. Cardinal Pole should be pardoned and brought home to join the king's council. These last two points hint at the hope of undoing the break with Rome and the dissolution of the monasteries.

The crown refused to make concessions, and the siege gave it time to bring up forces to regain control. The protesters resisted stoutly in a battle at Fenny Bridges on 29 July, but they were defeated at Clyst Bridge on 4–5 August and could not prevent the advance of the king's army to the relief of the city. The rising was finally crushed at its place of origin, Sampford Courtenay, on 29 August. This put an end to the rebellion as an organised movement. Many rebels died in the battles, others were executed locally, and seven were ceremonially hanged, drawn, and quartered in London. Robert Welsh was taken to his own church of St Thomas 'and, by a rope about his middle, drawn up to the top of the tower and there in chains hanged in his popish apparel and having a holy-water bucket, a sprinkle, a sacring bell, a pair of beads, and such other like popish trash hanged about him'. This account comes from John Hooker, who wrote later on from a Protestant point of view. Nevertheless, Hooker conceded that Welsh took his death 'very patiently', and thought that he would have been a useful member of society 'had not the weeds overgrown the good corn'.[86]

The suppression of the rising left the crown free to maintain the reforms it had made and to extend them further. The marriage of the clergy had already been permitted in 1548. In 1550, stone altars in churches were ordered to be removed and replaced by a single wooden table in the chancel for the purpose of communion. In 1552, the Prayer-Book was revised and reissued in a more radical form. Many details in the services were changed, with the broad effect that the medieval ceremonies retained in the 1549 book were mostly omitted, and services became static occasions involving the reading of Bible lessons and prayers. The communion service of 1549 had been said by a priest still wearing vestments and facing the high altar at the east end of the church. After this he put a piece of wafer bread directly into the mouth of each person as was traditional, and said 'The body of our Lord Jesus Christ . . . preserve thy body and soul unto everlasting life'. The chalice was then given with comparable words.[87]

These phrases enabled people to have different views about the sense in which the bread was Christ's body, not excluding the doctrine of transubstantiation. The Prayer-Book of 1552 took a deliberately different line. The new table was placed in the middle of the chancel on an east–west axis rather than the north–south orientation of the old high altar. The priest was told to wear only a surplice over his clothes and to stand on the north side of the table to say the communion prayers. Worshippers knelt around the table, and he put a piece of white loaf bread into each one's hands, saying 'Take and eat this in remembrance that Christ died for thee', with a similar phrase when he offered the chalice. This meant that the service was not like the old Latin mass. It was not a sacrifice and it did not create Christ's body in the form of bread, thereby giving you healing. Instead it commemorated Christ's Last Supper, reminding you of his sacrifice for you and teaching you to feed on him in a spiritual sense through faith.

Churchwardens' accounts show the parishes compliantly making the changes demanded of them, no doubt often reluctantly. At Ashburton, the rood and images were taken down in 1547–8, the new Prayer-Books acquired in 1549 and 1552, the altars removed in 1550, a communion table installed in the choir, and the roodloft (the gallery above the screen) demolished shortly afterwards.[88] There were similar changes at Morebath, although there a good deal of portable property such as vestments and ornaments was removed from the church and put into the care of lay people.[89] The crown was aware of such devices, and in 1552 it appointed commissioners to make inventories of church goods and take charge of them. Churches were to be left with only a surplice for the clergyman, tablecloths for the communion table, a cup for the communion, and one bell.[90] Four of the Morebath men who held the vestments had to take them to Exeter. The 'cope of blue satin', the 'cope of red velvet with spread eagles of gold', the 'silken tunicle of blue with branches of gold', the silver pax, and the paten of the smaller chalice were all handed over.[91] One further change should be mentioned, because it attracted a little support. At least three dozen clergy took advantage of the new permission to marry. Their boldness was to bring them into trouble.[92]

Throughout the religious changes from 1529 until the Prayer-Book rebellion, Bishop Veysey continued to rule the diocese. Courtly and careful, he followed the policy of limiting damage by complying with what was required. This did not prevent the crown making the changes it wished, and towards the end of Henry VIII's reign it began to plunder the estates of the bishopric: a process that continued under Edward VI. Writing about Veysey later on in the reign of Elizabeth I, Hooker was critical of the bishop for losing his property:

> How well so ever he deserved of noblemen and gentlemen, he deserved small commendment and thanks of his church and bishopric, for of thirty-four lordships and manors left unto him, he left unto his successors not above three or four, and of eleven houses but one, and that ruinated and encumbered, and of £1,800 yearly rent, he left about £320.[93]

This, though broadly true in financial terms, is most unfair to Veysey and was unfairly repeated by some later historians. The losses were the result of demands by the crown, and nobody could resist such demands in the middle of the sixteenth century.

The plunder began in 1545 with orders from Henry VIII that Veysey surrender the manor of Faringdon (Hants.) to the crown and lease the manors of Crediton and Paignton to courtiers. Further directives in 1546–7 extended the leases to Ashburton, Bishop's Nympton, Bishop's Tawton, Clyst, and Pawton (Cornwall).[94] When Henry died and the crown fell into the power of courtiers, the pressure grew worse. In 1548, the bishop was made to give up his London residence, Exeter Place, to Sir William Paget, and during the next two years he had to surrender absolutely all the properties mentioned above except for Bishop's Nympton, as well as Bishopsteignton, Bosham (Sussex), Chudleigh, Horsley (Surrey), and Morchard Bishop. By 1551, the government itself conceded that the bishop's annual income had fallen from the £1,566 of 1535 to only about £500.[95] This was about the minimum

Figure 38 Sampford Courtenay parish church, where the Commotion against The Book of Common Prayer began on 10 June 1549. The rising was finally crushed in the same parish on 29 August.

on which the bishop could live and pay his household and administrators. Oddly, the cathedral did not suffer in this way. It was not that the crown and aristocracy valued its worship, but they cherished its canonries: wealthy benefices with few duties, which could be given to their servants and relatives.

Having taken as much as it could of Veysey's property, the crown decided that it needed a more active Protestant to govern the diocese, and in 1551 the octogenarian bishop was told to resign. He was given a generous pension and retired to Sutton Coldfield. The man appointed in his place was Miles Coverdale: a translator of the Bible, a distinguished Reformer, and a married man, the first such bishop of Exeter.[96] For the next two years, Coverdale did what he could to forward the Reformation. In Hooker's view, he was an assiduous preacher and charitable to the poor but encountered dislike from ordinary people because he represented the new religious ways. Hooker claims that attempts were made to poison him at Totnes and at Bodmin in Cornwall. Still, Coverdale was able to win over two local opponents of change: the archdeacon of Barnstaple (John Pollard) and the vicar of Ipplepen (Walter Hele).[97] And, as we shall see, the Reformation was beginning to take root at the top of local society, however unpopular it might be lower down.

The Reign of Mary Tudor

Edward's death in July 1553 and the succession of his elder sister Mary were followed by a return to Catholicism, although it lasted for little more than five years. In the autumn of 1553, Parliament repealed the statutes of Edward that dealt with religion. This meant that the English Prayer-Book lapsed in favour of the old Latin ones, and it was lawful again to venerate saints and to pray for the dead. In 1554, the heresy laws were revived, the statutes of Henry VIII against the pope were repealed, and the Church received him as its head again. A clause of one of the new statutes calmed the fears of those who had acquired religious property by confirming their rights to what they held. This concession, needed to gain support for restoring Catholicism, made it difficult to revive the monasteries, and although a few were reinstated in England, none reappeared in Devon.[98]

Coverdale's position became impossible after Mary's accession. He was removed as bishop in September 1553 and escaped punishment only through the intervention of the king of Denmark, who arranged for him to go into exile. Veysey was then restored to power in spite of his age. He roused himself to travel to Exeter in November and stayed there for two months before returning to Sutton Coldfield, where he died in October 1554. Despite the shortness of his second term of office, it was marked by the expulsion of a number of Devon clergy from their benefices, chiefly in the summer of 1554. A few were singled out because of their support for the Reformation, but most were deprived for marrying. At the cathedral, the dean, the precentor, the archdeacon of Barnstaple, and three or four canons were turned out.[99] In the countryside, at least thirty-five men were evicted, and the number was probably higher. The records are not complete and some men may have resigned to forestall their removal like William Alley, the rector of Oakford, who took his wife to the North and became a schoolmaster and physician.[100]

This was the first time during the Reformation that people were penalised for having done what was legal at the time that they did it. The sole concession made to them was that they could be re-employed if they renounced their marriages and found a patron to present them. A few returned by this route. John Castlyn, having lost Holbeton, reappeared at Washfield. Anthony Hunt moved from Chawleigh to Knowstone and Molland, while George Carew, ejected from the cathedral precentorship, came back as archdeacon of Exeter. Whether their wives had died or had consented to have their marriages annulled, we do not know; the authorities did not trouble themselves with the wives.

Mary had problems in finding new bishops, given that so many senior clergy had consented to the changes of Edward's reign. After Veysey's death, the diocese was vacant for a year until the choice fell on James Turberville, who was consecrated as bishop in September 1555. He was a doctor of theology from a family of gentry in Dorset, had been a cathedral canon in recent times, and was not prominent in Church life. Hooker characterised him as 'very gentle and courteous' and 'most zealous in the Romish religion', but not personally 'cruel or bloody', although Hooker blamed him for his part in the persecution of Agnes Prest, to which we shall come. Little is known of Turberville's term as bishop. He was in power for less than four years, and his register does not record much more than the names of the clergy whom he ordained and instituted to benefices.[101]

The restoration of full Catholic worship was not straightforward. The clergy soon resumed the saying of mass, but much of the equipment of the old religion had disappeared, such as church silver, service books, and images, and had to be acquired afresh. The crown helped a little, since most of the church plate seized in 1552 was still being stored and this was returned. At the cathedral, there was an attempt to undo the iconoclasm of the last fourteen years, and a 'Dutchman' (German or Netherlander) was employed to repair the images, but not perhaps until about 1557–8.[102] At Ashburton, the high altar and two other altars were rebuilt in 1553–4; new service books were bought and the confiscated vestments fetched from London. This cost well over £6. It then took another four years to mend the roodloft, erase an inscription on it (presumably from the English Bible), replace Christ, Mary, and John above the loft, reinstate St Andrew beside the high altar, and purchase or restore a box to hold the bread and wine of the reserved sacrament, the organ, music books, a processional cross, banners, candles, and incense.[103]

The Morebath accounts tell a similar story, albeit a more impoverished one. The religious changes of 1553 coincided with a parish debt of over £6, and a voluntary collection produced only just under £4 to clear it. Nevertheless, there was support from local people for the revival of Catholic worship. The high altar was restored along with the canopy above it and the Easter sepulchre. One man gave money for a mass book, another donated a pyx, and the parish wives subscribed from 1*d.* to 6*d.* each to buy a manual. Other items were brought out of hiding, and the vicar later reminded his parishioners:

> Of John Williams of Bury we received again an image of Mary . . . And of William Morse at Loyton was received an image of John. And of the Widow Jordyn trails and knots [possibly trimmings of altar cloths or vestments]. And of divers other persons here was received pagines [writings] and books and divers other things concerning our rood loft. Like true and faithful Christian people this was restored to the church, by the which doings it showeth that they did like good Catholic men.

Even so, it was not until 1556 that the altar of St Sidwell was rebuilt, and only in 1558 was painting done around that altar and above the images on the roodloft. By the end of that year, Queen Mary would be dead.[104]

Her regime came close to restoring a former religious house at Crediton. Here in 1555, the governors appointed Hugh Deane, a former clerk of Exeter Cathedral, as 'chapel clerk' with a stipend of £8 per annum. This suggests the re-establishment of choral services in the Lady chapel with a choir of men and boys, probably serving on a part-time basis. In 1557, the bishop of Exeter took back the appointment of the clergyman of Crediton from the governors and appointed John Nicolles with the title of rector. It is likely that Nicolles was a committed Catholic, since he seems to have left the church soon after Mary's death. In the same year, Cardinal Pole, now archbishop of Canterbury, returned to Nicolles the tithes and offerings paid to the former college, worth £122 per annum, and there were plans to recreate what was virtually a small collegiate church with a rector, three assistant clergy, the schoolmaster, the chapel clerk, two parish clerks, four endowed grammar scholars, and four poor men. This scheme was not fully implemented because of Mary's death, but it continued in a modified form under Elizabeth I.[105]

Many people, like those of Morebath, gladly returned to Catholic practices. Others, having embraced the Reformation, remained estranged from them or doubtful about their future. There was a notable reluctance by young men to be ordained as clergy. In 1557 and 1558, only three and five candidates respectively were ordained as priests in the whole of Devon and Cornwall: not a good sign for the future of Catholicism.[106] Some of the leaders of local society were closely identified with the events of Edward's reign and the resistance to the rebels of 1549. Those of the gentry included the Carews of Mohun's Ottery, the Chudleighs of Ashton, a Courtenay of Powderham, and the Tremaynes of Collacombe among others. In the towns, John Bodley of Exeter and Peter Willis of Totnes stood out as former supporters of Edward's regime. Some of the gentry tried to organise a rising in Devon in 1554, and when it failed they went abroad, as did the Bodley family and Willis. Several of the exiles joined communities of like-minded English people in Aarau and Frankfurt in Germany and Geneva in Switzerland. When Mary died, they returned having experienced more radical forms of Protestantism than they had done in England.[107]

Lesser folk who favoured the Reformation but could not afford to leave home were obliged to conform and keep their beliefs to themselves. Agnes Prest was an exception.[108] This woman, a wife in her fifties from Northcott on the border of Cornwall and Devon, had listened to Protestant sermons under Edward. During the 1550s, she announced her disbelief in transubstantiation and the veneration of images, falling out with her husband and children and eventually leaving them. In due course, she was summoned to Exeter to be examined by the bishop and his chancellor, and was put into the bishop's prison there, but was transferred to the gaoler's private house on the grounds that she was naive rather than heretical. When she persisted in her beliefs and shared them with sympathetic visitors, the Church authorities resolved to deal with her, found her guilty, and gave her to the lay authorities for execution. She was burnt at Exeter in August 1558: the last of the three known people to have suffered this punishment in the South-West of England, and the only one in Mary's reign.

The Elizabethan Church Settlement, 1558–1560

Mary died and Elizabeth succeeded her on 17 November 1558. A new parliament assembled in January 1559 and, in a session lasting until May, enacted statutes restoring a Protestant Church of England. The Church was again made subject to the crown, with the more tactful use of the phrase 'supreme governor' to describe the monarch instead of 'supreme head'. The Prayer-Book was re-established in a form based on the second, more radical, version of 1552, with a few conservative alterations.[109] Most of the bishops, including Turberville, refused to work with the new regime and voted against the new legislation in Parliament. There were hopes of winning them over, and although they were suspended from power in the summer of 1559 and put into the Tower of London, it was not until March 1560 that the crown lost patience and appointed a new bishop of Exeter. This was William Alley, the former rector of Oakford, who was also a notable linguist and theologian. He was consecrated on 14 July.[110]

There were changes at the cathedral, as there had been after 1553. Mary had appointed a new dean in the person of Thomas Reynolds: a strong Catholic but a pluralist clergyman who was also warden of Merton College (Oxford). He was ousted in the summer of 1559 and sent to prison in London, where he died. During the next two years, the treasurer, John Blaxton, a well-known conservative who had dealt with Agnes Prest, lost his place with about six other canons. So did Gregory Bassett, now rector of Sowton.[111] Some of the dispossessed went to Herefordshire, where the crown became concerned about their activities. But Mary's reign had not instilled much fervour into the rank and file of the Devon clergy, and Elizabeth's government did not pursue them for what they had done in the past as long as they obeyed it in the present.[112] The vast majority did so, and adapted yet again to religious change, like Christopher Trychay at Morebath. A particularly outstanding 'vicar of Bray' was the cathedral chancellor, William Leyson. A Catholic by preference, he nevertheless conformed to Protestantism under Edward VI and Elizabeth, and served under all four of the Reformation monarchs from 1537 until his death in 1582.

Meanwhile, in September 1559, a fresh royal visitation of the Church took place throughout England. New teams of commissioners addressed articles of enquiry to the local clergy, issued injunctions, and exacted oaths of allegiance to the queen as supreme governor.[113] Bishop Jewel of Salisbury, who took part in the visitation of Exeter diocese and came from north Devon himself, said after it was finished that he and his companions found people everywhere 'well disposed towards religion', in other words to its reformed variety, 'even in those quarters where we expected most difficulty'. He complained, on the other hand, of the wilderness of superstition that had sprung up in Mary's reign. 'We found in all places votive relics of saints, nails with which the infatuated people dreamed that Christ had been pierced, and I know not what small fragments of the sacred cross.'[114] Jewel was probably over-optimistic; many older people still clung mentally to the religion of their childhood. Still, in 1564, when Bishop Alley had to make a report on conservative local worthies unsuitable to act as justices of the peace, he could find only five in Devon: mostly in the Exeter area and fewer than in Cornwall.[115]

The injunctions of 1559 embodied a return to the policies of Henry VIII and Edward VI in many respects. Orders were given that worship be done in English, English Bibles placed in churches, parish registers and poor boxes restored, and shrines and images abolished. The clergy were again allowed to marry. At the same time, the authorities did not reinstate the Church of England to the high point of Protestantism that it had reached in the final year of Edward's reign. True, the new edition of the Prayer-Book issued in the spring of 1559 was mainly based on that of 1552, and Sunday worship resumed a form like that of the end of Edward's reign.[116] But the Elizabethan government ordered the communion table, when it was not in use, to stand where the high altar had formerly been. When communion took place, the bread and wine given to the congregation were again considered

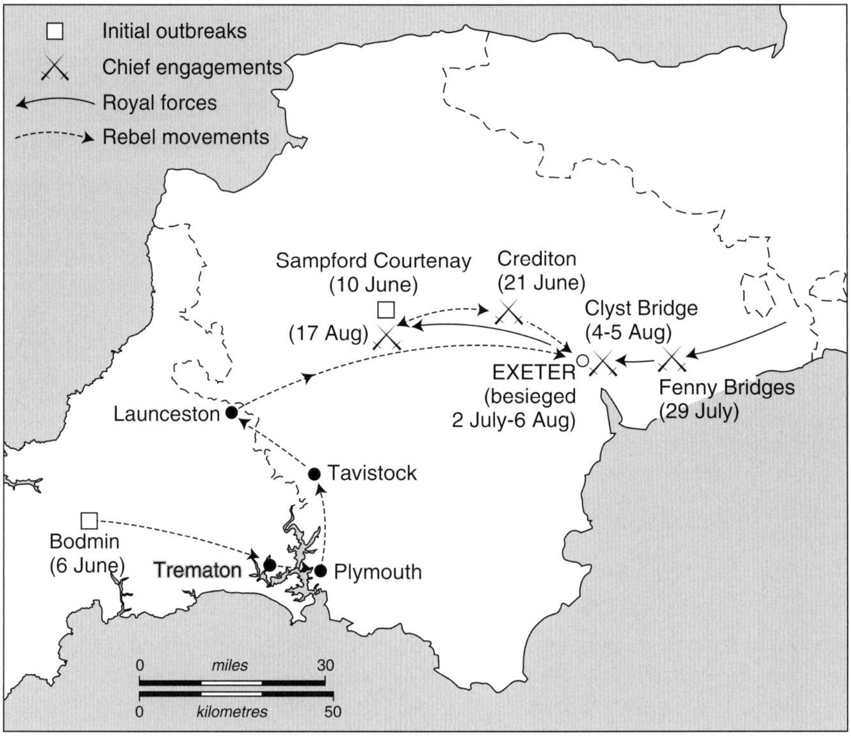

Figure 39 The Commotion of 1549, showing the principal routes of the rival forces and the sites of the major battles.

to be consecrated objects, not merely symbols of the Last Supper. A London clergyman got into trouble in 1573 when he ran out of communion wine and dispensed more without praying over it.[117] The communion bread returned to the traditional form of wafers, rather than the fine loaf bread of 1552, and the priest in giving out the wafers said the words of both 1549 and 1552: 'the body of our Lord Jesus Christ' and 'take and eat this in remembrance', and similarly with the wine.

The injunctions also declared that music in parish churches was lawful. Choirs of men and boys could be organised again, and an anthem sung at the end of a service provided that it was in English. In practice, however, music in Elizabethan churches tended to centre on the singing of the psalms by the congregation in metrical versions like 'All people that on earth do dwell', rather than the chanting of psalms in the choir as in the Middle Ages. Worshippers were told again to bow at the name of Jesus, and although processions in general remained forbidden, an exception was made for Rogationtide. Permission resumed for clergy and laity to make their customary tours around their parishes on one of the Rogation days, saying Psalm

103 and other prayers, and such processions continued to be accompanied by eating and drinking as they had been until the 1540s.[118]

Once more, clergy and parishioners had to reorder their churches to accord with the new regime, and to bear the expenses. As in 1553, the most essential changes were carried out fairly quickly. At Ashburton in 1559–60, the Prayer-Book was purchased, the altars demolished, and the images on the roodscreen and elsewhere removed 'to be burnt'. A communion table was reinstated and eventually, in 1563–4, the whole roodloft was dismantled, although here and elsewhere the rest of the roodscreen survived.[119] Morebath got rid of its altars in 1559 and bought the Prayer-Book, the English Bible, the new Protestant book of homilies, and Erasmus's *Paraphrases* or explanations of the gospels. Two years later, its roodloft was taken down. The Morebath accounts refer to a vestment and a mass book as being in private hands, and it is not impossible that some items were hidden as they had been in Edward's reign. But this time they would never come back into use.[120]

In November 1561, Bishop Alley carried out a survey of the beneficed clergy of his diocese which produced more detailed evidence about them than has been available to us hitherto.[121] The survey is not as complete and orderly as one would wish, reflecting the difficulty even for a Reformation bishop of locating information, so the statistics extracted here are only approximate ones. About 140 parishes in the diocese, well over one third, had no resident rector or vicar. In many of these, the incumbent was absent because he held more than one benefice, served the king or a nobleman, or was at university. In others, a monastery had served the benefice through a brother or chaplain, and the lay landlord who bought the church from Henry VIII continued to employ a mere curate. The survey succeeded in identifying 218 resident clergy, on the other hand, and it provided six pieces of information about each one: whether he was a graduate, married, learned, resident, hospitable, and a preacher.

Thirty-one of these clergy were graduates, mainly MAs and probably almost entirely from Oxford. A few others styled themselves as 'Master' and may have done some study, but were classified as non-graduates. The vast majority were unmarried; only 23 had wives, but that is not surprising given the long tradition of celibacy and the troubles that marriage had caused in Mary's reign. In terms of learning, the survey had four main categories. The lowest was 'studious, not learned in Latin', which applied to 29 clergy, and presumably meant that they could (and did) read English but not Latin. A further three were 'not learned in Latin'; how these 32 had coped with the Latin liturgy can only be imagined. The next category upwards was 'moderately learned in Latin', in which there were 104 clergy, and above that, 'adequately learned in Latin', which applied to 63. Finally, 12 clergy were reckoned as 'good' or 'well taught'. 'Adequately' was evidently commendable because some of the graduates were placed in this group, and it seems that most of the beneficed clergy knew some Latin and had done so before the Reformation. If the survey had been extended to the poorer clergy with the status of curates and chaplains, the number of inadequate Latinists would probably have grown.

Where the clergy were resident, they were almost all found to be 'hospitable', that is to say that they kept house and could entertain travellers and give charity to the poor as their duty had been since at least the thirteenth century. What they were not were preachers. Only 11 held the bishop's licence to preach, which meant that they were trusted to do so throughout the diocese, and one of these was too old to practise. A further 12 were recorded as preaching without a licence, sometimes with the rider that they did so in their own church or parish. One of these was Christopher Trychay. Since any incumbent could lawfully preach to his parishioners, this indicates that hardly anyone claimed to do so in a serious way. They might have explained the Lord's Prayer, the Creed, or the sins and virtues as they had long been required to do, or have enlarged on a Bible reading as the Reformation injunctions required. They were again expected to read aloud the official book of *Homilies*. But their work had traditionally centred on liturgy and ceremonial, not on teaching, and this was still manifest after thirty years of changes in religion.

Bishop Alley's survey shows how difficult it was to reform the Church at a local level. Destruction, like that of monasteries, altars, and images was relatively easy. Altering the ways of the clergy and their people could only be a slow process. The survey also demonstrates how the Reformation failed to solve the ancient problems of the parochial system. The parishes that had been served by brothers and chaplains sent from monasteries were not reconstituted as rectories or vicarages. They now became 'donatives', whose proprietors (like the monasteries) appointed curates without reference to the bishop and paid them pittances. Pluralism and non-residence remained rife, and bishops were no stronger than they had been to resist the encroachments of powerful lay people. Nearly all the peculiar jurisdictions of the Middle Ages remained in place: in Exeter, the exemption enjoyed by the Dominican friars passed to the earls of Bedford who took over their buildings. The Church of England was to live with all these anomalies until the Victorians, with more energy, abolished them.

The Reformation: an Assessment

How different was the Church in Devon in the 1560s from what it had been like in the 1520s? This question can be answered in three respects: landscape, worship, and people. By Elizabeth's reign, the Devon landscape was not quite the same. In five of the towns – Barnstaple, Exeter, Plymouth, Plympton, and Totnes – large churches that once dominated the skyline had been pulled down or converted for other purposes (Figure 42, p. 195). In the countryside, another eight substantial monasteries had disappeared or been put to new uses (Figure 41, p. 193). Most of the chapels had been demolished or turned into barns or dwellings, and crosses in churchyards were disappearing or would do so during the seventeenth century because of their connections with Catholic worship. Only holy wells and lesser wayside crosses remained because they were smaller and not so conspicuous.

As a result, the Devon landscape looked less religious. The parish churches were now its only spiritual features along with their clergy houses and glebes. Their rivals – religious houses and chapels – were gone. No other places existed at which to worship or be buried, except for the cathedral. As landscape elements, however, the churches stopped growing altogether. Rebuilding petered out in the middle of the sixteenth century. The outsides of the buildings became frozen in time. For the next three hundred years, the characteristic church of the Devon landscape (and indeed that of England in general) was one rebuilt or remodelled during the fifteenth and early sixteenth centuries, usually with a tower and aisles (Figures 2, p. 7, 6, p. 21, and 9, p. 34). What was built at that time became what people thought churches should be, an understanding that is still with us.

Churchscapes, the insides of churches, did not freeze in this way. Their walls and pillars remained the same, and so did some important parts of their furnishings. Chancels continued to be divided from naves by screens. Pulpits survived: no longer for reciting the bede-roll but for reading the *Homilies* and later for the preaching of original sermons. Naves kept the seating that had appeared or had been upgraded during the fifteenth and early sixteenth centuries. Yet much else changed between the 1530s and the 1560s. Holy objects were removed: altars, lights, and nearly every image, whether sculpted or painted on walls. Such images as survived did so chiefly in stained-glass windows or as carvings in lofty places.

Nevertheless such images were no longer objects of devotion. Churches now lacked anything that could be venerated apart from whatever respect people might pay to the communion table or font. Visual aids still had a place in church, but chiefly as texts: the Lord's Prayer, the Creed, the Ten Commandments, inscriptions on tombs, or boards describing local charities. Texts, as we have seen, originated long before the Reformation, so their proliferation after it was not something wholly new. By Elizabeth's reign, the royal coat of arms began to be displayed as well, expressing the fact that the monarch was the ruler of Church and state. Even this had antecedents in the popularity of royal emblems during the early sixteenth century.

The parish church also changed inside by expressing religious uniformity. Before the Reformation, it had consisted of two or more rooms containing several areas of devotion and activity: the chancel, the nave, the side chapels and altars, images, the font, and the porch. These had specific uses on different occasions. Now there was a single place of worship: the church as a whole, focussing on the area in front of the chancel screen. In most churches, the clergyman and clerk moved from the chancel to the nave side of the screen, where reading desks and a pulpit were provided for them. Nearly every service was centred here except for christenings at the font. The chancel came to be used only on the rare occasions of holy communion, and even then only for the prayers immediately before the communion and for the distribution of the bread and wine.

Other parts of the church ceased to have spiritual functions. The porch was reduced to a shelter, and the side chapels were filled with benches or tombs. But the church remained a divided place in one important respect: that of seating. This continued to be based on rank and sometimes on the payment of fees. At Ashburton, certain people were now paying *6d.* or *8d.* for a seat, perhaps with the right to keep it as long as they lived.[122] It has already been suggested that the medieval gentry occupied part of the chancel or some of the side chapels. They certainly did so after the Reformation: appropriating such areas as private spaces where they built pews of a larger kind, buried their family members under the floor, and placed tombs and hatchments (funeral coats of arms) to display their importance.

Services in church after 1559 had several resemblances to the old Latin ones. There was continuity in terms of timing. Morning prayer, beginning at about 9.00, consisted of matins followed by the litany (a series of prayers of intercession, said kneeling), and the first part of the communion service including a homily or sermon. This sequence lasted for about two hours. In the afternoon at 3.00, there was evening prayer which took about three quarters of an hour. The missing element was the celebration of the eucharist or holy communion. Thomas Cranmer may have hoped for this every Sunday when he planned the Prayer-Book of 1549, but he was unwilling for the priest alone to consume the bread and wine and wished him to be joined by at least some of the congregation for their spiritual benefit. At the same time, he was aware of people's reluctance to come forward. They were used to receiving communion only at Easter or on their death-beds, not as a part of their regular worship. Accordingly, in 1549, Cranmer laid down that if nobody was willing to receive communion, the service must be concluded after the offertory and before the prayer of consecration. In 1552 and 1559, this notional quorum of one lay person was raised to 'a goodly number', and the celebration of communion remained rare.[123] In the end, the Church's leaders managed only to increase the number of communions from one at Easter to four, including Christmas Day, Pentecost, and a Sunday in the autumn. These were the days when most people came to church to make their quarterly offerings of money.

Because the service was in English, the congregation could now understand its contents. They began to hear more of the Bible. The morning services included an

Figure 40 The city walls of Exeter defeated the Commotion, whose followers surrounded the city but could not capture it. Whether from fear or conviction, the people of Exeter saved the Reformation in Devon.

Old Testament lesson, a New Testament lesson, some psalms, a reading from the epistles and from the gospels, and that of the afternoon two further lessons and more psalms. But the laity did not have much more to do in church than they had done before. There were as yet no hymns, their nearest equivalent being the metrical psalms. Lack of books meant that the psalms were sung by a choir or by the parish clerk singing one line at a time and everyone repeating it: a lengthy process. The clerk also said the 'amens' to the prayers. Any prayer that the congregation was required to say would be read by the clergyman line by line while they followed him. Only the Lord's Prayer and the Apostles' Creed would be well enough known for people to say them straight through. No lay person normally read a lesson until the nineteenth century, and there was no scope for anyone to lead prayers. The people were still largely spectators rather than participants.

Most of the material at services was repeated on every occasion. Only the psalms, the Bible readings, and the homilies ran through a sequence, although later, as preaching developed, the sermon became something fresh and individual. Every church did the same, so that those who ignored the requirement to attend their own church had nothing to gain by attending another, unless a sermon was preached or they visited the cathedral. Whereas the medieval mass had been something to watch and adore rather than to understand, the services of the Church of England were times of instruction. The churchscape came to resemble a schoolroom. The clergyman read the service from a special seat, like that of a schoolmaster. The parishioners sat on benches as if they were pupils, with written texts on the walls. They were taught about the nature of God, the history of his relationship with the world, the promises that he had made to his people, and the duties that he required in return.

Outside church, much about the clergy remained traditional. In Elizabeth's reign, they were still addressed as 'Sir' John or whatever their forename was, and they were still the chief spiritual persons in their parishes. They retained their glebe and tithes, although they were more heavily taxed than before the 1530s. Their status even improved in some respects. The Tudor monarchs turned the parish into a unit of civil government. During the mid and late sixteenth century, they gave it responsibility for poor relief, roads and bridges, and some military matters. The clergyman became the leader of what became the 'vestry' or parish administration for these purposes. In this way he gained powers over his parish that his predecessors had not held before the Reformation. He was also free of competition from monks, friars, guild priests, and chantry priests. There were now fewer clergy than before, and they were less of an 'estate', a widely assorted group, than they had been before the Reformation. In future they would come closer to being a profession with uniform ways of life and public roles.

Lay people had a parallel experience of change and continuity. Much stayed the same for them. They still entered the Church, like it or not, by baptism, now usually done on the Sunday after the birth rather than on the birthday itself. They remained subject to the Church's laws: laws supported as before by the power of the crown. They were still expected to learn the basic prayers, to be confirmed (although that was now less easy to achieve), to attend church on Sundays, to keep the Church's times and seasons including the Lenten fast, and to be buried in the parish church or churchyard. They paid tithes and offerings as before, although they no longer had to make private confessions. Inside church, they sat by social rank. Senior parishioners continued to act as churchwardens and these officers, like the clergyman, acquired new parish responsibilities. There were still Church courts to police tithe-paying and moral behaviour, especially slander and sexual immorality.

In short, most people in the 1560s, from the crown and the Church authorities down to ordinary parishioners, still thought in terms of everyone belonging to a single Church and following similar rules, as they had done in the Middle Ages. Only a small minority of Catholics held aloof. But the insistence of the Reformation on uniformity would strain this consensus and eventually break it. Within eighty years, the Civil War would bring a time of confusion that allowed secessions, and it would never again be possible to hold everyone inside the same religious community.

Chapter 6

A Thousand Years of Christianity

What may we learn from the Church history of Devon? Is it simply the history of the Church in England, or has it features of its own? In many respects, the religious history of any English county is identical with that of the nation and indeed of western Europe. The texts, doctrines, and worship of Christianity are found in every place. So are the standard institutions of the Church: a diocese and bishop, archdeaconries, rural deaneries, parishes, churches, guilds, stores, and so on. When Devon acquired religious houses, they were of kinds found commonly elsewhere: minsters from the seventh century, Benedictine monasteries from the tenth, alien priories from the eleventh and twelfth, and subsequently most of the major orders of monks and friars.

At the same time, every English county is distinctive in its geography, economy, and population, and this is true of Devon. Its spanning of the highland and lowland zones has affected its religious history. The highland zone had fewer towns and monasteries; the lowland zone had more. The parishes of the highlands, with their scattered populations, were sometimes poorer than those of the lowlands, as we have seen by comparing Morebath and Ashburton. Both kinds of parishes might have stores, companies, and guilds, but it is probable that a scattered and poorer community worked in somewhat different ways from a richer more compact one. Then there is Devon's peripheral status as an outlying part of England and one of less political importance. This also left its mark upon the Church. Exeter Cathedral was not one of the richest or most influential cathedrals in England. Devon had no major saint or religious shrine. It does not seem to have been greatly affected by Lollardy, and its people were reputed to be religious conservatives at the time of the Reformation.

Nevertheless, one can hardly judge Devon as remote in religious terms. It was well integrated with the rest of the Church in England. Most of its bishops came from elsewhere, especially the Midlands and the North.[1] They brought with them clergy from their homelands who ran their administrations, received cathedral canonries, and occupied parish benefices. The Devon monasteries belonged to religious orders whose members met together, enacted laws, evolved common policies, and inspected each other's houses. Students from Devon went to Oxford, where Exeter College and Hart Hall specialised in lodging and maintaining them. Although the county had no famous shrine, it was traversed by pilgrims journeying to its ports en route for Compostella or passing overland to St Michael's Mount. Its people travelled to holy places in England such as Canterbury and Windsor.

Devon's westerly neighbour was also a periphery, and a comparison between the two is illuminating. Cornwall was more insular than Devon.[2] It was distinctive in preserving traces of its Brittonic past, notably in the survival of the Cornish language in the west of the county down to the eighteenth century. It retained at least two features of Christianity from before the Anglo-Saxon conquest in the ninth and tenth centuries. One was the situation of its churches in isolated places, possibly based on ancient burial grounds. The other was the association of many of these churches with Brittonic saints: some local, some shared with Brittany and Wales, whose medieval legends placed their lives (rightly or wrongly) in these countries and in Ireland, not in England. Even after its integration with England in the tenth century, it was notably lacking in houses of the great religious orders. It gained three Augustinian priories, some alien Benedictine cells, two friaries, and a small preceptory of the Order of St John. But the Cistercians and Premonstratensians never settled there, and there was no major Benedictine monastery.

At the same time, the two counties had much in common. Eastern Cornwall lost the Cornish language by the eleventh or twelfth centuries, and its dialect of English would have come close to that of Devon. Although the Tamar formed a substantial boundary with few crossing places, the countryside of north-east Cornwall did not differ greatly in character from that of north-west Devon. The isolated churches of both counties may have had different origins, but both were typical of the highland zone in England as a whole. Both counties shared a bishop after 1050, and he and the cathedral came to own many of the churches of Cornwall and to choose their incumbents. The parish churches contained the same kinds of stores, guilds, and companies, venerating the same kinds of saints: the Virgin Mary, the apostles, the Roman martyrs, and Thomas Becket. Chapels in large numbers were also a common feature, with features and ministries of a similar kind, as were holy wells.

A survey of a thousand years of history makes it appropriate to reflect on the pattern of this history. What will now be said about Devon is largely true of England as a whole. The history of the Church in the county from 400 to 1560 was linked by many continuities, especially by the presence of the parish churches, their worship, and their social functions from about 900 onwards. But there were also changes, and the term 'Middle Ages' is misleading if it suggests that religion was always

Figure 41 The ruins of Frithelstock Priory, one of the few remaining traces of a religious house in Devon. So remote was the place that even the stone was not taken for use elsewhere.

much the same. Each century added something new and sometimes experienced losses. During the tenth and eleventh, the domination of the county by minsters gave way to that of the smaller parish churches. The eleventh saw the arrival of a French governing class, the first grants of property to French abbeys, and the earliest alien priories.

The twelfth century was an age of law-making, which united Devon more firmly with the rest of the western Church in doctrines and moral codes. Church organisation grew stronger and bishops more ambitious to rule both clergy and laity. In the thirteenth, literacy began to make an impact, especially on the devotions of the wealthier in society. The fourteenth was marked by growing nationalism, which rebuffed some of the claims of the papacy and caused the decline of the alien priories. Coincidentally, population changes affected the wealth of the religious houses and the numbers of parish clergy. The fifteenth and sixteenth centuries were characterised by much church building, modifying the nature of the places where people worshipped, and the Reformation of the sixteenth brought about large alterations in a fairly short space of time.

A feature of these changes, shared by Devon and by the rest of England, was an oscillation between insularity on the one hand and integration with the Continent on the other. The late Anglo-Saxon period was one of relative insularity, partly because of the disruption to communications by the Vikings. The Norman Conquest began a period of integration, in which ties with Normandy were followed by the wider associations of the new religious orders. In turn, insularity revived in the late thirteenth and fourteenth centuries. The crown exerted more power over the Church in terms of law and taxation. The French abbeys gradually lost their properties. The English language became more widely used for literary purposes, and the distinctive Perpendicular style evolved in buildings. This insularity relaxed again in and after the late fifteenth century. English schools followed Continental ones by teaching classical Latin. Printing enabled texts to travel more frequently across the English Channel. By the 1520s, the Reformation in Germany began to make an impact on England, although much of the English Reformation was influenced by a still potent insularity, notably in the creation of a distinctive Church of England.

The causes of change are also worth considering. Church historians have traditionally attributed them to the top of society: popes, councils, bishops, scholars, kings, and parliaments. Those in authority were undoubtedly influential. Kings and noblemen enabled Christianity to take root in the first place, founded religious houses and parish churches, and provided most of their endowments. Popes, councils, and bishops created and administered Church law, to be enforced upon the whole population. Yet one is struck by the relatively limited involvement of the popes in Church life at a local level, apart from the granting of licences to (generally wealthy) individuals for special privileges. Even bishops had only occasional contact with their parishes: chiefly through instituting clergy and dealing with outstanding cases of crime. Parish clergy experienced obstacles in running their churches and dealing with their parishioners, and the lack of surviving evidence of this should not lead us to assume that they had no problems. The Church claimed to be superior to the lay powers of kings, noblemen, and town councils, but at all levels struggled to translate its claims into outcomes. It was itself a movement of individuals rather than an organisation. Its clergy owed as much to the laity as to their clerical superiors, and might side with the former against the latter, as they did very markedly during the Reformation.

At the same time, change came from the bottom of society. While churches might be founded from the top, their functioning depended on the willingness of ordinary people to support them with tithes, offerings, and contributions to the maintenance of buildings. Those in authority were responsible for the presence of clergy providing pastoral care, but parishioners took the initiative in forming guilds and companies, in paying for stores, and sometimes in founding chapels. The development of church buildings to encompass aisles and chapels was due in part to the need to accommodate these activities. The erection of roodscreens with fine embellishments reflected the desire of congregations to have church fittings as good as their neighbours. Seats were the creation of such people as well, since they were never required by those in authority but came into existence through local initiatives. In the *Book of Common Prayer*, the top-down imposition of Reformed doctrine and practice was matched by a concern to keep services in a form familiar to ordinary

Figure 42 St Nicholas Priory, Exeter. Another relic of a religious house, adapted in this case to become the dwelling of a city merchant.

people. And the failure of the Book to maintain communion services every Sunday came about because of the refusal of congregations to receive communion so frequently.

History is a sequence; it is less certainly a progress. On the whole, the later the time, the greater the evidence. Church history therefore appears to have evolved from simplicity to complexity. It is indeed probable that the Church had more institutions in 1400 than it possessed a thousand years previously, but it had many of those by the Norman Conquest that we think of as typical of the later Middle Ages. The existence of numerous guilds in the Exeter region in about 1100 shows that Church congregations were already dividing into separate groups with their own social bases, sometimes excluding others and possibly having their own religious habits or allegiances, at least with regard to the saints they venerated. We know too little about the churches of Anglo-Saxon and Norman England and their fittings to be able to say with safety that they were simpler in their worship and social dispositions than those of the fourteenth and fifteenth centuries.

One view of progress needs to be treated with caution. This is that the Church evolves from godliness to worldliness: a development that has been particularly influential in the understanding of monastic history. The belief goes back to the Middle Ages themselves, when the world was regarded as having been made by God in a perfect way. From this, human affairs could only deteriorate, requiring periodic reforms to return things to wellbeing. There was an undoubted fervour for monasticism in the twelfth century, but we know too little about the monasteries at that time to estimate their faults and limitations. In the later Middle Ages, in contrast, surviving records tell us more of the shortcomings than of the virtues. We cannot compare like with like. There is an assumption today that medieval people were more religious than people are now. That is true in terms of the understanding of science and medicine, in church attendance, and in some social practices. But no census exists of how many people went to church, and contemporary writers were more struck by people's spiritual and social faults than by their merits.

At first sight, the Church of the Middle Ages seems very far away from modern life. Its unfamiliar beliefs, strange ceremonies, religious communities, popular observances, and the repression of dissent leave an exotic and sometimes distasteful impression. Yet the Church was composed of human beings like ourselves, faced by similar challenges and possibilities, and with the same strengths and weaknesses. Authorities framed policies but struggled to impose them on a diverse and often resistant society. Local agents – the clergy in this case – varied in their commitment and effectiveness. The community of the parish achieved a good deal, but its records reflect the enthusiasm of the devout, not the disengagement of the irreverent and marginalised. Social factors and economic resources affected what could be done. Unity of belief and practice was achieved at the price of allowing a good deal of individual choice and of asking for what people could be expected to tolerate. We know more than our ancestors, but we are not necessarily different or better in how we behave.

Guide to Technical Terms

abbey – an important and well-endowed monastery or nunnery, ruled by an abbot or abbess.

advowson – the right to choose and present the clergyman of a parish church and present him to the bishop for **institution**, or to be involved in choosing the head of a religious house. The owner of the right was known as the **patron**.

aisle – a subdivision of a church, usually alongside and parallel with the **nave** and **chancel** or **choir**.

alien priory – a priory in England owned and ruled by an abbey in France.

altar – a stone table at which **mass** was celebrated. The high altar was the principal altar of a church, placed at the east end of the **chancel** or **choir**.

altarage – the offerings made to the high altar of a parish church, the perquisite of the rector or vicar. Sometimes the altarage was considered to include the small **tithes**.

anchorite – a man or woman who took vows to live celibately and permanently in an enclosed room or house, as opposed to having freedom of movement like a **hermit**.

anniversary – *see* **obit**.

annuellar – the original name for a chantry priest.

antiphon – a piece of music sung in church before and after a psalm, or as an anthem in its own right.

appropriation – the practice by which a bishop or religious house was allowed to become rector of a parish and to take **tithes** from the parish.

arcade – a row of arches, usually separating a **nave** from an **aisle**.

archdeacon – the clergyman in charge of an archdeaconry, a subdivision of a **diocese**.

archpriest – a title sometimes given to the cleric in charge of a small **college** of priests.

benefice – a Church post with an income, held by a cleric such as a **rector**, **vicar**, or secular **canon**, who are therefore known as 'beneficed clergy'.

bishop – the Church leader in overall charge of a **diocese** with the sole power to confirm and ordain. See also **suffragan**.

breviary – a book containing the daily offices or services said by the clergy.

canon – a cleric living in a community. A secular canon belonged to a **minster**, **college**, or some **cathedrals** and was similar to a **rector** or **vicar** in way of life but without parish duties. A regular canon belonged to an abbey or priory that followed the Rule of St Augustine or comparable rules, and was similar to a **monk** in way of life.

canon law – the law of the Church.

cathedral – the chief church of the bishop of the diocese. Exeter Cathedral was staffed by secular **canons** and **vicars choral**.

cell – a small religious house owned and ruled by an abbey or priory elsewhere.

chalice – the cup used for wine in the communion service or **mass**.

chancel – the eastern part of a parish church where services were said by the clergy, and sometimes accommodating important laity. In cathedrals, monasteries, and colleges the word **choir** is generally used instead.

chantry – the saying of a daily mass by a priest for the well-being of a living person, or the soul of a dead one, either for a limited period or perpetually. The term is also used for the endowment that paid the priest, and for the place where the masses were said, such as a chapel inside a church.

chantry priest – the priest of a chantry, also known in Devon and Cornwall as an **annuellar**.

chapel – an enclosed area within a church containing an **altar**, or a separate building with an altar that did not have the status of a parish church. A chapel of ease served a community a long way from a parish church. A free chapel was free of some or all of the authority of the local parish clergyman and his church.

chaplain – a term used in the Middle Ages for a priest who worked in a parish as an assistant or deputy to a **rector** or **vicar**, or in a private household.

choir – the eastern part of a cathedral, monastery, or college where services were said: the equivalent of the **chancel** of a parish church. Also the collective term for the clergy who performed the service in that part of the church.

chorister – a boy singer in a cathedral, minster, or collegiate church. Similar singers in monasteries were usually called 'boys'.

chrism – a mixture of oil and balm used in baptism and in other rites.

church ale – ale brewed to help make profit for a church and sold at social functions or to individual people.

church house – a house built by parishioners close to a parish church and used for social functions.

churching – a ceremony by which a mother gave thanks after a birth, and was led back into the parish church by its clergyman.

civil law – Roman law (as distinct from **canon law** and **common law**).

clerestory – the upper part of a church, usually above an **arcade**, carrying a row of windows to light the church.

clerk – a term generally meaning a cleric who was not a priest but of lower status.

collation – *see* **institution**.

college, collegiate church – a church staffed by a resident group of **secular clergy** who governed it together. In the Middle Ages, the word meant a collection of clergy and did not imply any academic functions.

commendation, ***'in commendam'*** – the grant of a benefice to somebody as a temporary measure, pending the appointment of a permanent occupant.

common law – the law of the courts of the king of England.

communion – *see* **mass**.

compulsion – an order by the bishop requiring a chaplain (often a chantry priest) to accept employment as an assistant priest in a parish.

confession – the process of confessing one's sins to the rector or vicar of the parish at least once a year during Lent.

consistory – the court of the bishop of the diocese.

corrody – a pension charged on a monastery, which had to provide the pensioner with board and lodging for life.

crossing – the part of a church at the east end of the nave, between the transepts.

curate – originally the **rector** or **vicar** of a parish who exercised the **cure of souls**. After the Reformation the term came to mean a priest who assisted or deputised for a rector or vicar, but until the middle of the sixteenth century such men were usually known as **chaplains**.

cure of souls – the right and duty to care for the souls of the inhabitants of a parish.

dean – the title given to the chief clergyman of a **cathedral** and of some **colleges**, as well as the presiding cleric of a **rural deanery**.

dedication festival – the celebration of the day when the church building was dedicated, to be distinguished from the **patronal festival**.

diocese – the territory ruled by a bishop. The diocese of Exeter covered Cornwall and Devon.

dispensation – the relaxation of a Church law for the benefit of a particular person.

excommunication – a punishment imposed by a cleric, usually a bishop, which forbade a sinner to attend church, receive the sacraments, or mix with other people until the sinner submitted to the Church.

friar – a cleric living in a community supported by voluntary donations, unlike monks and parish clergy who received their support from lands and other endowments.

glebe – land belonging to the **rector** or **vicar** of a parish; an alternative word was **sanctuary**.

guild – a society formed to promote religion or a craft, but the craft guilds also supported religious activities in the Middle Ages.

hermit – a person, invariably male, who took a vow of celibacy and lived alone but was able to travel about unlike an **anchorite**.

high altar – *see* **altar**.

holywater clerk – *see* **parish clerk**.

hospital – in the Middle Ages a religious or semi-religious institution offering long-term care for lepers or the infirm, or short-term accommodation for the sick, rather than medical treatment.

incumbent – the occupant of a **benefice**, such as a **rector** or **vicar**.

induction – the ceremony by which a rector or vicar, after his **institution** by the bishop, was given possession of his parish church and its property.

indulgence (or **pardon**) – the forgiving of **penance** by a pope or a bishop in return for doing a good deed such as a crusade, pilgrimage, prayer, or contribution to a church or a hospital.

institution (or **admission**) – the act by which a bishop approved the appointment to a **benefice** of a clergyman presented to him by a **patron**. When the bishop was himself the patron of the benefice and therefore both presented and instituted, the act was known as a collation.

ledger-stone – a flat stone laid over a grave in a church.

Lent – the forty weekdays (plus Sundays) from Ash Wednesday until the day before Easter, a time of fasting and penitence for sins; also an **indulgence** of forty days of penance.

manual – a book containing the pastoral services done by clergy, such as baptisms, marriages, and funerals, so called because they took it around in their hands for these purposes.

mass – the service of the eucharist or holy communion.

mendicant – a **friar**; the term means a beggar.

minster – in modern use, a church (especially in the tenth, eleventh, and twelfth centuries) staffed by a group of secular **canons**, **priests**, or **clerks**, rather than **monks**. In later centuries such churches are often known as **colleges** or collegiate churches.

missal – a book containing the service of the mass.

monastery – a church served by a group of **monks** or regular **canons**.

monk – a cleric who lived in a monastery that observed the Rule of St Benedict, or another similar rule.

mortuary – a due paid to a **rector** or **vicar** after someone's death.

nave – the western part of a church, also called the 'body', open to lay people.

nun – the female equivalent of a monk, living in a nunnery.

obit – a mass celebrated on the anniversary of someone's death, also known as an anniversary.

official – the deputy of a bishop or archdeacon who managed their legal affairs.

ordain, **ordination** – the rite by which a bishop confers religious status on a person. There were several grades of ordination, the highest of which was **priest**.

palm-cross – a name sometimes given to standing crosses in churchyards.

pardon, **pardoner** – an **indulgence** and the person who advertised it.

parish – the area belonging to a parish church, whose inhabitants had the duty to support that church and its clergyman and the right to receive care in return.

parish clerk – the assistant of a rector or vicar at the services in a parish church, usually a young man until the fifteenth century.

paten – a small metal plate for holding the bread in the **mass**.

patron – the person who held the right to appoint or be involved with the appointment of the **rector** or **vicar** of a parish church, or the head of a religious house. This right was known as an **advowson** and could be held by clergy or lay people.

patronal festival – the feast day of the patron saint of the church, to be distinguished from the **dedication festival**.

peculiar, peculiar jurisdiction – a territory consisting of one or more parishes which had its own system of administration for Church purposes, separate from the normal administration of the diocese.

penance – the punishment incurred by a sin, which had to be endured before the sin would be obliterated.

penitentiary – a cleric appointed by the bishop to hear the confessions of other clergy and those of lay people who had committed sins too serious to be dealt with by their parish priests.

piscina – a drain in a church wall for disposing of holy water.

polyphony – music sung in harmony by voices following different parts.

portionary church – a church whose revenues supported two or more clergyman known as portionists, who had parish duties but did not live together as a community.

prebend – a share of the income of a church, equivalent to a **stipend** or salary.

prebendal church – a church similar to a **portionary church** but whose clergymen did not normally have parish duties.

prebendary – the holder of a **prebend**, a member of the **secular clergy** similar to a secular **canon**, differing from a **rector** or **vicar** in not usually having parish duties.

presbytery – the eastern part of a choir of a church, near the high altar, where the clergy celebrated **mass**.

priest – a cleric with the power to say mass, baptise, and administer most other **sacraments**. **Rectors**, **vicars**, and **chaplains** were normally priests, and by the later Middle Ages so were **monks, canons**, and **friars**.

prior – the head of a **priory**, sometimes of a **hospital**.

priory – a monastery, generally less large and wealthy than an **abbey**.

proctor – a legal representative or agent.

provision, papal provision – an appointment of a bishop, abbot, prior, cathedral canon, rector, or vicar by the pope instead of by the **patron** normally responsible for making the appointment. Such appointments were common in fourteenth-century England, but only replaced the rights of other clergy, never challenging those of lay patrons.

rector – the clergyman of a parish who received all its revenues; his **benefice** and house were known as a rectory.

regular clergy – **monks**, regular **canons**, **friars**, and **nuns**, so called because they all followed written codes of rules.

religious house – any church served by a group of clergy, such as a **cathedral**, **monastery**, **friary**, **college**, or **hospital**.

reliquary – a wooden or metal container holding bones or other relics of Christ or the saints.

requiem – a **mass** including prayers for the soul of a dead person.

retrochoir – the area behind the high altar of a large church, similar to a choir **aisle**.

rood – a large image of Christ on the cross, placed on the roodscreen: a screen (normally of wood) between the chancel and the nave.

rural deanery – a group of parishes administered by a rural **dean**, also known as a 'deanery of Christianity'.

sacraments – one of seven solemn rites of the medieval Church: baptism, confirmation, marriage, confession, communion, ordination, and the anointing of the sick.

sacristan – *see* **sexton**.

sanctuary – the part of the church around the high altar at the east end of the chancel or choir; also a privilege by which people accused of a crime could take refuge in a church or on certain pieces of Church property; also an alternative name for **glebe**.

Sarum, Use of – **breviaries**, **manuals**, **missals**, and other service books following the usages of Salisbury Cathedral, commonly used in southern England in the fourteenth, fifteenth, and early sixteenth centuries.

secular clergy – clergy who did not follow the monastic life, such as parish clergy and the **canons** of **cathedrals** and **colleges**.

sexton – a form of 'sacristan', a lowly clerical or lay assistant who helped with the running of a parish church and churchyard, eventually coming to mean someone who did physical tasks like ringing bells and digging graves.

Sir – a title given to all priests, as well as to knights; it did not signify possession of a university degree.

stipend – the income of a **benefice** received by the cleric who held it.

suffragan – an assistant bishop.

tithe – the obligation of all householders to pay the rector of their parish one tenth of the produce of their land, including all crops and young animals. Fish, dairy products, and the milling of grain were also tithed. Tithes of grain were known as 'great tithes' or 'garb tithes'; other tithes as 'small tithes'. In towns, tithes were replaced by monetary payments.

tympanum – a panel within an archway above a church door or between the chancel and the nave.

vicar – the clergyman of an **appropriated** parish, who received part not all of its revenues; his **benefice** and house were known as a vicarage.

vicar choral – a clergyman in a **cathedral** or **college** who deputised for a **canon** in saying the daily services.

vicar general – the deputy of a bishop, with general responsibility for administering his affairs in his absence other than confirmations and ordinations which were done by a **suffragan**.

Notes and Abbreviations

Works not fully cited here are listed in the Bibliography

Abbreviations

×	An unknown date somewhere between two known dates
BRUO, i–iii	A. B. Emden, *A Biographical Register of the University of Oxford to A.D. 1500*
BRUO, iv	A. B. Emden, *A Biographical Register of the University of Oxford A.D. 1501 to 1540*
CCR	*Calendar of Close Rolls*
CPL	*Calendar of Papal Letters*
CPR	*Calendar of Patent Rolls*
DA	*Reports and Transactions of the Devonshire Association*
D&C	Exeter Cathedral Archives, Dean and Chapter documents
DCNQ	*Devon and Cornwall Notes and Queries*
DCRS	Devon and Cornwall Record Society
DRO	Devon Record Office, Sowton, Exeter
LPFD	*Letters and Papers, Foreign and Domestic, Henry VIII*
ODNB	*Oxford Dictionary of National Biography*
OED	*Oxford English Dictionary*
TNA	The National Archives, Kew

Chapter 1. From the Romans to Domesday Book

1 *Reg. Grandisson*, i, 97–8.
2 On Devon's historical geography, see Kain and Ravenhill, *Historical Atlas of South-West England*.
3 Aileen Fox, *South-West England 3500BC–AD600*, 2nd edn (Newton Abbot, 1973), 193–4.
4 P. T. Bidwell and others. *The Legionary Bath-House and Basilica and Forum at Exeter* (Exeter, 1979), 2, 111–13.
5 Okasha, *Early Christian Inscribed Stones*, 79–81, 100–8, 154–73, 193–4, 208–10, 260–3, 268–87, 338–40.
6 Gildas, *Ruin of Britain*, 29–30, 99–100 (chapters 28–9).
7 K. Barker, D. A. Hinton, and A. Hunt (ed.), *St Wulsige and Sherborne* (Oxford, 2005), 136–7.
8 P. Weddell. 'The Excavation of a Post-Roman Cemetery near Kenn, South Devon', *Devon Archaeological Society Proceedings*, 58 (2000), 93–126.
9 Orme, *Saints of Cornwall*, 156–8.
10 Orme, *Nicholas Roscarrock's Lives of the Saints*, 137–9.
11 J. M. Bately (ed.), *The Anglo-Saxon Chronicle: a Collaborative Edition*, vol. iii (Cambridge, 1986), 27, 30; Whitelock, *Anglo-Saxon Chronicle*, 16, 21. Dates quoted from the Chronicle are as adjusted by the editors. *Peonnan* is often regarded as Penselwood (Somt.) but Pinhoe is a possibility and might explain why Exeter had a monastery with an English abbot only a couple of decades later.
12 Bately, *Anglo-Saxon Chronicle*, 32; Whitelock, *Anglo-Saxon Chronicle*, 23.
13 W. Levison (ed.), *Vitae Sancti Bonifacii*, Monumenta Germaniae Historica, Scriptores Rerum Germanicarum 57 (Hannover, 1905), 6; C. H. Talbot, *The Anglo-Saxon Missionaries in Germany* (London, 1954), 28.
14 F. L. Attenborough (ed.), *The Laws of the Earliest English Kings* (Cambridge, 1922), 43, 45, 47, 51, 55, 61.
15 Sawyer, *Charters*, nos. 1676, 255; Hooke, *Charter-Bounds*, 83, 86–99.
16 Aldhelm, *Omnia Opera*, ed. R. Ehwald, Monumenta Germaniae Historica, Auctores Antiquissimi, 15 (Berlin, 1913–19), 480–6; Aldhelm, *The Prose Works*, trans. M. Lapidge and M. Herren (Cambridge, 1979), 155–60.
17 Aldhelm, *Omnia Opera*, 524–8; Aldhelm, *The Poetic Works*, trans. M. Lapidge and I. L. Rosier (Cambridge, 1985), 177–9.
18 *Asser's Life of King Alfred*, ed. W. H. Stevenson (Oxford, 1959), 68; Keynes and Lapidge, *Alfred the Great*, 50–1, 97, 264–5.
19 Orme, *Exeter Cathedral*, 8–10, 75–6.
20 Sawyer, *Charters*, no. 380; Hooke, *Charter-Bounds*, 113.
21 Whitelock, *Anglo-Saxon Chronicle*, 55–6.
22 *Councils and Synods I*, i, 169–73.
23 Sawyer, *Charters*, no. 1021; Hooke, *Charter-Bounds*, 187–8.
24 On minsters, see Blair, *Church in Anglo-Saxon Society*, 3–4 and passim.
25 Levison, *Vitae Sancti Bonifatii*, 5–7; Talbot, *Anglo-Saxon Missionaries in Germany*, 27–8.
26 Sawyer, *Charters*, nos. 386–90.
27 C. G. Henderson and P. T. Bidwell, 'The Saxon Minster at Exeter', in S. M. Pearce (ed.), *The Early Church in Western Britain and Ireland* (Oxford, British Archaeological Reports, 1982), 145–75 at 152–6.

28 Sawyer, *Charters*, no. 255; Hooke, *Charter-Bounds*, 86–99.
29 Sawyer, *Charters*, no. 1695, Hooke, *Charter-Bounds*, 102 (Braunton); Sawyer, *Charters*, no. 1507, Hooke, *Charter-Bounds*, 103–4 (Exminster); Sawyer, *Charters*, no. 380, Hooke, *Charter-Bounds*, 113 (Plympton).
30 Sawyer, *Charters*, no. 838; Finberg, *Tavistock Abbey*, 21–3; J. Stéphan, *Buckfast Abbey: a short history and guide*, revised edn (Buckfast, 1962), 7.
31 Searle, *Chronicle of Battle Abbey*, 80–3, discussed in *Regesta Regum Anglo-Normannorum*, 2nd edn, i, 162–5.
32 Sawyer, *Charters*, no. 1236.
33 *Domesday Book: Additamenta* (Exon Domesday); *Domesday Book: Devon* (Exchequer Domesday).
34 *Domesday Book: Additamenta*, f. 456r–v (Hartland); *Domesday Book: Devon*, 1/17 (Plympton); 13a/1 (South Molton); 17/58 (Totnes); 1/18 (Yealmpton).
35 *Domesday Book: Devon*, 2/5–8.
36 Ibid., 2/2.
37 Ibid., 1/12–13, 1/33, 1/52.
38 Ibid., 52/50.
39 *Domesday Book: Additamenta*, f. 65r (Hartland, Hollacombe, Newton St Petrock); 66r (South Molton); 70r (*Alentona*, Modbury, *Niuuentona*, Plympton).
40 Orme, 'The Church from *c.*1300 to the Reformation', in Kain and Ravenhill, *Historical Atlas of South-West England*, 215.
41 *Reg. Bronescombe*, ed. Hingeston-Randolph, 454.
42 *Valor Ecclesiasticus*, ii, 350.
43 Whitelock, *Anglo-Saxon Chronicle*, 30–1; Sawyer, *Charters*, no. 1161; Hooke, *Charter-Bounds*, 189.
44 Sawyer, *Charters*, no. 1507; Hooke, *Charter-Bounds*, 103–4.
45 *Domesday Book: Devon*, 1/11 (Axminster); 1/6, 13a/1 (South Molton); 1/17 (Plympton); 17/1 (Totnes); 1/18 (Yealmpton).
46 *Domesday Book: Devon*, 1/34 (Chillington); 1/16 (West Alvington); 1/33 (Woodbury).
47 D. Hill and A. R. Rumble. *The Defence of Wessex: the Burghal Hidage and Anglo-Saxon Fortifications* (Manchester, 1996), 26–7, 202–5, 208–9, 213–14.
48 T. J. Miles. 'The Excavation of a Saxon Cemetery and Part of the Norman Castle at North Walk, Barnstaple', *Devon Archaeological Society Proceedings*, 44 (1986), 59–84.
49 Orme, 'Two Unusual Devon Saints', 10–13; Orme, *English Church Dedications*, 144, 162, 204–5.
50 Orme, 'Medieval Chapels of Heavitree', 121–9.
51 There are three parallel cases of churches in Cornwall holding land without record of a community of clergy: Constantine, Goran, and Lansallos (Orme, *Victoria County History of Cornwall*, ii, 19, 128, 130, 132).
52 Attenborough, *Laws of the Earliest English Kings*, 36–7.
53 Ibid.
54 Finberg, *Tavistock Abbey*, 21–3; Stéphan, *Buckfast Abbey*, 7.
55 R. R. Darlington and P. McGurk (ed.), *The Chronicle of John of Worcester*, vol. ii (Oxford, 1995), 418–19.
56 *Domesday Book: Devon*, 5/1–15.
57 Ibid., 2/2, 6–8, 12–13, 15–17, 22, as interpreted in Orme, *Exeter Cathedral*, 9–10.

58 *Domesday Book: Devon*, 6/1–13 (Buckfast).
59 Ibid., 45/3 (Hartland); 1/17 (Plympton); 1/18 (Yealmpton); 1/11 (Axminster).
60 Ibid., 13a/1 (South Molton); 17/58 (Totnes); 13a/3 (Braunton).
61 The number of 24 is first mentioned in 1268, when it was believed to date from the foundation of the cathedral in 1050 (*Reg. Bronescombe*, ed. Robinson, iii, 65).
62 A. S. Napier and W. H. Stevenson, *The Crawford Collection of Early Charters and Documents now in the Bodleian Library* (Oxford, 1895), 29–31.
63 *Domesday Book: Additamenta*, f. 456r–v.
64 Finberg, *Tavistock Abbey*, 220.
65 Oliver, *Monasticon*, 317–18.
66 Leland, *Itinerary*, i, 215.
67 Searle, *Chronicle of Battle Abbey*, 80–3.
68 *Domesday Book: Devon*, 13a/1.
69 *Reg. Bronescombe*, ed. Hingeston-Randolph, 454.
70 A. S. Napier (ed.), *The Old English Version of the Enlarged Rule of Chrodegang*, Early English Text Society, original series, 150 (1916).
71 Orme, 'Church in Crediton', 100, 102; Leland, *Itinerary*, i, 215.
72 Orme, *Exeter Cathedral*, 95.
73 Blair, *Church in Anglo-Saxon Society*, 519–22.
74 Searle, *Chronicle of Battle Abbey*, 80–3.
75 Orme, 'Church in Crediton', 100–1.
76 Ibid. For the complicated arrangements at Probus (Cornwall), see Orme, *Victoria County History of Cornwall*, ii, 264.
77 Conner, *Anglo-Saxon Exeter*, 171–209.
78 Ibid., 33–147.
79 Napier and Stevenson, *The Crawford Collection*, 23–4, 125–33.
80 Blair, *Church in Anglo-Saxon Society*, 446–504.
81 *Councils and Synods I*, i, 97–9.
82 Sawyer, *Charters*, no. 795; Hooke, *Charter-Bounds*, 172–5.
83 Sawyer, *Charters*, no. 963; Hooke, *Charter-Bounds*, 197–9.
84 Sawyer, *Charters*, no. 1003; Hooke, *Charter-Bounds*, 204.
85 DRO, Exeter City Archives, Book 53A, f. 36r.
86 *Domesday Book: Devon*, 6/10 (Charford); 52/11 (Cheriton Bishop); 36/19 (Cheriton Fitzpaine); 34/15 (Cheriton in Brendon); 20/4 (Churchill in East Down); 17/30 (Churston Ferrers); 16/27 (Honeychurch); and 35/29 (Whitchurch).
87 On what follows, see Orme, *English Church Dedications*, passim.
88 Ibid. On Holne, see Orme, *English Church Dedications*, Supplement No. 1, 305–7.
89 Orme, *English Church Dedications*, 242. The chapels were in Charles parish, St Petrox (Dartmouth), and Petton in Bampton parish (Orme, *Saints of Cornwall*, 218).
90 For a list, see Orme, 'Christianity in Devon', 30–4 (St Martin [Exeter] was omitted by mistake).
91 See above, pp. 53–4.
92 Sawyer, *Charters*, no. 1507; Hooke, *Charter-Bounds*, 103–4 (Whitchurch); *Domesday Book: Devon*, 1/12–13 (Colyton, Kingskerswell).
93 Sawyer, *Charters*, no. 498; Hooke, *Charter-Bounds*, 147–9.
94 Turner, *Making a Christian Landscape*; idem, *Medieval Devon and Cornwall*.

95 Blair, *Church in Anglo-Saxon Society*, 521.
96 Orme, *Saints of Cornwall*, 226–7.
97 Ibid., 218.
98 Ibid., 159–60.
99 Ibid., 257–9.
100 Ibid., 102–3.
101 Ibid., 218.
102 Orme, *Medieval Schools*, 39–40.
103 Orme, *Medieval Children*, 22–4.
104 Blair, *Church in Anglo-Saxon Society*, 434–40.
105 Conner, *Anglo-Saxon Exeter*, 168–9; Whitelock, *English Historical Documents*, 605.
106 Lepine and Orme, *Death and Memory*, 259–61.
107 There was a guild of twenty members in Exeter *c.*1200 (Orme, 'The Kalendar Brethren', 154).
108 Napier and Stevenson, *Crawford Collection*, 23–4, 125–33; Whitelock, *English Historical Documents*, 580–1.
109 *Domesday Book: Devon*, 3/7, 15/7, 16/51, 16/129, 16/135, 25/19, 34/17, 34/50, 42/14, 42/23, 45/2, 51/6.
110 British Library, Cotton MS Tiberius B v, f. 75v; Hooke, *Charter-Bounds*, 225.
111 N. Orchard (ed.), *The Leofric Missal*, 2 vols, Henry Bradshaw Society, 113–14 (2002), ii, 14–15; Hooke, *Charter-Bounds*, 225–6.
112 *Councils and Synods I*, i, 208, 321–2, 483.
113 Gover, Mawer, and Stenton, *Place-Names of Devon*, i, 141, 250, 323.

Chapter 2. From 1086 to 1300

1 *Domesday Book: Devon*, 2/1–24, 4/1–8/1.
2 On Osbern and the other bishops discussed here, see the biographies by Frank Barlow in *English Episcopal Acta*, i, pp. xxxii–liv, and in *ODNB*.
3 Above, p. 72.
4 On the Cornish estates, see Orme, *Victoria County History of Cornwall*, ii, 23–4.
5 Muriel E. Curtis, *Some Disputes between the City and the Cathedral Authorities of Exeter* (Manchester, 1932), 9–19.
6 *Domesday Book: Devon*, 2/1–24; Barlow, *English Episcopal Acta*, i, p. xxix.
7 Barlow, *English Episcopal Acta*, ii, 196–7; John Stow, *A Survey of London*, ed. C. L. Kingsford, 2 vols (Oxford, 1908), ii, 92.
8 Barlow, *English Episcopal Acta*, ii, 291–300.
9 *Councils and Synods II*, i, 227–37.
10 Ibid., i, 227.
11 Ibid., ii, 982–1077; order relating to copies of the summary on p. 1077.
12 *Reg. Bronescombe*, ed. Hingeston-Randolph; ed. Robinson.
13 However, the ordination records of Bishop Grandisson (1327–69) have been lost.
14 Above, pp. 59–62.
15 D&C 3672A. The cathedral's figures are only for tithes of grain, but the valuations of these parishes in 1291 must have had a similar basis.

16 The best current edition of the Taxation for Devon is in *Reg. Bronescombe*, ed. Hingeston-Randolph, 450–81.
17 Barlow, *English Episcopal Acta*, ii, 306–10.
18 Ethel Lega-Weekes, *Some Studies in the Topography of the Cathedral Close Exeter* (Exeter, 1915), 108–114, 129–35, 147–64.
19 Coulton, 'Visitation of Totnes', 108–24.
20 E.g. Barlow, *English Episcopal Acta*, 311.
21 The earliest list of the deaneries and the parishes in them dates from 1291 (*Reg. Bronescombe*, ed. Hingeston-Randolph, 450–67).
22 Barlow, *English Episcopal Acta*, i, 123.
23 *Reg. Brantyngham*, ii, 706 (election); *Reg. Stafford*, 244, 310 (serving in turn); *Reg. Lacy*, ed. Dunstan, iii, 307 (serving in turn or election).
24 Oliver, *Monasticon*, 95–6, 103–4; Finberg, *Tavistock Abbey*, 235–6; *LPFD*, iii part 1, p. 153.
25 *Reg. Bronescombe*, ed. Hingeston-Randolph, 465–6; Peskett, *Registers of Devon and Cornwall*, passim.
26 Above, p. 142.
27 On the Jews in Exeter, see Adler, 'Medieval Jews of Exeter', 221–40, and now Hillaby, *The Palgrave Dictionary of Medieval Anglo-Jewish History*. The following account is based on the present author's contribution to Orme, *Unity and Variety*, 46–8.
28 *Councils and Synods II*, ii, 1044–5.
29 Orme, *Education in the West of England*, 47.
30 Those reported to the king ('significations of excommunication') are recorded in TNA, C 85.
31 On the cathedral, see Orme, *Exeter Cathedral*, 37–42, 94–104.
32 The following information about religious houses is largely based on Knowles and Hadcock, *Medieval Religious Houses*, although this work badly needs updating and improving in its data.
33 Larking, *Knights Hospitallers in England*, 13–14. The Order also owned the church of Halwill and property in Chulmleigh.
34 The Templars also held the manor of Cove in Tiverton parish, the churches of Brendon and Clayhanger, and some minor properties (*Records of the Templars in England in the Twelfth Century*, ed. Beatrice A. Lees [London, 1935], pp. cxxxii–iii, 59–60). These were administered by their preceptory at Templecombe (Somt.), which duly passed to the Hospitallers who then gave Cove to Bodmiscombe.
35 *CCR 1231–4*, 101; DRO, Exeter City Archives, ED/SJ/2.
36 TNA, C 143/12 no. 3; *CPR 1292–1301*, 205; *CPR 1381–5*, 295, 399.
37 *CPR 1330–4*, 46; *Reg. Grandisson*, ii, 787–8, 1027–31.
38 *Reg. Grandisson*, ii, 1047; *CPR 1350–4*, 528.
39 On hospitals in Devon, see Orme and Webster, *The English Hospital*, 215–66.
40 Ibid., 170–7.
41 *CPR 1330–4*, 97.
42 Oliver, *Monasticon*, 363.
43 Oxford, Bodleian Library, MS Digby 81, ff. 66r–88v (Tavistock); *Ungedruckte Anglo-Normannische Geschichtsquellen*, ed. F. Liebermann (Strasbourg, 1897), 25–30 (Plympton); Grosjean, 'Vie de S. Rumon . . . Nectan', 361–75, 393–402 (Tavistock), 376–97, 402–14 (Hartland); Oliver, *Monasticon*, 341–6 (Forde), 362–4 (Newenham).

44 *ODNB*, Baldwin of Forde; John of Forde; Roger of Forde.
45 E. St J. Brooks, 'Unpublished Charters Relating to Ireland, 1177–82, from the Archives of the City of Exeter', *Proceedings of the Royal Irish Academy*, 43 (1935–7), 313–66.
46 Orme, *English Church Dedications*, passim. Most church dedications to Thomas Becket are actually conjectures of the eighteenth century (ibid., pp. 48–9).
47 *Reg. Bronescombe*, ed. Hingeston-Randolph, 450–81.
48 The borders of Devon in 1291 were slightly different from what they are now. During the nineteenth and twentieth centuries, the county lost North Petherwin and Werrington to Cornwall, Thorncombe to Dorset, and Churchstanton to Somerset, but acquired Chardstock, Hawkchurch, and Stockland from Dorset.
49 For the map, produced by the present writer, see Kain and Ravenhill, *Historical Atlas of South West England*, 215.
50 *Ordinale Exon*, i, p. xxi.
51 D&C 2111 (St Cuthbert); DRO, Exeter City Archives, Book 53A, f. 8v (St John); *John Lydford's Book*, ed. Dorothy M. Owen, DCRS, 20 (1974), 105 (St Mary Minor).
52 Coulton, 'Visitation of Totnes', 108–24; for the cathedral visitations, see D&C 2672A (unprinted); D&C 3673, printed in *Reg. Stapeldon*, passim, under the churches concerned; and D&C 2852, printed in *Reg. Grandisson*, i, 570–9.
53 D&C 3672A; see also above, p. 35.
54 *Councils and Synods II*, ii, 1006.
55 On roodscreens, see above, p. 111.
56 *Councils and Synods II*, ii, 1007–8.
57 Above, pp. 115–16.
58 *Councils and Synods II*, ii, 1005–8.
59 D&C 3672A.
60 Barlow, *English Episcopal Acta*, ii, 308, 310; *ODNB*, Baldwin of Forde.
61 *Reg. Bronescombe*, ed. Hingeston-Randolph; ed. Robinson, passim.
62 Orme, *Education in the West of England*, 103.
63 Above, p. 25.
64 *Councils and Synods II*, ii, 1026–7.
65 D&C 3672A.
66 *ODNB*, Bartholomew; Baldwin of Forde; Joseph of Exeter.
67 *ODNB*, John of Seccheville; Henry of Bracton.
68 Lepine and Orme, *Death and Memory*, 139–67.
69 On chapels, see above, pp. 119–24.
70 Orme, 'Indulgences in the Diocese of Exeter', 15–32.
71 Barlow, *English Episcopal Acta*, ii, 217–18; Orme, 'Church in Crediton', 118.
72 Grosjean, 'Vie de S. Rumon . . . Nectan', 414; F. Rose-Troup, *Exeter Vignettes* (Exeter, 1942), 15–18.
73 *Materials for the History of Thomas Becket*, ed. J. C. Robertson, 7 vols (London, Rolls Series, 1875–85), i, 193–5, 351–2, 407–8, 457, 472–4; ii, 210–11.
74 Grosjean, 'Vie de S. Rumon . . . Nectan', 411–12.
75 On the Kalendars guild, see Orme, 'Kalendar Brethren', 153–69, and Lepine and Orme, *Death and Memory*, 235–7, 263–71.
76 Grosjean, 'Vie de S. Rumon . . . Nectan', 408–9.

Chapter 3. The Later Middle Ages: the Clergy

1 Orme, 'Mortality in Early Fourteenth-Century Exeter', 195–9.
2 *Reg. Grandisson*, ii, 1076; Oliver, *Monasticon*, 364.
3 *Reg. Lacy*, ed. Dunstan, ii, 217.
4 On the hospital, see Orme and Webster, *The English Hospital*, 217–22; Orme, 'A Medieval Almshouse for the Clergy', 1–15; and Orme, 'Clergy of Clyst Gabriel', 115–18.
5 *Reg. Grandisson*, iii, 1338–1403.
6 Above, p. 142.
7 *Reg. Bronescombe*, ed. Hingeston-Randolph, 202; ed. Robinson, ii, 74; *Reg. Stapeldon*, 384.
8 For a provisional list, see Fryde, *Handbook of British Chronology*, 284–7.
9 *Valor Ecclesiasticus*, ii, 29–391.
10 Ibid., ii, 319.
11 Ibid., ii, 376–7; i, 219.
12 *Reg. Stapeldon*, 227.
13 On St James, see Rose-Troup, *Lost Chapels*, 33–4; on Affeton, *Reg. Lacy*, ed. Dunstan, ii, 146–8; and on Oldridge, the nineteenth-century county directories.
14 Documents granting independence to chapels are rare. The evidence comes mainly from the institution of a rector to the church in the bishop's register.
15 Orme, 'Warland Hospital, Totnes', 41–8; Orme and Webster, *The English Hospital*, 223, 266.
16 In general, see New, *History of the Alien Priories* and Matthew, *The Norman Monasteries*.
17 Yeo, *Monks of Cowick*, 16–25.
18 McHardy and Orme, 'The Defence of an Alien Priory', 303–12.
19 The figures are based, as before, on those in Knowles and Hadcock, *Medieval Religious Houses*, passim.
20 *Reg. Grandisson*, ii, 996–8.
21 *Reg. Brantyngham*, ii, 667–71.
22 *Reg. Lacy*, ed. Dunstan, iii, 215–35.
23 *The Register of John Morton, Archbishop of Canterbury 1486–1500*, ed. C. Harper-Bill, vol. ii, Canterbury and York Society, 77 (1991), 75–83.
24 Orme, *Education in the West of England*, 203, 205, 212.
25 Orme, *Medieval Schools*, 278–83.
26 Ibid., 266–75.
27 *ODNB*, William Slade; Richard Sharpe, *A Handlist of the Latin Writers of Great Britain and Ireland before 1540* (Turnhout, 1997), 810.
28 John Leland, *Collectanea*, ed. T. Hearne, 2nd edn (London, 1774; repr. Farnborough, 1970), iv, 150–3.
29 Cartularies and registers survive or are recorded from Buckfast, Dunkeswell, St Nicholas and St John (Exeter), Forde, Modbury, Newenham, Otterton, Plympton, Tavistock, and Torre (G. R. C. Davis, *Medieval Cartularies of Great Britain* [London, 1958]).
30 Heale, *Dependent Priories*, passim.
31 Larking, *Knights Hospitallers*, 13–14.
32 Yeo, *Monks of Cowick*, 4, 13–14; Orme, 'Saint Walter of Cowick', 1–7.
33 Orme and Webster, *The English Hospital*, 236–7.
34 *BRUO*, i, 389–90.

35 *Reg. Stapeldon*, 95; Oliver, *Monasticon*, 225–6, 236.
36 *Reg. Stapeldon*, 95–6, 316–18.
37 *Reg. Grandisson*, ii, 724.
38 Ker, *Medieval Libraries*, 28–9; *Reg. Stafford*, 419.
39 TNA, C 1/44/227.
40 Little and Easterling, *Franciscans and Dominicans*, 40–6.
41 *CPL*, iv, 404; *Reg. Brantyngham*, ii, 576, 588, 723; *CPR 1401–5*, 103.
42 *CPL*, vi, 223–4; *Reg. Stafford*, 376.
43 Ker, *Medieval Libraries of Great Britain*, 86.
44 A. G. Little, 'Educational Organisation of the Mendicant Friars in England (Dominicans and Franciscans)', *Transactions of the Royal Historical Society*, new series, 8 (1894), 49–70.
45 *Reg. Stapeldon*, 317; *BRUO*, iii, 1518, 2008.
46 *BRUO*, iii, 2060; i, 359.
47 *Reg. Lacy*, ed. Dunstan, v, 75, 160.
48 D&C 3773, f. 13r.
49 *Reg. Stapeldon*, 111.
50 *LPFD*, iv (i), 341.
51 *Reg. Grandisson*, i, 558; ii, 954.
52 *Reg. Brantyngham*, i, 382, 430–1.
53 Little and Easterling, *Franciscans and Dominicans*, 15; *Reg. Stapeldon*, 317.
54 *Register of Edward the Black Prince* (London, 1930–3), ii, 36, 62.
55 Little and Easterling, *Franciscans and Dominicans*, 39.
56 TNA, E 36/115, p. 121.
57 Lepine and Orme, *Death and Memory*, 44–119.
58 Hale and Ellacombe, *Accounts of the Executors*, 28, 30, 39, 43; *Reg. Grandisson*, iii, 1517–18; *Reg. Brantyngham*, ii, 743.
59 Lepine and Orme, *Death and Memory*, 140–67, 189; *Reg. Stafford*, 340, 390, 399, 416–17; *Reg. Lacy*, ed. Dunstan, iv, 1–58.
60 *Reg. Lacy*, ed. Dunstan, iv, 7, 31, 46.
61 Orme, *Cornish Wills*, index p. 281.
62 *Reg. Stafford*, 390; *Reg. Lacy*, ed. Dunstan, iv, 1.
63 *CPR 1350–4*, 183; *CPR 1381–5*, 256.
64 R. L. Poole and Mary Bateson (ed.), *Index Britanniae Scriptorum: John Bale's Index of British and other Writers*, 2nd edn (London, 1990), pp. xxv, 104.
65 DRO, Exeter City Archives, Receivers' Rolls, 9–10 Henry IV.
66 Worcester, *Itineraries*, 124–5; Orme, *Cathedral Cat*, 78–9.
67 On the cathedral in this period, see Orme, *Exeter Cathedral*, especially 45–54.
68 Orme, 'Church in Crediton', especially 103–9.
69 Orme, *Victoria County History of Cornwall*, ii, 244–62.
70 A new history of the college is about to be published by J. R. Maddicott.
71 On the scholarships, see also above, pp. 146–7.
72 It has been said that Exeter College did not admit its members until they had spent a year or two at Oxford, but this seems less likely than that Stapledon planned a seamless path from school to graduation.
73 Nigel Saul, 'The Pre-history of an Oxford College: Hart Hall and its neighbours in the Middle Ages', *Oxoniensia*, 54 (1989), 327–43.

74 *Reg. Grandisson*, ii, 731–4 (Bere Ferrers); ibid., ii, 852–5 (Haccombe); *Reg. Stapeldon*, 402–5 (Whitchurch); Oliver, *Monasticon*, 322–30 (Slapton).
75 Dalton, *Collegiate Church of Ottery St Mary*.
76 Orme, *Exeter Cathedral*, 100–3.
77 Above, p. 145.
78 *Reg. Lacy*, ed. Dunstan, iv, 52; Ker, *Medieval Libraries*, 141.
79 Ker, *Medieval Libraries*, 55.
80 *BRUO*, ii, 801; Orme, *Nicholas Roscarrock's Lives of the Saints*, 171.
81 Nicholas Orme, *Education and Society in Medieval and Renaissance England* (London, 1989), 259–70; *ODNB*, Alexander Barclay.
82 On what follows, see Orme and Webster, *The English Hospital*, 181–4, 215–66.
83 Ibid., 221–2.
84 Lepine and Orme, *Death and Memory*, 39–43.
85 Other places included Dartmouth, Eggesford, Newton Bushell, Pilton, Plymouth, Tavistock, and Torrington (Orme and Webster, *The English Hospital*, 215–66).
86 Rotha Mary Clay, *The Hermits and Anchorites of England* (London, 1914); Anne Warren, *Anchorites and their Patrons in Medieval England* (Berkeley, Calif., 1986).
87 There is a list of Devon anchorites and hermits, in need of expansion and correction, in Clay, *Hermits and Anchorites*, 212–13.
88 On the grammar schools of the later Middle Ages, see above, pp. 146–9.
89 Most of the known members of Oxford in the Middle Ages are listed in *BRUO*, i–iv, and those of Cambridge in Emden, *Biographical Register of Cambridge*.
90 *Reg. Stapeldon*, 446–56, 523–4.
91 *Reg. Brantyngham*, ii, 787.
92 DRO, Chanter XIII and XIV, ordination lists (registers of Bishops Oldham and Veysey).
93 Papal provisions are listed in the *CPL* and *Calendar of Papal Petitions*; the subject is discussed in detail by W. E. Lunt, *Financial Relations of the Papacy with England to 1327* (Cambridge, Mass., 1939) and *Financial Relations of the Papacy with England 1327–1534* (Cambridge, Mass., 1962).
94 *Reg. Lacy*, ed. Dunstan, i, 6–7, and other examples.
95 London, Lambeth Palace Library, MS 721, ff. 63r–79v.
96 See also above, pp. 153–4.
97 D&C 2912.
98 Orme, 'Dissolution of the Chantries in Devon', 102–14.
99 Above, pp. 153–4.
100 *Councils and Synods II*, i, 236; ii, 1026; three chaplains at St Marychurch were each paid £3 in 1281 (D&C 3672A).
101 *Statutes of the Realm*, i, 373–4; ii, 188; William Lyndwood, *Provinciale* (Oxford, 1679, repr. Farnborough, 1968), 240.
102 Above, p. 25.
103 Orme, *Medieval Children*, 229–31; Orme, *Medieval Schools*, 39–40, 205–7.
104 Orme, *Cornish Wills*, 62. I now think that this will relates to Tiverton rather than Sheviock.
105 *Reg. Lacy*, ed. Dunstan, ii, 214.
106 Orme, *English School Exercises*, section 5 no. 26.
107 Hanham, *Churchwardens' Accounts of Ashburton*, p. xvii; Duffy, *Voices of Morebath*, 54–64.
108 Lyndwood, *Provinciale*, 142–3.

109 Duffy, *Voices of Morebath*, 55.
110 *Councils and Synods II*, ii, 1011–15, 1022–3.
111 Ibid., ii, 1018–20.
112 Coulton, 'Visitation of Totnes', 120, and see the case of John Hay, above, p. 105.
113 *Reg. Stapeldon*, 109.
114 E.g. ibid., 346.
115 *Reg. Lacy*, ed. Dunstan, iv, 3–4.
116 *Councils and Synods II*, ii, 1014.
117 Coulton, 'Visitation of Totnes', 118.
118 *Reg. Lacy*, ed. Dunstan, iv, 1–50.
119 *Reg. Brantyngham*, i, 412; *Reg. Stafford*, 134; *Reg. Lacy*, ed. Dunstan, i, 158–9.
120 *Reg. Brantyngham*, ii, 656.
121 *Reg. Lacy*, ed. Dunstan, ii, 8–10.
122 D&C 3673; *Reg. Stapeldon*, 107, 109–10, 111–12, 130–1, 132–3, 337–8, 345–6, 368–9, 378–80, 380–1. See also *Reg. Grandisson*, i, 570–9.
123 On what follows, see Orme, 'Sufferings of the Clergy', 62–73.
124 *Reg. Stapeldon*, 108.
125 Ibid., 107.
126 Tristram Risdon, *The Chorographical Description . . . of Devon* (London, 1714), 79; Orme, *Exeter Cathedral*, 113.

Chapter 4. The Later Middle Ages: the Laity

1 Coulton, 'Visitation of Totnes', 110–24.
2 Ibid., 111, 120.
3 Ibid., 119.
4 Ibid., 111, 120–4.
5 Ibid., 116, 118.
6 *The Register of Henry Chichele, Archbishop of Canterbury*, ed. E. F. Jacob, vol. ii, Canterbury and York Society, 42 (1937), 290.
7 Leland, *Itinerary*, i, 213.
8 Above, p. 61.
9 On the history of church seating, see Cooper and Brown, *Pews, Benches and Chairs*.
10 Athene Reiss, *The Sunday Christ: sabbatarianism in English medieval wall painting* (Oxford, 2000). There are no surviving examples in Devon.
11 F. Bligh Bond and Bede Camm, *Roodscreens and Roodlofts*, 2 vols (London, 1909), ii, 275–365; Michael A. Williams, 'Medieval English Roodscreens'.
12 TNA, PROB 11/21, f. 202v; Hanham, *Churchwardens' Accounts of Ashburton*, p. x.
13 *Councils and Synods II*, ii, 1017.
14 Above, p. 185.
15 *Reg. Stafford*, 419.
16 Orme, 'History of Brampford Speke', 62–3.
17 Above, pp. 97–8.
18 It should be added that there is no evidence that altars in churches were placed so as to be visible from one another by priests celebrating mass; multiple celebrations at the same time would have been unusual, if not unknown.

19 Hanham, *Churchwardens' Accounts of Ashburton*, 26, 88, 90, 118–26, 191.
20 On bells, see Ellacombe, *Church Bells*; on that of Crediton, Oxford, Bodleian Library, MS Bodley 832, f. 106r–v.
21 Hanham, *Churchwardens' Accounts of Ashburton*, 48.
22 Ibid., p. viii.
23 For an edition based on the later printed versions, see *Missale ad Usum . . . Ecclesiae Sarum*, ed. F. H. Dickinson (Burntisland, 1861–83).
24 TNA, C 1/363/39.
25 On chapels in medieval England, see Orme, 'Church and Chapel', 75–102, and 'The Other Parish Churches', 78–94; and on those of Devon, Jeanne James, 'Medieval Chapels in Devon' and Coulter, *Ancient Chapels of North Devon*.
26 Above, p. 19; the castle chapel ('canons of St Mary') existed by 1086 (*Domesday Book: Devon*, 16/89–92). Anglo-Saxon burials have been found in the vicinity.
27 James, 'Medieval Chapels in Devon', 8 and passim.
28 Thus there is no recorded licence for the chapel of Upcott Barton (Cheriton Fitzpaine), mentioned in 1455 (R. L. Storey, *The End of the House of Lancaster* [London, 1966], p. 169).
29 Orme, 'Medieval Chapels of Heavitree', 124.
30 Raymond J. Skinner, 'The "Declaration" of Ley: his pedigree', *DCNQ*, 37 part 2 (1992), 61.
31 *Reg. Lacy*, ed. Dunstan, iii, 50.
32 Orme, 'Medieval Chapels of Heavitree', 124–7.
33 J. Allan, R. A. Higham, and G. Young, 'The Medieval Chapel at Fardel Manor, Cornwood, and its Context', *Devon Archaeological Society Proceedings*, 66 (2008), 85–116.
34 *Reg. Lacy*, ed. Dunstan, i, 9, 35.
35 Orme, 'Church and Chapel', 94–100.
36 Orme, 'Bishop Grandisson and Popular Religion', 109–13.
37 Orme, 'Church in Crediton', 120.
38 *Reg. Lacy*, ed. Dunstan, ii, 150–1, 153–5, 174–5, 211–21.
39 Above, p. 75.
40 Snell, *Chantry Certificates*, 28, 30, 38, 52, 57, 59.
41 On Devon holy wells, see Theo Brown, 'Holy and Notable Wells of Devon', *DA*, 89 (1957), 205–15; 90 (1958), 60–1, whose evidence is mostly post-1750, and Nicholas Orme, 'Medieval Holy Wells in Devon', *DA*, 145 (2013).
42 Above, p. 27.
43 Gover, Mawer, and Stenton, *Place-Names of Devon*, i, 67, 109, 122, 245, 249, 309, 327; ii, 483, 537.
44 P. Grosjean, 'Legenda S. Sativolae Exoniensis', *Analecta Bollandiana*, 53 (1935), 359–65; Grosjean, 'Vie de St Rumon . . . Nectan', 399, 401; Orme, *Nicholas Roscarrock's Lives of the Saints*, 138.
45 *Reg. Brantyngham*, i, 391; Orme, 'Medieval Chapels of Heavitree', 125; *Reg. Lacy*, ed. Dunstan, iii, 136.
46 Nicholas Orme, 'Medieval Holy Wells in Devon'.
47 On crosses, see W. Crossing, *The Ancient Stone Crosses of Dartmoor and its Borderland* (Exeter, 1902), and Phillips, 'Ancient Stone Crosses of Devon', passim. The fullest inventory is in the Heritage Environment Register (Devon County Council).
48 Oliver, *Monasticon*, 378.

49 Orme, *Cornish Wills*, 77.
50 See, for example, the anonymous play of *c*.1600, *The Merry Devil of Edmonton*, I.i.58–61.
51 *Missale ad Usum . . . Ecclesiae Sarum*, ed. Dickinson, 262.
52 Hanham, *Churchwardens' Accounts of Ashburton*, 139; Osborne, *Church Wardens' Accounts of Chagford*, 180; Binney, *Accounts of Morebath*, 246; *OED*, s.n. 'palm-cross'.
53 Walsham, *Reformation of the Landscape*, 100–30, to which add Frere and Kennedy, *Visitation Articles*, iii, 289–91, 323, etc.
54 Phillips, 'Ancient Stone Crosses', 263. Plymtree churchyard cross was believed in *c*.1755 to have been removed during the Civil War (Bodleian Library, MS Top. Devon b.2 f. 110r).
55 *Councils and Synods II*, ii, 1008.
56 The parishes are listed in Whiting, *The Blind Devotion of the People*, 5; Holne should be added.
57 On what follows, see Orme, 'Confession in a Fifteenth-Century Devon Parish', 57–68.
58 *Records of Early English Drama: Devon*, ed. J. M. Wasson (Toronto, 1986), 83, 357.
59 On Rogationtide processions, see Orme, 'Parish Processions in Medieval and Tudor Cornwall', 73–82.
60 *Reg. Lacy*, ed. Dunstan, iii, 156–7.
61 Ibid., i, 34.
62 Orme, *Medieval Children*, 187–9.
63 *Councils and Synods II*, i, 231–2, 409.
64 Copeland, 'Devonshire Church Houses', passim.
65 Hanham, *Churchwardens' Accounts of Ashburton*, p. xiii.
66 *Reprint of the Barnstaple Records*, ed. J. R. Chanter and T. Wainwright, 2 vols (Barnstaple, 1900), ii, 16–35.
67 Snell, *Chantry Certificates*, passim; Orme, 'Dissolution of the Chantries in Devon', 75–123.
68 Barnstaple, North Devon Record Office, 1500A, PW 1, ff. 1r–2v; Duffy, *Voices of Morebath*, 24–7.
69 TNA, PROB 11/18, f. 103r (will of John Hewe); PROB 11/22, f. 191v (will of Thomas Legh); Hanham, *Churchwardens' Accounts of Ashburton*, pp. xii–xiii.
70 Orme, *Saints of Cornwall*, 197–200, 234–5.
71 Orme, 'Church and Chapel', 89.
72 *Reg. Lacy*, ed. Dunstan, iii, 50; Orme, *English Church Dedications*, 202.
73 Orme and Webster, *The English Hospital*, 247–8.
74 *Councils and Synods I*, i, 208, 321–2, 483.
75 *Reg. Brantyngham*, i, 344.
76 *A Relation . . . of the Island of England*, ed. Charlotte A. Sneyd, Camden Society, 37 (1847), 23.
77 On what follows, see Orme, 'Two Early Prayer Books', 345–50.
78 E.g. *Reports on the Manuscripts of Lord Middleton*, Historical Manuscripts Commission (London, 1911), 330–86.
79 *Reg. Stafford*, 383–420 passim; *Reg. Lacy*, ed. Dunstan, iv, 16–56 passim.
80 On indulgences, see Swanson, *Indulgences in Late Medieval England*.
81 Orme, 'Indulgences in the Diocese of Exeter', 15–32.
82 Oliver, *Lives of the Bishops*, 249.
83 Above, p. 67.

84 TNA, C 1/81/19.
85 *The Apologye of Syr Thomas More*, ed. A. I. Taft, London, Early English Text Society, ordinary series, 180 (1930), 82.
86 Orme, *Exeter Cathedral*, 8, 10, 71–2, 172.
87 Orme, 'Two Saint Bishops', 403–11.
88 Ibid., 412–18.
89 Orme, *Nicholas Roscarrock's Lives of the Saints*, 170–2.
90 Ibid., pp. 117–18, 137–9, 157–9, 175–6; above, p. 83.
91 F. W. Weaver, *Wells Wills* (London, 1890), 97–8.
92 Orme, 'Bishop Grandisson and Popular Religion', 113–15.
93 P. Grosjean, *Henrici VI Angliae Regis Miracula Postuma*, Subsidia Hagiographica, 22 (Brussels, 1935), 224–6, 275–6, 291–3.
94 C. M. Storrs, *Jacobean Pilgrims from England to St. James of Compostella: from the early twelfth to the late fifteenth century* (London, 1998), 173–82.
95 *The English Hospice at Rome*, 2nd edn (Leominster, 2005), 127, 131.
96 *Reg. Brantyngham*, i, 85, 158, 480–1; *BRUO*, iii, 1772.
97 K. B. McFarlane, *Lancastrian Kings and Lollard Knights* (Oxford, 1972), 216.
98 D&C 3508, f. 8v; Orme, *Cathedral Cat*, 71.
99 Examples may be found in TNA, C 85/78–82, passim.
100 TNA, C 85/79 no. 25.
101 Coulton, 'Visitation of Totnes', 110; Binney, *Accounts of Morebath*, 64.
102 *Ordinale Exon*, ed. Dalton and Doble, ii, 548.
103 On almonry boys, see above, p. 82.
104 Hanham, *Churchwardens' Accounts of Ashburton*, 26, 88, 90, 118–26, 191; Orme, *Education in the West of England*, 111.
105 D&C, Fabric Rolls, years 1513–14.
106 Orme, 'Early Musicians of Exeter Cathedral', 395–410; *The New Grove Dictionary of Music and Musicians*, ed. Stanley Sadie, 2nd edn, 29 vols (London, 2001), s.n. John Dark, Thomas Pack; Orme, 'Church in Crediton', 115.
107 British Library, Additional MS 5665.
108 D&C 3779, ff. 129v, 144v.
109 Power, *Medieval English Nunneries*, 237–84, 568–81.
110 Orme, *Education in the West of England*, 42–55.
111 Ibid., passim.
112 Above, p. 90.
113 Orme, *Education in the West of England*, 48–9.
114 Ibid., 112.
115 David Thomson, *A Descriptive Catalogue of Middle English Grammatical Texts* (New York and London, 1979), 141–7, 290–315; Orme, *English School Exercises*, sections 4–5.
116 Michael Clanchy, *From Memory to Written Record*, 2nd edn (Oxford, 1993).
117 *Letters and Papers of John Shillingford*, ed. Stuart A. Moore, Camden Society, new series, 2 (1871); *Kingsford's Stonor Letters and Papers 1290–1483*, ed. Christine Carpenter (Cambridge, 1996).
118 A. McIntosh, M. L. Samuels, and M. Benskin, *A Linguistic Atlas of Late Mediaeval English*, 4 vols (Aberdeen, 1986), i, 187.
119 *ODNB*, John Fortescue.

Chapter 5. The Reformation

1 *Valor Ecclesiasticus*, ii, 289–91.
2 *ODNB*, John Arundell; Hugh Oldham; John Veysey; by the present author.
3 Leland, *Itinerary*, i, 171.
4 *Valor Ecclesiasticus*, ii, 292–7.
5 *Tudor Exeter*, ed. Margery M. Rowe, DCRS, new series, 22 (1977), 30–3.
6 Allan, 'College of the Vicars Choral at Exeter', 29–43.
7 Orme, *Exeter Cathedral*, 189–91.
8 Above, p. 39; *LPFD*, i part 2, p. 1146.
9 *BRUO*, iv, passim.
10 *LPFD*, vi, p. 547; the proposed date, 1533, is too late.
11 Above, pp. 55, 74–5.
12 *Valor Ecclesiasticus*, ii, 289–391.
13 Frances Rose-Troup, 'Lists Relating to Persons Ejected from Religious Houses', *DCNQ*, 17 (1932–3), 81–96, 143–4, 191–2, 238–40, 285–8.
14 TNA E 36/64, pp. 19–28, 32–4, 46–52.
15 Orme, *Minor Clergy of Exeter Cathedral: Biographies*, passim (but Henry Bant should warn against complacency about ex-cathedral members).
16 Most of the graduate Devon clergy of the early sixteenth century are listed in *BRUO*, iv.
17 On what follows, see Duffy, *Voices of Morebath* and, on Trychay's appointment, Orme, 'New Light on Christopher Trychay', 35–6. Duffy's book is based on the churchwardens' accounts published as Binney, *The Accounts of Morebath*.
18 Duffy, *Voices of Morebath*, 32–46.
19 Hanham, *Churchwardens' Accounts of Ashburton*, pp. xv–xvii and passim.
20 *LPFD*, ix, pp. 391–2; Youings, *Dissolution of the Monasteries*, 139–41. By 1539, Shaugh and Wembury had canons assigned to serve them (*LPFD*, xiv part 1, p. 168).
21 Cherry and Pevsner, *Devon*, 46–9 and passim.
22 Ursula M. Radford, 'The Wax Images Found in Exeter Cathedral', *The Antiquaries Journal*, 29 (1949), 164–8.
23 Orme, *Nicholas Roscarrock's Lives of the Saints*, 138–9; TNA, E 315/126 nos. 16–17.
24 Orme, *Minor Clergy of Exeter Cathedral: Biographies*, s.nn.
25 Foxe, *Acts and Monuments*, v, 469.
26 G. W. Bernard, *The Late Medieval English Church* (New Haven and London, 2012), 33–40.
27 Orme, *Exeter Cathedral*, 70; Worcester, *Itineraries*, 110–11.
28 Orme, 'Martin Coeffin, the First Exeter Publisher', 220–30.
29 A. W. Pollard and G. R. Redgrave, *A Short-Title Catalogue of Books Printed in England*, 2nd edn, 3 vols (London, 1976–91), nos. 3200, 6795.6.
30 DRO, Chanter XIII, ff. 144v–145r.
31 Ibid., ff. 179v–181r.
32 Orme, *Exeter Cathedral*, 191–3; Orme, 'Medieval Chapels of Heavitree', 127.
33 TNA, E 25, printed in *Report of the Deputy Keeper of the Public Record Office*, vii (London, 1846), appendix ii, 279–306; E 36/64, pp. 19–28, 32–4, 46–52.
34 *Statutes of the Realm*, iii, 493–9.
35 *Valor Ecclesiasticus*, ii, 289–391.
36 Foxe, *Acts and Monuments*, v, 20.

37 DRO, Exeter City Archives, Book 51, f. 342r–v.
38 *LPFD*, vii, 107–8.
39 *Statutes of the Realm*, iii, 663–6.
40 DRO, ED/M/1036.
41 Frere and Kennedy, *Visitation Articles*, ii, 1–11.
42 D. Wilkins (ed.), *Concilia Magnae Britanniae et Hiberniae*, 4 vols (London, 1737), iii, 823–4 (holy days).
43 Frere and Kennedy, *Visitation Articles*, ii, 61–4.
44 Ibid., ii, 34–43.
45 P. L. Hughes and J. F. Larkin (ed.) *Tudor Royal Proclamations*, 3 vols (New Haven and London, 1964–9), i, 275–6.
46 *ODNB*, Simon Heynes; Orme, *Exeter Cathedral*, 197–204.
47 DRO, Exeter City Archives, Book 51, f. 344r; Leland, *Itinerary*, i, 227.
48 Radford, 'The Wax Images Found in Exeter Cathedral', 164–8.
49 Orme, *Nicholas Roscarrock's Lives of the Saints*, 139; TNA, E 315/126, nos. 16–17.
50 DRO, Exeter City Archives, Book 51, ff. 342r, 346v.
51 *ODNB*, John Cardmaker.
52 *BRUO*, iv, 30; Foxe, *Acts and Monuments*, v, 20.
53 *LPFD*, vii, pp. 640–1; viii, pp. 215, 343, 387; David M. Smith, *The Heads of Religious Houses, England and Wales: III, 1377–1540* (Cambridge, 2008), 437.
54 Orme, 'The Last Medieval Abbot of Buckfast', 97–103.
55 *LPFD*, ix, p. 268.
56 Wilkins, *Concilia*, iii, 786–91.
57 *Statutes of the Realm*, iii, 575–8.
58 DRO, Exeter City Archives, Book 51, f. 343r.
59 *LPFD*, xiii part 2, pp. 139, 148, 150.
60 No prior of Kerswell is mentioned at the surrender of Montacute (ibid., xiv part 1, p. 225).
61 Ibid., xiv part 1, pp. 115–84.
62 *Statutes of the Realm*, iii, 733–9.
63 Ibid., iii, 778–81.
64 Youings, *Devon Monastic Lands*, pp. xx–xxix.
65 Oliver, *Monasticon*, 301.
66 Binney, *Accounts of Morebath*, 91.
67 Shakespeare, *Sonnets*, 73 line 4.
68 *Statutes of the Realm*, iii, 739–43.
69 Snell, *Chantry Certificates*, 62–3; *LPFD*, xx part ii, p. 354.
70 *LPFD*, xx part ii, p. 543; Oliver, *Monasticon*, 417–21.
71 Orme, 'Church in Crediton', 123–4.
72 *Statutes of the Realm*, iii, 988–93.
73 The 'chantry certificates' of 1546 are edited by Snell, *Chantry Certificates,* and discussed by Orme, 'Dissolution of the Chantries in Devon', 78–81.
74 Frere and Kennedy, *Visitation Articles*, ii, 103–30.
75 *Statutes of the Realm*, iv part i, 24–33.
76 All that is known of the survey is discussed in Orme, 'Dissolution of the Chantries', 81–4, 92–114.

77 Ibid., 114–23.
78 Oliver, *Lives of the Bishops*, 488–93.
79 Orme, *Education in the West of England*, 112–13.
80 Leland, *Itinerary*, i, 169, 173, 240.
81 *BRUO*, iv, 155–6, 400.
82 *Statutes of the Realm*, iv part 1, 18–22 (repeal of heresy laws); Duffy, *Stripping of the Altars*, 547–8 (royal orders of 1548) and 476–7 (church goods).
83 *Statutes of the Realm*, iv part 1, 37–9. The best edition of the 1549 Prayer-Book is F. E. Brightman (ed.), *The English Rite*, 2nd edn (London, 1970).
84 On the rising, see Rose-Troup, *Western Rebellion*, and A. L. Rowse, *Tudor Cornwall* (London, 1941), 253–90.
85 It defies credibility to accept Eamon Duffy's argument (*Voices of Morebath*, 134–9) that the vicar of Morebath recorded payments in the churchwardens' accounts to three young men to take part in the rising. In an age of ferocious punishments for treason, nobody would have written such evidence down!
86 John Hooker, *The Description of the Citie of Excester*, ed. W. J. Harte and others, 3 parts, DCRS (1919–47), ii, 91–4; *ODNB*, Robert Welsh.
87 *Statutes of the Realm*, iv part i, 67, 146–7 (clergy marriage); Frere and Kennedy, *Visitation Articles*, ii, 242–4 (altar removal); *Statutes of the Realm*, iv part i, 130–1 (act imposing Prayer-Book of 1552); and Brightman, *English Rite* (text of 1552 Prayer-Book).
88 Hanham, *Churchwardens' Accounts of Ashburton*, 119–28.
89 Binney, *Accounts of Morebath*, 165.
90 Duffy, *Stripping of the Altars*, 476–7; Beatrix Cresswell, 'The Church Goods Commission in Devon (1549–1552)', *DA*, 43 (1911), 237–55; and idem, *The Edwardian Inventories for the City and County of Exeter*, Alcuin Club, 20 (1916).
91 Binney, *Accounts of Morebath*, 172.
92 See above, pp. 178–9.
93 DRO, Exeter City Archives, Book 51, f. 351r; John Hooker, *A Catalog of the Bishops of Excester* (London, 1584), sig. Hii verso–Iii recto.
94 *LPFD*, xx part 1, p. 282; xx part 2, p. 444; xxi part 1, pp. 143, 248, 473, 758; xxi part 2, p. 381.
95 *CPR 1547–8*, 295; *1548–9*, 16, 170, 402–3; *1549–51*, 7, 50, 164; *1559–63*, 36–7.
96 *ODNB*, Miles Coverdale.
97 DRO, Exeter City Archives, Book 51, f. 350r; Hooker, *Catalog of the Bishops*, sig. Ii recto–Iii recto. On Hele and Pollard, see *BRUO*, iv, 279, 456.
98 *Statutes of the Realm*, iv part i, 202 (repeal of 1553); ibid., 246–54 (repeal of 1554).
99 Le Neve, *Fasti Ecclesiae Anglicanae 1541–1857:* xii, passim.
100 DRO, Chanter XVI, ff. 16v–30v; *Calendar of Institutions by the Chapter of Canterbury Sede Vacante*, ed. C. E. Woodruff and Irene Churchill, Kent Archaeological Society, Records Branch, 8 (1924), 51, 68, 94; DRO, Chanter XVIII, ff. 4r–v. Not all institutions of clergy in this period state what had happened to the previous incumbent, and the records after October 1554 are less informative. On Alley, see also above, p. 181.
101 On Turberville, see *BRUO*, iv, 579; *ODNB*; and Hooker, *Catalog of the Bishops*, sig. Iii verso. His bishop's register is DRO, Chanter XVIII–XIX.
102 Foxe, *Acts and Monuments*, viii, 500.

103 Hanham, *Churchwardens' Accounts of Ashburton*, 129–40; compare Osborne, *Church Wardens' Accounts of Chagford*, 178–92.
104 Binney, *Accounts of Morebath*, 173–202.
105 Orme, 'Church in Crediton', 125.
106 DRO, Chanter XVIII, ff. 86r–87v.
107 Christina H. Garrett, *The Marian Exiles* (Cambridge, 1938), 70, 92–4, 104–8, 118–21, 131–2, 198–9, 203, 209, 236–7, 272–3, 309–12, 337.
108 On what follows, see Foxe, *Acts and Monuments*, viii, 497–503, and DRO, Exeter City Archives, Book 51, f. 352r.
109 *Statutes of the Realm*, iv part i, 350–8, 359–64, 397–400.
110 *ODNB*, William Alley. Turberville died in the Tower of London in about 1570.
111 Le Neve, *Fasti Ecclesiae Anglicanae 1541–1857*, passim; *BRUO*, iv, 30.
112 It is noteworthy that Baldwin Flear, an ex-cathedral secondary and Oxford MA, who was one of the few priests ordained in Devon under Mary, appears in 1561 as the married rector of Lezant in Cornwall (Orme, *Minor Clergy of Exeter Cathedral: Biographies*, s.n.).
113 Frere and Kennedy, *Visitation Articles*, iii, 1–29.
114 John Jewel, *Works*, ed. J. Ayre, 4 vols, Parker Society (1847–50), iv, 1216–18.
115 'A Collection of Original Letters from the Bishops to the Privy Council, 1514', ed. Mary Bateson, *The Camden Miscellany IX*, Camden Society, new series, 53 (1895), 69–70.
116 Modern editions of the 1559 Prayer-Book are W. K. Clay (ed.), *Liturgies and Occasional Forms of Prayer set forth in the reign of Queen Elizabeth*, Parker Society (1847), 23–245, 272–98, and E. Benham (ed.), *The Prayer-Book of Queen Elizabeth 1559* (Edinburgh, 1890).
117 *ODNB*, Robert Johnson (died 1574), case of 1573.
118 Frere and Kennedy, *Visitation Articles*, iii, 15 (processions), 22–3 (singing), 25 (bowing). On post-Reformation Rogation processions, see Cox, *Churchwardens' Accounts*, 264–5.
119 Hanham, *Churchwardens' Accounts of Ashburton*, 142–52; compare Osborne, *Church Wardens' Accounts of Chagford*, 195.
120 Binney, *Accounts of Morebath*, 202–13.
121 Cambridge, Corpus Christi College, MS 97.
122 Hanham, *Churchwardens' Accounts of Ashburton*, pp. viii–ix, 123–87.
123 Brightman, *English Rite*, ii, 714–15.

Chapter 6. A Thousand Years of Christianity

1 Notably Grandisson, Brantingham, Stafford, Lacy, Nevill, Bothe, Fox, Redman, Oldham, and Veysey.
2 On Cornwall, see Nicholas Orme, *Victoria County History of Cornwall*, vol. ii, the first part of which is presented in a more simple form in Orme, *Cornwall and the Cross: Christianity 500–1560*.

Bibliography

This is a list of the printed works that are cited several times in the footnotes of this book, together with others that are useful for further reading or research on Devon. For abbreviations, see above, p. 205.

Adler, M. 'The Medieval Jews of Exeter', *DA*, 63 (1931), 221–40.

Allan, John. 'The College of the Vicars Choral of Exeter', in *Vicars Choral at English Cathedrals*, ed. Richard Hall and David Stocker (Oxford, 2005), 29–43.

Barlow, Frank. *The English Church 1000–1066*, 2nd edn (London, 1979).

Barlow, Frank. (ed.) *English Episcopal Acta*, vol. xi: *Exeter 1046–1184* (London and Oxford, 1996).

Barlow, Frank. (ed.) *English Episcopal Acta*, vol. xii: *Exeter 1186–1257* (London and Oxford, 1996).

Barlow, Frank, and others. *Leofric of Exeter* (Exeter, 1972).

Binney, J. Erskine. *The Accounts of the Wardens of the Parish of Morebath, Devon, 1520–1573* (Exeter, 1904).

Blair, John. *The Church in Anglo-Saxon Society* (Oxford, 2005).

Blair, John, and Orme, Nicholas. 'The Anglo-Saxon Minster and Cathedral at Exeter: twin churches?', *Friends of Exeter Cathedral, Annual Report*, 65 (1995), 24–6.

Boase, C. W. *Registrum Collegii Exoniensis*, Oxford Historical Society, 27 (1894).

Calendar of Close Rolls, 47 vols (London, Public Record Office, 1892–1963).

Calendar of Papal Letters (London, Public Record Office, and Dublin, Irish Historical Manuscripts Commission, 1894–, in progress).

Calendar of Papal Petitions, vol. i (London, Public Record Office, 1897).

Calendar of Patent Rolls (London, Public Record Office, 1891–, in progress).

Chambers, D. S. *Faculty Office Registers 1534–1549* (Oxford, 1966).

Cherry, Bridget, and Pevsner, Nikolaus. *Devon, The Buildings of England*, 2nd edn (London, 1989).

Chope, R. Pearse. *The Book of Hartland* (Torquay, 1940).

Conner, Patrick W. *Anglo-Saxon Exeter: a tenth-century cultural history* (Woodbridge, 1993).

Cooper, Trevor, and Brown, Sarah (ed.) *Pews, Benches and Chairs: church seating in English parish churches from the fourteenth century to the present* (London, 2011).

Copeland, G. W. 'Devonshire Church Houses', *DA*, 92 (1960), 116–41; 93 (1961), 250–65; 94 (1962), 427–39; 95 (1963), 135–55; 96 (1964), 202–7; 98 (1966), 157–67; 99 (1967), 263–8.

Coulter, James. *The Ancient Chapels of North Devon* (Yarnscombe, 1993).

Coulton, G. G. 'A Visitation of the Archdeaconry of Totnes in 1342', *English Historical Review*, 26 (1911), 108–24.

Councils and Synods I: A.D. 871–1204, ed. Dorothy Whitelock, M. Brett, and C. N. L. Brooke, 2 vols (Oxford, 1981).

Councils and Synods II: A.D. 1205–1313, ed. F. M. Powicke and C. R. Cheney, 2 vols (Oxford, 1964).

Cox, J. C. *Churchwardens' Accounts* (London, 1913).

Cox, J. C., and Harvey, Alfred. *English Church Furniture*, 2nd edn (London, 1908).

Dalton, J. N. *The Collegiate Church of Ottery St Mary* (Cambridge, 1917).

Dickens, A. G. *The English Reformation*, 2nd edn (London, 1989).

Domesday Book, IX: *Devon*, 2 vols, ed. C. and F. Thorn (Chichester, 1985). Original text and translation of the Exchequer Domesday.

Domesday Book: Additamenta, ed. H. Ellis (London, Record Commission, 1816). Original text of the Exon Domesday.

Duffy, Eamon. *The Stripping of the Altars: traditional religion in England 1400–1600* (New Haven and London, 1992).

Duffy, Eamon. *The Voices of Morebath: Reformation and rebellion in an English village* (New Haven and London, 2001).

Ellacombe, H. T. *The Church Bells of Devon* (Exeter, 1872).

Emden, A. B. *A Biographical Register of the University of Oxford to A.D. 1500*, 3 vols (Oxford, 1957–9).

Emden, A. B. *A Biographical Register of the University of Cambridge to 1500* (Cambridge, 1963).

Emden, A. B. *A Survey of Dominicans in England*, Institutum Historicum FF. Praedicatorum, Dissertationes Historicae, 18 (Rome, 1967).

Emden, A. B. *A Biographical Register of the University of Oxford A.D. 1501 to 1540* (Oxford, 1974).

The English Parish Church through the Centuries (University of York, cd rom, 2010). Several of the articles are by the author of this book.

Finberg, H. P. R. *Tavistock Abbey: a study in the social and economic history of Devon*, 2nd edn (Newton Abbot, 1969).

Fizzard, Allison D. *Plympton Priory* (Leiden, 2008).

Foxe, John. *Acts and Monuments*, ed. J. Pratt, 4th edn, 8 vols, (London, 1877).

Frere, W. H., and Kennedy, W. M. (ed.) *Visitation Articles and Injunctions of the Period of the Reformation*, 3 vols, Alcuin Club 14–16 (1908–10).

Fryde, E. B., Greenway, D. E., Porter, S., and Roy, I. (ed.) *Handbook of British Chronology*, 3rd edn (London, Royal Historical Society, 1986).

Gildas. *The Ruin of Britain and Other Works*, ed. M. Winterbottom (London, 1978).

Gover, J. E. B., Mawer, A., and Stenton, F. M. *The Place-Names of Devon*, 2 vols, English Place-Name Society, 8–9 (1931).

Grosjean, P. 'Vie de S. Rumon, Vie . . . de S. Nectan', *Analecta Bollandiana*, 71 (1953), 361–414.

Hale, W. H., and Ellacombe, H. T. (ed.) *Accounts of the Executors of Richard Bishop of London 1303, and of the Executors of Thomas Bishop of Exeter 1310*, Camden Society, new series, 10 (1874).

Hanham, Alison (ed.) *Churchwardens' Accounts of Ashburton, 1479–1580*, DCRS, new series, 15 (1970).

Heale, Martin. *The Dependent Priories of Medieval English Monasteries* (Woodbridge, 2004).

Heale, Martin. *Monasticism in Late Medieval England c.1300–1535* (Manchester, 2009).

Higham, R. A. *Making Anglo-Saxon Devon: emergence of a shire* (Exeter, 2008).

Hillaby, J. and C. *The Palgrave Dictionary of Medieval Anglo-Jewish History* (Basingstoke, 2013).

Hooke, Della. *Pre-Conquest Charter-Bounds of Devon and Cornwall* (Woodbridge, 1994).

James, Jeanne. 'Medieval Chapels in Devon', University of Exeter, unpublished MPhil thesis (1997).

Jeffery, Paul. *The Collegiate Churches of England and Wales* (London, 2004).

Jenkins, John C. 'Torre Abbey: locality, community, and society in medieval Devon', University of Oxford, unpublished DPhil thesis (2010).

Jones, Anthea. *A Thousand Years of the English Parish* (Moreton-in-Marsh, 2000).

Kain, R. J. P., and Oliver, R. R. *The Tithe Maps of England and Wales: a cartographic analysis and county-by-county catalogue* (Cambridge, 1995).

Kain, R. J. P., and Prince, H. C. *The Tithe Surveys of England and Wales* (Cambridge, 1985).

Kain, R. J. P., and Prince, H. C. *Tithe Surveys for Historians* (Chichester, 2000).

Kain, R. J. P., and Ravenhill, W. L. D. (ed.) *Historical Atlas of South-West England* (Exeter, 1999).

Ker, N. R. *Medieval Libraries of Great Britain*, 2nd edn (London, 1964); *Supplement to the Second Edition*, ed. A. G. Watson (London, 1987).

Keynes, S., and Lapidge, M. (ed.) *Alfred the Great: Asser's life of King Alfred and other contemporary sources* (Harmondsworth, 1983).

Knowles, David. *The Religious Orders in England*, 3 vols (Cambridge, 1948–59).

Knowles, David. *The Monastic Order in England, 940–1216*, 2nd edn (Cambridge, 1963).

Knowles, David, and Hadcock, R. N. *Medieval Religious Houses: England and Wales*, 2nd edn (London, 1971).

Larking, Lambert B. *The Knights Hospitallers in England*, Camden Society, 65 (1857).

Le Neve, J. *Fasti Ecclesiae Anglicanae 1066–1300*, vol. x: *Exeter*, ed. Diane E. Greenway (London, 2005).

Le Neve, J. *Fasti Ecclesiae Anglicanae 1300–1541*, vol. ix: *Exeter Diocese*, ed. J. M. Horn (London, 1964).

Le Neve, J. *Fasti Ecclesiae Anglicanae 1541–1857*, vol. xii: *Exeter Diocese*, ed. W. H. Campbell (London, 2007).

Leland, John. *The Itinerary of John Leland*, ed. L. Toulmin Smith, 5 vols (London, 1907–10).

Lepine, D. *A Brotherhood of Canons Serving God: English secular cathedrals in the later middle ages* (Woodbridge, 1995).

Lepine, David, and Orme, Nicholas. *Death and Memory in Medieval Exeter*, DCRS, new series, 46 (2003).

Letters and Papers, Foreign and Domestic, Henry VIII, ed. J. S. Brewer, J. Gairdner, and R. H. Brodie, 21 vols in 33 parts (London, 1864–1932).

Little, A. G., and Easterling, R. C. *The Franciscans and Dominicans of Exeter* (Exeter, 1927).

Matthew, D. J. A. *The Norman Monasteries and Their English Possessions* (London, 1962).

McHardy, Alison, and Orme, Nicholas. 'The Defence of an Alien Priory: Modbury (Devon) in the 1450s', *The Journal of Ecclesiastical History*, 50 (1999), 303–12.

New, C. W. *History of the Alien Priories in England to the Confiscation of Henry V* (Chicago, 1916).

Okasha, Elizabeth. *Corpus of Early Christian Inscribed Stones of South-West Britain* (London, 1993).

Okasha, Elizabeth. 'A Supplement to Corpus of Early Christian Inscribed Stones of South-West Britain', *Cornish Archaeology* 37–8 (1998–9), 137–52.

Oliver, George. *Monasticon Dioecesis Exoniensis*, with supplement (Exeter and London, 1846).

Oliver, George. *Additional Supplement to the Monasticon Dioecesis Exoniensis* (Exeter, 1854).

Oliver, George. *Lives of the Bishops of Exeter and a History of the Cathedral* (Exeter, 1861).

Ordinale Exon, ed. J. N. Dalton and G. H. Doble, 4 vols, Henry Bradshaw Society, 37–8, 63, 79 (1909–40).

Orme, Nicholas. *Education in the West of England, 1066–1548* (Exeter, 1976); 'Education in the West of England: Additions', *DCNQ*, 34 (1978), 22–5.

Orme, Nicholas. 'The Kalendar Brethren of the City of Exeter', *DA*, 109 (1977), 153–69.

Orme, Nicholas. 'The Early Musicians of Exeter Cathedral', *Music and Letters*, 59 (1978), 395–410.

Orme, Nicholas. *The Minor Clergy of Exeter Cathedral* (Exeter, 1979).

Orme, Nicholas. 'The Dissolution of the Chantries in Devon, 1546–8', *DA*, 111 (1979), 75–123.

Orme, Nicholas. 'The Church in Crediton from St Boniface to the Reformation', in *The Greatest Englishman*, ed. T. A. Reuter (Exeter, 1980), 97–131.

Orme, Nicholas. 'Education and Learning at a Medieval English Cathedral: Exeter, 1380–1548', *The Journal of Ecclesiastical History*, 32 (1981), 265–83.

Orme, Nicholas. 'The Medieval Clergy of Exeter Cathedral: I, the Vicars Choral and Annuellars', *DA*, 113 (1981), 79–102.

Orme, Nicholas. 'The Medieval Chantries of Exeter Cathedral', *DCNQ*, 34 (1981), 319–26; 35 (1982), 12–21, 67–71.

Orme, Nicholas. 'The Medieval Clergy of Exeter Cathedral: II, the Secondaries and Choristers', *DA*, 115 (1983), 79–100.

Orme, Nicholas. 'Two Saint-Bishops of Exeter', *Analecta Bollandiana*, 104 (1986), 403–18.

Orme, Nicholas. 'Sir John Speke and His Chapel in Exeter Cathedral', *DA*, 118 (1986), 25–41.

Orme, Nicholas. 'Rawridge Chapel, Upottery', *DCNQ*, 35 (1986), 327–31.

Orme, Nicholas, 'The Lost Parish of Dotton', *DCNQ*, 36 (1987), 1–5.

Orme, Nicholas. 'Warland Hospital, Totnes, and the Trinitarian Friars in Devon', *DCNQ*, 36 (1987), 41–8.

Orme, Nicholas. 'Indulgences in the Diocese of Exeter', *DA*, 120 (1988), 15–32.

Orme, Nicholas. 'A Medieval Almshouse for the Clergy: Clyst Gabriel', *The Journal of Ecclesiastical History*, 39 (1988), 1–15.

Orme, Nicholas. 'Martin Coeffin, the First Exeter Publisher', *The Library*, 6th series, 10 (1988), 220–30.

Orme, Nicholas. 'Mortality in Early Fourteenth-Century Exeter', *Medical History*, 32 (1988), 195–203.

Orme, Nicholas. 'The History of Brampford Speke', *DA*, 121 (1989), 53–86.

Orme, Nicholas. 'A Letter of St Roche', *DCNQ*, 36 (1989), 153–9.

Orme, Nicholas. 'Saint Walter of Cowick', *Analecta Bollandiana*, 108 (1990), 1–7.

Orme, Nicholas. (ed.) *Unity and Variety: a history of the Church in Devon and Cornwall* (Exeter, 1991).

Orme, Nicholas. 'Sufferings of the Clergy: illness and old age in Exeter diocese, 1300–1540', in *Life, Death, and the Elderly: historical perspectives*, ed. M. Pelling and R. M. Smith (London, 1991), 62–73.

Orme, Nicholas. 'The Charnel Chapel of Exeter Cathedral', in *Medieval Art and Architecture at Exeter Cathedral*, ed. F. Kelly, The British Archaeological Association, Conference Transactions, 11 (1991), 162–71.

Orme, Nicholas. 'Two Early Prayer-Books from North Devon', *DCNQ*, 36 (1991), 345–50.

Orme, Nicholas. *Nicholas Roscarrock's Lives of the Saints: Cornwall and Devon*, DCRS, new series, 35 (1992).

Orme, Nicholas. 'Bishop Grandisson and Popular Religion', *DA*, 124 (1992), 107–18.

Orme, Nicholas. 'Henry de Berbilond, d. 1296, a Vicar Choral of Exeter Cathedral', *DCNQ*, 37 (1992), 1–7.

Orme, Nicholas. 'Denis not Disen: the real patron saint of Bradninch', *DCNQ*, 37 (1992), 45–7.

Orme, Nicholas. 'The Medieval Chapels of Heavitree Parish', *Devon Archaeological Society Transactions*, 49 (1991, publ. 1993), 121–9.

Orme, Nicholas. 'The Clergy of Clyst Gabriel, 1312–1508', *DA*, 126 (1994), 107–21.

Orme, Nicholas. 'Church Dedications in North Devon', *DCNQ*, 37/8 (Autumn, 1995), 249–50.

Orme, Nicholas. 'Two Unusual Devon Saints', *The Devon Historian*, 51 (October 1995), 10–13.

Orme, Nicholas. *English Church Dedications* (Exeter, 1996); 'English Church Dedications: Supplement No. 1', *DCNQ*, 38/10 (Autumn, 2001), 305–7; 'English Church Dedications: Supplement No. 2', *DCNQ*, 40 part 2 (Autumn 2007), 40.

Orme, Nicholas. 'Church and Chapel in Medieval England', *Transactions of the Royal Historical Society*, 6th series, 6 (1996), 75–102.

Orme, Nicholas. *The Saints of Cornwall* (Oxford, 2000).

Orme, Nicholas. *Medieval Children* (New Haven and London, 2001).

Orme, Nicholas. 'The Last Medieval Abbot of Buckfast', *DA*, 133 (2001), 97–107.

Orme, Nicholas. 'William Elyot, a Fifteenth-Century Registrar and His Books', *Archives*, 26 (2001), 112–17.

Orme, Nicholas. 'Confession in a Fifteenth-Century Devon Parish' [i.e. Bere Ferrers], *DA*, 134 (2002), 57–68.

Orme, Nicholas. 'A Country Parish in the 1450s' [i.e. Mortehoe], *Friends of Exeter Cathedral, Annual Report*, 72 (2002), 16–24.

Orme, Nicholas. *Medieval Schools* (New Haven and London, 2006).

Orme, Nicholas. 'The Other Parish Churches: chapels in late medieval England', in *Parish Churches in Late Medieval England*, ed. Clive Burgess and Eamon Duffy (Donington, 2006), 78–94.

Orme, Nicholas. *Cornwall and the Cross: Christianity 500–1560* (Chichester and London, 2007).

Orme, Nicholas. (ed.) *Cornish Wills 1342–1540*, Devon and Cornwall Record Society, new series, 50 (2007).

Orme, Nicholas. 'Access and Exclusion: Exeter Cathedral, 1300–1540', in *Freedom of Movement in the Middle Ages*, ed. P. Hordern (Donington, 2007), 267–86.

Orme, Nicholas. 'New Light on Christopher Trychay, Vicar of Morebath', *DCNQ*, 40 part 2 (2007), 35–6.

Orme, Nicholas. *The Cathedral Cat: stories from Exeter Cathedral* (Exeter, 2008).

Orme, Nicholas. 'A Church of Two Thousand Years', 'Understanding Devon's Churches', in *The Pilgrim's Guide to Devon Churches* (Exeter, 2008).

Orme, Nicholas. *Exeter Cathedral: the first thousand years* (Exeter, 2009).

Orme, Nicholas. *A History of the County of Cornwall:* vol. ii: *Religious History, 500–1560* (Victoria County History, Woodbridge and London, 2010).

Orme, Nicholas. 'The Medieval Church in North Devon', *DA*, 142 (2010), 49–71.

Orme, Nicholas. 'Christianity in Devon to 1086', *DA*, 143 (2011), 1–39.

Orme, Nicholas. 'Parish Processions in Medieval and Tudor Cornwall', *Journal of the Royal Institution of Cornwall* (2011), 73–82.

Orme, Nicholas. 'The Augustinian Canons and Education', in *The Regular Canons in the Medieval British Isles*, ed. Janet Burton and Karen Stöber (Turnhout, Brepols, 2012), 213–32.

Orme, Nicholas. *English School Exercises, c.1420–c.1520* (Toronto, Pontifical Institute of Mediaeval Studies, 2013).

Orme, Nicholas. *The Minor Clergy of Exeter Cathedral: Biographies, 1250–1548*, DCRS, new series, 54 (2013).

Orme, Nicholas. 'Medieval Holy Wells in Devon', *DA*, 145 (2013).

Orme, Nicholas. 'The Dominican Friars of Exeter', *Exeter Archaeology Reports, forthcoming.*

Orme, Nicholas. 'The Franciscan Friars of Exeter', *Exeter Archaeology Reports, forthcoming.*

Orme, Nicholas, and Good, Jonathan. 'Edward I and the Churches of Devon, 1297', *The Devon Historian*, 67 (2003), 3–9.

Orme, Nicholas, and Webster, Margaret. *The English Hospital, 1070–1570* (New Haven and London, 1995).

Osborne, F. M. (ed.) *The Church Wardens' Accounts of St. Michael's Church Chagford, 1480–1600* (Chagford, 1979).

The Oxford Dictionary of National Biography, ed. C. Matthew and B. Harrison, 60 vols (Oxford, 2004); updated electronic edition (including further biographies): http://www.oxforddnb.com. Several of the articles relating to the Church in Devon are by the present author.

The Oxford English Dictionary, ed. J. Simpson and E. S. C. Weiner, 40 vols, 2nd edn (Oxford, 1989).

Pearce, Susan. M. (ed.) *The Early Church in Western Britain and Ireland*, British Archaeological Reports, British Series, 102 (Oxford, 1982).

Peskett, Hugh. *Guide to the Parish and Non-Parochial Registers of Devon and Cornwall 1538–1837*, DCRS, extra series, 2 (1979).

Phillips, E. Masson. 'The Ancient Stone Crosses of Devon', *DA*, 69 (1937), 289–342; 70 (1938), 299–340; 71 (1939), 231–41; 72 (1940), 265–72; 75 (1948), 259–66; 91 (1959), 83–91.

The Pilgrim's Guide to Devon Churches (Cloister Books, Exeter, 2008).

Power, Eileen. *Medieval English Nunneries c.1275–1535* (Cambridge, 1922).

Regesta Regum Anglo-Normannorum, ed. H. W. C. Davis et al., 4 vols (Oxford, 1913–59); 2nd edn, vol. i, ed. David Bates (Oxford, 1998).

The Register of Thomas de Brantyngham, Bishop of Exeter, ed. F. C. Hingeston-Randolph, 2 vols (London and Exeter, 1901–6).

The Registers of Walter Bronescombe and Peter Quivil, Bishops of Exeter, ed. F. C. Hingeston-Randolph (London and Exeter, 1889).

The Register of Walter Bronescombe Bishop of Exeter 1258–1280, ed. O. F. Robinson, 3 vols, Canterbury and York Society, 82, 87, 94 (1995–2003).

The Register of John de Grandisson, Bishop of Exeter, ed. F. C. Hingeston-Randolph, 3 vols (London and Exeter, 1894–9).

The Register of Edmund Lacy, Bishop of Exeter, ed. F. C. Hingeston-Randolph, 2 vols (London and Exeter, 1901–15). Vol. ii is now superseded by the edition of G. R. Dunstan, next following.

The Register of Edmund Lacy, Bishop of Exeter: Registrum Commune, ed. G. R. Dunstan, 5 vols, DCRS, new series, 7, 10, 13, 16, 18 (1963–72).

The Register of Edmund Stafford, ed. F. C. Hingeston-Randolph (London and Exeter, 1886).

The Register of Walter de Stapeldon, Bishop of Exeter, ed. F. C. Hingeston-Randolph (London and Exeter, 1892).

Rose-Troup, Frances. *The Western Rebellion of 1549* (London, 1913).

Rose-Troup, Frances. *Lost Chapels of Exeter* (Exeter, 1923).

Sawyer, P. H. *Anglo-Saxon Charters: an annotated list and bibliography* (London, Royal Historical Society, 1968); online updated version http://www.trin.cam.ac.uk/sdk13/chartwww/charthome.html

Searle, Eleanor. (ed.) *The Chronicle of Battle Abbey* (Oxford, 1980).

Sharpe, Richard. *A Handlist of the Latin Writers of Great Britain and Ireland before 1540* (Brussels, 1997).

Snell, L. S. *The Chantry Certificates for Devon and the City of Exeter* (Exeter, 1960).

The Statutes of the Realm, from Magna Carta to the end of the reign of Queen Anne, 10 vols (London, Record Commission, 1810–24).

Storrs, C. M. *Jacobean Pilgrims from England to St. James of Compostella* (Compostella, 1994; reprinted London, 1998).

Swanson, R. N. *Church and Society in Late Medieval England* (Oxford, 1989).

Swanson, R. N. *Indulgences in Late Medieval England* (Cambridge, 2007).

Thompson, A. Hamilton. 'Diocesan Organization in the Middle Ages: archdeacons and rural deans', *Proceedings of the British Academy*, 29 (1943), 153–94.

Thompson, A. Hamilton. *The English Clergy and their Organization in the Later Middle Ages* (Oxford, 1947).

Tinti, F. (ed.) *Pastoral Care in Late Anglo-Saxon England* (Woodbridge, 2005).

Turner, Sam. *Making a Christian Landscape: the countryside in early medieval Cornwall, Devon and Wessex* (Exeter, 2006).

Turner, Sam. (ed.) *Medieval Devon and Cornwall: shaping an ancient countryside* (Macclesfield, 2006).

Valor Ecclesiasticus tempore Henrici VIII auctoritate regia institutus, ed. J. Caley, 6 vols (London, Record Commission, 1810–24).

The Victoria County History of Cornwall – see Orme, Nicholas (2007).

Walsham, Alexandra. *The Reformation of the Landscape: religion, identity, and memory in early modern Britain and Ireland* (Oxford, 2011).

Whitelock, Dorothy. (ed.) *The Anglo-Saxon Chronicle* (London, 1965).

Whitelock, Dorothy. (ed.) *English Historical Documents c.500–1042*, 2nd edn (London, 1979).

Whiting, Robert. *The Blind Devotion of the People: popular religion and the English Reformation* (Cambridge, 1989).

Williams, Michael A. 'Medieval English Roodscreens with Special Reference to Devon', University of Exeter, unpublished PhD thesis (2008).

Worcester, William. *Itineraries*, ed. J. H. Harvey (Oxford, 1969).

Wright, A. R. *British Calendar Customs: England*, ed. T. E. Lones, 3 vols, Folk-Lore Society, 97, 102, 106 (1936–40).

Yeo, Geoffrey. *The Monks of Cowick* (Exeter, 1987).

Yorke, Barbara. *Wessex in the Early Middle Ages* (London, 1995).

Youings, Joyce. (ed.) *Devon Monastic Lands: calendar of particulars for grants 1536–1558*, Devon and Cornwall Record Society, new series, 1 (1955).

Youings, Joyce. *The Dissolution of the Monasteries* (London and New York, 1971).

Index

Places are in Devon unless otherwise stated

Abbot's Bickington 59, 74
advowsons *see* parish churches: patrons
Ælfwold, bishop 18, 27
Æthelheard, king 5, 8–9
Æthelstan, king 18, 140
Affeton 74–5
Aldhelm, saint 6
Alfred, king 6, 8, 13, 22
alien priories 42–3, 76–7, 193
Alley, William, bishop 179, 181–2, 184–5
almonry boys 82, 145
almshouses 92–3, 138, 160, 180, 184
Alphington 44, 59
altars *see* parish churches
anchorites 93
annuellars 97
appropriated benefices *see* parish churches: appropriated
Apulia, Simon of, bishop 32, 57
archdeacons and archdeaconries 37, 42, 60, 63, 71, 74, 159, 178–9
Arundell, John, bishop 76, 151
Ashburton 1, 147, 171, 176
  church (to 1500) 36, 60–1, 64, 110–12, 114, 116, 120, 127, 133–4, 145, 156
  church (1500–60) 99, 175, 179, 184, 187, 191
Ashford 55, 75
Ashton 111, 117, 181
Ash Wednesday 128, 171
Asser, bishop 6–8
Atherington 111
Atwill, John, dissenter 159
Augustinian canons 43–5, 48, 76
Augustinian friars *see* friars
Axminster 9, 12–13, 15–17, 22–3, 48, 58, 60, 157
Axmouth 26
Aylesbeare 164
Ayshford 123

Baldwin, abbot and archbishop 53, 63–4
Bale, John, bibliographer 88
Bampton (Devon) 98, 208
Bampton (Oxon.) 32
baptism 25, 99, 102, 110, 121, 129, 163, 173, 187, 190
Barclay, Alexander, poet 92
Barlinch (Somt.), priory 74, 168
Barnstaple 1, 47, 60, 133, 141, 146–7
  chapels 120, 122, 124, 130, 171
  church 13, 15, 37, 48–9, 52, 60, 114, 127
  hospital 47, 92
  priory 43, 76–7, 152, 165
Bartholomew, bishop 32, 40, 44, 49, 64, 67
Bassett, Gregory, friar 164, 182
Battle (Sussex), abbey 42
bede-rolls 113, 118, 186
bells *see* parish churches
Benedictine monks 43, 76
benefit of clergy 158
Benet, Thomas, dissenter 160–1
Berdon, William, student 147
Bere Ferrers 91, 109, 122, 128
Berkeley, James, bishop 72, 140
Berry Pomeroy 67, 174

Bible and Bible reading 163, 165, 170, 172, 178–9, 182, 184, 187–9
Bideford 120
Bigbury 120, 134
bishops
  Anglo-Saxon period 6–8
  consistory courts 73
  parishes of 39
  personal origins 32, 71–2, 151, 191
  property and income 32, 42, 151, 176
  registers 35, 54, 62, 70, 119, 137, 153–4
  role of 33–5, 67, 71–4, 128–9, 138, 194
  suffragan 73, 83
Bishop's Clyst 32, 72, 120, 176
Bishop's Nympton 32, 55, 57, 72, 176
Bishop's Tawton 32, 34, 55, 72, 114, 151, 176
Bishopsteignton 32–3, 55, 60, 176
Bitton, Thomas, bishop 35, 87
Blackborough 58, 124
Black Death 47, 70–1, 76
Blaxton, John, cleric 182
Bodley family 181
Bodmin (Corn.) 12, 24, 32, 70–1, 173, 178
Bodmiscombe 39, 45, 76, 82, 210
Bondleigh 60
Boniface, saint 5, 9
Book of Common Prayer 173–5, 178, 181–2, 184, 194
books and writings 83, 85, 91, 149
  hagiography 53, 92
  history 53, 83, 158
  literature 64, 88, 92, 149
  liturgy 18–19, 27, 100, 103, 106, 118, 136, 158, 179, 184
  printed 158
  scholarship 18–19, 53, 64–5, 82–3, 85, 103
Bosham (Sussex) 32, 176
Bow 120; *see also* Nymet Tracey
boy bishop 132
Bracton or Bratton, Henry of, lawyer 65
Bradninch 53, 122, 133
Bradstone 27
Bradworthy 57
Brampford Speke 22, 57, 75, 113
Branscombe 36, 60–1, 164
Brantingham, Thomas, bishop 71–2, 78–9, 85–7, 91, 96, 119, 142, 151
Braunton 4, 7–9, 13, 15–16, 22–3, 39, 55, 60
Brendon 20, 210
Brentor 120, 122
Brewer, William, bishop 32–3, 35, 132, 141
Brewer, William, magnate 49
Bridestowe 19, 23
Bridford 26
bridges 137–8, 157, 162, 171
Brightley, abbey 48–9
Brixton 27, 124, 157
Broadclyst 86, 157
Broad Nymet 75
Broke, Thomas, gentleman 142
Bronescombe, Walter, bishop 35, 38, 88, 90
Buckfast, abbey 9, 11, 15–17, 22, 31, 41, 43, 49, 76, 82, 104, 152–3, 164, 167
Buckland, abbey 43, 48–9, 71, 76, 82, 152–3, 167–8
Buckland Brewer 133
Buckland-in-the-Moor 97
Bulkworthy 59, 110
burhs 13
burials *see* death
Burlescombe 123

Cadbury 37, 59
calendar observances 128–32, 157, 190
Calverleigh 75
Cambridge, university of 85, 160, 164
  King's College 77
canon law 34–5, 59, 190, 193
Canonsleigh, priory 44, 49, 76, 81, 83–4, 152, 165, 167
Canterbury (Kent)
  archbishop of 81; *see also* Cranmer; Pole
  pilgrimage to 67, 141, 192
Cardmaker, John, reformer 164
Carew family 179, 181
Carmelites *see* friars
Carslegh, Peter, cleric 164
Carthusian monks 48
cartularies 82, 212
Caxton, William, printer 158
cemeteries *see* death
Centwine, king 5
Cenwealh, king 9
Chagford 1
Challacombe 120
change in Church history 192–6
chantries 97–8, 113, 169–71, 174
  chantry priests *see* parish clergy

chapels
  of ease 120, 122, 171
  free (of control) 124
  free-standing 119–24, 171; mentioned 57, 67, 75, 93, 130, 138, 143, 157, 192
  in parish churches *see* parish churches
Chard, Thomas, abbot 152
Chard, Thomas, prior and bishop 83
Chardstock 211
charity *see* poor people
Charles 208
Charleton 120
charnel chapels 130
Chaucer, Geoffrey, poet 63
Chawleigh 179
Cheldon 99
Cheristow 120
Cheriton Bishop 20, 141
Cheriton Fitzpaine 20, 216
Chichester, Sir John 127
children 39, 44, 85, 94, 132, 140, 145–6, 156–7; *see also* baptism; choristers; confirmation; schools
Chittlehampton 5, 8, 13, 15, 23, 57, 114, 124, 157, 164
Chivelstone 12
choristers 91, 145
Christmas 128
Christow 23
Chudleigh 32–3, 55, 57, 72, 120, 176
Chudleigh family 181
Chulmleigh 12, 41, 60, 124, 131, 134, 171, 210
church courts 37, 73, 143, 159
church houses 132
churching of women 110, 157, 173
Churchstanton (now Somt.) 211
Churchstow 59, 87, 102
churchwardens 127, 190
  accounts kept by 127, 134, 154–7, 175–6
churchyards *see* death
Churston Ferrers 20
Cistercian monks 39, 43, 45, 76
Clannaborough 57–8, 75
Clayhanger 45, 210
clocks and clock time 115, 127
Clony (Ivybridge?), hospital 47, 92
Cluniac monks 43, 76
Clyst Bridge, battle 174
Clyst Gabriel, hospital 70, 92, 107, 152
Clyst Honiton 36, 60, 105–6
Clyst St Lawrence 125
Clyst St Mary 70
Cnut, king 16
Coeffin, Martin, publisher 158
Colaton Raleigh 26
Colcombe 124
Coldridge 157
Colebrooke 19, 26, 60, 64, 100, 105
Collacombe 181
colleges and collegiate churches 89–92, 169
Colyford 93
Colyton 11–12, 15, 19, 22, 26, 60, 86, 93, 102–3, 105, 111, 125, 157
'Commotion' (rising of 1549) 173–5, 177, 182–3, 188
communion, holy (eucharist, mass)
  before the Reformation 39, 61, 97, 100, 114, 116–19, 122, 129, 163, 169
  from the Reformation 170–3, 175, 179, 182–3, 187–9
Compostella (Spain) 68, 138, 141, 192
compulsions 97
confession 86, 102, 128–9, 135, 138, 163, 169, 190
confirmation 79, 173
confraternities *see* guilds
Constantine, ruler 4
Copplestone 19, 125
Corbin, Otto, dissenter 159
Cornwall 12, 23–5, 32, 85, 87, 90, 117, 131, 134, 141, 165, 167, 173–4, 176, 178, 182, 192, 207–8
  holy wells in 125
Cornworthy, parish, church and priory 44, 76, 83–4, 110, 123, 165
Corpus Christi 129
councils and synods, church 33, 35, 40, 61, 63, 99–100, 110, 113–14, 127–8, 132, 194
Courtenay family 83, 86, 153, 181
  Peter, bishop 71
Cove 210
Coverdale, Miles, bishop 178
Cowick, priory 39, 49, 75–7, 82–3, 110, 140, 153
Cranmer, Thomas, archbishop 162, 170, 173, 187

Crediton 33, 54, 57, 72, 93, 94–6, 120, 174, 176
  hospital 47–8, 76, 92, 152
  minster and cathedral (to 1050) 8–9, 15, 19, 23
  minster (after 1050) 10–12, 16–18, 22, 31–2, 41, 58, 60, 67, 77, 89, 91, 123–4, 138, 143, 145, 152
  minster (during Reformation) 169, 180
  school 146
Crispin, Richard, cleric 171, 174
Cromwell, Thomas 160–4, 169
crosses, standing 4, 125–7, 186
crusades 36, 39, 45, 69, 82, 138
Cullompton 11, 13, 15, 17–18, 42, 98, 110–11, 133, 157
  almshouse 93
Culmstock 36, 60–1, 154

Dartington 111
Dartmouth 1, 20, 47, 63, 92, 141, 146, 159, 208
Dawlish 36, 60–1, 105
Deane, Hugh, musician 180
death *see also* Black Death
  burials and tombs 25, 47, 84–5, 87, 92, 107, 116, 127, 137, 158, 187, 190
  cemeteries and churchyards 4–5, 9, 13, 19, 124
  funerals 25, 47, 70, 125, 137, 156–7, 170, 173
dedications *see* parish churches
Devon
  borders of 211
  nature of 1–2, 191–3
Diptford 114
dissent, religious 141–3, 159; *see also* heresy
Dittisham 124
Dodbrooke 54, 93
Doddiscombsleigh 26
Domesday Book 11–12, 14, 16, 22, 27, 32, 41
Dominicans *see* friars
Dotton 25, 57
Dowland 157
Down St Mary 19, 60, 62
Dumnonii 3–5
Dunchideock 74
Dunkeswell 37
  abbey 31, 43, 48–9, 52, 76, 152, 167
Dunne, Gabriel, abbot 164
Dunster (Somt.) 67

East Allington 157
East Budleigh 111, 123
East Down 20
Easter 129
East Horsley (Surrey) 72, 176
East Portlemouth 24
East Teignmouth 19–20, 60, 119
East Worlington 59
Edgar, king 16, 19, 22
education *see* schools; universities
Edward the Confessor, king 8, 13, 31, 42
Edward the Elder, king 8
Edward I, king 40
Edward II, king 72
Edward III, king 85, 87
Edward IV, king 151
Edward VI, king 170–8
Edward, the Black Prince 86
Egg Buckland 20
Eggesford 136
Elizabeth I, queen 181–5
Erasmus, *Paraphrases* 184
Ermington 149
Eton (Bucks.), college 77
evensong *see* matins and evensong
Exeter, cathedral, previously minster
  (before 1066) 8, 11, 18, 22, 31, 41
  (1066–1300) 32, 36–7, 39, 41, 46, 60–1, 64, 67, 70, 97
  (1300–1500) 73, 75, 84–6, 88–9, 91, 97–8, 104–5, 107, 114, 131, 138–141, 143, 145
  (1500–1560) 151–2, 154–8, 162–4, 171, 178–82, 188
Exeter, city of 1–3, 6, 26, 40, 86, 120, 129, 134, 138, 158–60, 162, 174, 176
  almshouses and hospitals 47, 87, 93, 134; *see also* St John
  castle chapel 41, 119, 171
  chapels 120, 122
  friaries 45, 67, 84–8, 153, 162, 164, 167, 169
  guilds 26, 66, 68, 120
  mayor and council of 88, 133, 149, 165–7
  St James, priory 11, 13, 15, 19, 41, 43, 49, 52, 77
  St John, hospital 47–8, 57, 67, 83, 92–3, 104, 147, 152, 165, 167–8
  St Nicholas, priory 13, 43, 49, 53, 76, 81, 152, 165, 169, 195
  schools 63, 90, 92, 96, 99, 146–9
  wells, holy 124–5

Exeter, Joseph of, poet 64
Exeter, marquess of *see* Courtenay family
Exeter, parish churches
  St Cuthbert 57, 67
  St David 25
  St George 19
  St James, South Street 57, 67, 74–5
  St Kerrian 24, 67
  St Laurence 57, 102–3
  St Leonard 93
  St Martin 19, 21, 57, 152
  St Mary Arches 58–9
  St Mary Major 3, 102
  St Mary Minor 57
  St Mary Steps 20, 67
  St Olave 11, 13, 15, 42
  St Sidwell 13, 23, 67, 124–5, 140
  St Thomas 54, 75, 174–5; *see also* Cowick
  Trinity 74–5
Exminster 9, 13, 15, 23

Fardel 123
Faringdon (Hants.) 32, 72, 176
Farway 59
fasting 25, 128, 131, 137, 190
Fenny Bridges, battle 174
Forde, abbey 31, 43, 49, 53, 63, 76, 82, 152–3, 167, 169
Fortescue, Sir John, lawyer 149
Fox, Richard, bishop 72
France 42–3, 53, 64–5, 69, 76–7, 110, 119, 193–4
Franciscan friars *see* friars
Fremington 124
friars 39, 45–7, 52, 67, 84–8, 104–5, 137, 153–4, 162, 164, 167, 192
Frithelstock, priory 44, 48, 52, 76, 104, 122–3, 152, 165, 169, 193
funerals *see* death

gentry *see* nobility and gentry
Gerent, king 5–6
Germany 53, 86, 158–9, 163, 179, 181
Gildas 4
Glasney (Corn.), college 90
Glastonbury (Somt.) 5
glebes 12, 22, 31, 74, 189
Grandisson, John, bishop 1, 70–3, 78, 83, 85–7, 89, 91–2, 119, 123, 143, 146
graves *see* burials
Great Torrington *see* Torrington
Greenway, John, merchant 110, 161
Grenville, Sir Richard, 168
guilds and confraternities 133–4, 170–1; mentioned 26, 66, 68, 87, 97, 122, 127, 137, 192, 196
Gytha, countess 11

Haccombe 55, 75, 91, 102
Hailes (Gloucs.), abbey 141
Halberton 67, 133
Halsford 26
Halwell 13, 23, 27, 124–5
Halwill 23, 27, 124, 210
Hankford, Sir William 110
Harberton 111, 124
Harewode family 136
Hartland 120
  abbey 41, 44, 48–9, 52–3, 67, 75–6, 78, 152–3, 164, 167
  early minster 4, 8, 11–13, 15–17, 23, 33, 41, 57
  parish and church 57, 67–8, 75, 114, 122, 124, 157
harvest 131–2
Hatherleigh 133
Hawkchurch 59, 211
Heanton Punchardon 120
Heavitree 13, 60, 87, 142, 160
Hele, Walter, cleric 178
Henry I, king 32
Henry II, king 32
Henry III, king 32
Henry VI, king 141, 157
Henry VII, king 106, 151, 173
Henry VIII, king 74, 151, 158, 160–2, 168–70, 172, 176
heresy 142, 159, 164, 171, 178, 181
hermits 93
Heynes, Simon, reformer 164
Highampton 55
High Bickington 111
High Bray 57
Holbeton 60, 122, 157, 179
Hollacombe 11–12, 15, 20, 24
Holne 20
Holsworthy 113
Holy Week 129, 171
Homilies, book of 170, 184–6
Honeychurch 20, 59

Honiton 1, 47, 87, 92, 134, 141, 157
Hooker, John, historian 162, 175–6, 179
hospitality 102, 185
hospitals 47–8, 70, 90, 92–3, 107, 124, 137–8
Howe, John, prior 153
Hundred Years War 69, 76–7
Huxham 58

iconoclasm 127, 143, 164, 170, 179, 186
Iddesleigh 134
Ilfracombe 60, 122, 141, 157
images 111, 140, 162–4, 170, 179–81, 186
indulgences or pardons 67, 88, 138, 157
Ine, king 5, 25
injunctions, Reformation 162–3, 165, 170, 182
Instow 19, 23, 124
insularity 193–4
Ipplepen, church and priory 43, 77, 178
Ireland 53, 85, 93
Italy 85, 136; *see also* papacy; Rome
Ivybridge 47

Jacobstow 23, 75
James, Jeanne, historian 119
Jerusalem 33, 138, 141
Jewel, John, bishop 182
Jews in Devon 39–40
John, king 32, 49

Kenn 5, 57
Kennerleigh 120
Kentisbeare 124
Kentisbury 134
Kenton 58
Kerswell, priory 43, 49, 52, 76–7, 83, 152, 165, 167
King, Oliver, bishop 72
Kingskerswell 11–12, 15, 19, 22
Kingsteignton 157
Knowstone 74, 179

Lacy, Edmund, bishop 71–2, 80, 94, 97, 102, 119, 123, 137, 139–41, 157, 164
laity *see also* children; merchant class; nobility and gentry; poor people; women
  charity to the poor 67, 163
  duties of 62, 65, 163
  guild members *see* guilds
  impact of 194–5
  religion of (before 1086) 25–6
  religion of (1086–1300) 65–8
  religion of (1300–1500) 109–49
  religion of (1500–1530) 156–9
  religion of (1530–1560) 162–90, 185–90
Lammas 131
Landcross 5, 8, 57
Landkey 5, 9
landscape 22–3, 59, 122, 185–6
Lane, John, merchant 110
Langtree 125
Latimer, Hugh, reformer 162
Launceston (Corn.) 32, 174
Leland, John, antiquary 17, 82, 171
Lent 128–9, 132
Leofric, bishop 8, 31–2, 41
leprosy and lepers 47, 92
Lewdown 122
Ley, Henry, gentleman 122
Leyson, William, cleric 182
Lifton 13, 15, 131, 142
literacy 149, 158, 193
Littleham (Bideford) 20
Littleham (Exmouth) 60
Little Torrington 102; *see also* Taddiport
Lollards 39, 71, 142
London 33, 85, 88, 104, 142, 164, 171, 181–2
  bishops' houses in 33, 72, 176
Lundy 4, 55, 57, 74
Luppitt 50
Luther, Martin 159–60, 164
Lydford 12–13, 15, 20, 22
Lympstone 57

maidens, church companies of 133–4, 157
Malborough 12
Malmesbury (Wilts.), abbey 42
Manaton 124
Mariansleigh 74
marriage
  clergy *see* parish clergy
  laity 102, 110, 128, 143, 173
Marsh Barton (Alphington) *see* St Mary Marsh
Marshal, Henry, bishop 32–3
Mary I, queen 164, 178–81
Marystow 23
Mary Tavy 59, 109
mass *see* communion

matins and evensong 116–17, 170, 173, 187
Meavy 19
Meddon 120
merchant class and religion 63, 65–7, 94, 110, 137, 161, 181
Merton 120
Meshaw 99
Midsummer Day 131
Milton Abbey (Dorset) 104
Minchin Buckland (Somt.), priory 76
minsters 9–19, 22, 33, 40–1, 88–9
Modbury, church and priory 11, 13, 15, 37, 43, 77, 114
Mohun family 49
Mohun's Ottery 181
Molland 74, 179
monasteries 9, 16–17, 42–53, 70, 76–83, 104, 137, 192, 196
  dissolution of 164–9, 174, 178
  education in 78, 81–2, 145
  functions and activities of 53, 78–83, 196
  incomes of 50–2, 71
  patrons of 49
  personnel of 52, 71, 77–8
Monkleigh 110
Montacute (Somt.), priory 76–7, 167
Morchard Bishop 32, 176
More, Sir Thomas 138
Morebath 99, 111, 124, 127, 134, 140, 143, 154–6, 168, 175–6, 180, 184, 191, 221
Moreman, John, cleric 171, 174
Moretonhampstead 105, 122
music, religious 81–2, 91, 100, 114, 145, 153, 180, 183
  musicians (named) 145, 180

Nether Exe 75
Newenham, abbey 43, 48–50, 53, 70, 76, 152, 167
Newport (Barnstaple) 120, 143
Newton Ferrers 11, 15, 102, 109, 120
Newton Poppleford 120
Newton St Cyres 53, 59
Newton St Petrock 11–12, 15, 20, 24
Newton Tracey 55
Nicolles, John, cleric 180
nobility and gentry 67, 84, 86–7, 96, 136–7, 142
  careers as clergy 63, 83, 94
  chapels in houses of 120, 123
  charity by 27, 137
  founders of minsters, parish churches, chapels 15–16, 22, 122
  founders of monasteries 49, 53, 65
  privileges in churches 61, 114, 187
  Reformation and 168, 181
Norman Conquest 31
Northam 42
North Bovey 143
Northcott 181
Northlew 125, 157
North Molton 57–8
North Petherwin (now Corn.) 211
North Tawton 67
nuns and nunneries 44, 76–7, 81, 83–4, 93, 137, 165–8
Nutwell 26, 120
Nymet Rowland 75
Nymet Tracey 122; *see also* Bow

Oakford 179
'officials' 37
Offwell 59
Okehampton 47, 92, 120
Oldham, Hugh, bishop 92, 151–2, 155
Oldridge 58, 75
Ordgar, nobleman 15, 27
ordination 94–6, 98–9, 180
Osbern, bishop 31–2
Otterton, priory 42–3, 49, 52, 77
Ottery St Mary 93, 120, 171
  church 42, 84, 91–2, 107, 109, 111, 143, 145–6, 152, 157, 166, 169
Oxford, university of 64–5, 82, 85, 104, 142, 153–4, 182, 184, 192
  Exeter College 90, 146, 192, 213

Paget, William, royal servant 167, 176
Paignton 32–3, 72, 120, 159, 176
Pancrasweek 125
papacy 1, 25, 32, 35–6, 39, 45, 67, 69, 72, 85, 138, 193–4
  and the Reformation 154, 160, 174, 178
papal provisions 96
pardoners 138
parish churches
  altars in 61, 112–13, 175, 179–80, 186, 215
  appropriated 55–6, 59, 168
  bells 60, 115, 127, 176

buildings 23, 59–61, 100, 109–16, 127, 157, 166, 186, 193
chapels in 98, 113, 157, 187
churchyards *see* death
dedications of buildings 131–2, 163
dedications to saints 20, 23, 53–4
equipment and furnishings 26, 61–2, 127–8, 173, 175–6, 179–80, 184
numbers 54–5, 96, 153
origins 19–25
parishioners *see* laity
patrons of 33, 35, 56, 75, 96, 168, 184
pulpits and preaching 111–13, 186
rectories and vicarages 55–6
roodscreens and lofts 61, 111, 180, 184, 186
seating 62, 110–11, 114–16, 157, 186
services *see* communion; matins
towers 60, 114, 157

parish clergy
activities and duties 100–5, 189
chaplains, chantry priests, curates 44, 56, 63, 94, 97, 105, 113, 122, 153–6, 167, 184
education 63–4, 94, 154, 184–5
housing 102, 120
income and wages 57–8, 98
lifestyle 62–5, 103, 184–5, 189
married 33, 35, 175–6, 178–9, 182, 184
numbers 52, 70–1, 94–8
old age and death 105–7
origins 22, 25, 27
pensions 105–6
period (1066 to 1300) 31, 62–5
period (1300 to 1500) 94–8
period (1500 to 1560) 153–7, 184–5
rectors and vicars 55–6, 61, 153, 184–5
taxation 36, 160–2

parish clerks 98–9, 101; mentioned 25, 61, 63, 67, 94, 118, 126

parishes
boundaries, sizes, shapes 12, 22, 56–7, 131
new creations 75, 124
numbers 54–5, 74–5, 153
united with others 57, 74–5
wealth 57–8, 160–2

parish registers 163, 182
Parracombe 124
Peasants' Revolt 71, 173
peculiar jurisdictions 37–9, 42, 185
penance 129, 138
penitentiaries 128–9, 142
Penselwood (Somt.) 206
Peter Tavy 57, 59
Petrockstow 20
Petton 208
Philham 120
Piers Plowman, poem 86
pilgrimage 26–7, 67–8, 88, 100, 140–1, 157, 163, 192

Pilton 1
chapels, hospital, anchorite 47, 92–3, 122, 157, 164
parish church and priory 13, 15, 41, 43, 48, 52, 76, 152, 165, 168–9

Pinhoe 11, 19, 206

Plymouth 1, 63, 141, 147, 174
chapels, hermits, hospital, school 47, 63, 93, 105, 120–2, 146
church 18, 23, 47, 74, 85, 110, 120, 122, 141
friaries 45–7, 84–8, 167

Plympton 125
anchorite, hospital, school 47, 63, 92–3, 146
minster 9, 11–13, 15–18, 23, 33
parish and church 37, 57
priory 32, 41, 44, 48–53, 74, 76, 81–2, 152–3, 156–7, 167

Plymstock 157
Plymtree 217
Pole, Reginald, cardinal 163, 174, 180
Pollard, John, cleric 178
Pollard, Walter, student 147–8
Polsloe, priory 44, 76, 83, 86, 104, 165, 167
polyphony *see* music

poor people 63–4, 99, 117
charity to 67, 104, 137–8, 170, 180, 182

pope *see* papacy
population changes 69–70
Powderham 120, 181
prayer 27, 100, 105, 116–19, 123, 125, 136–7, 145, 163, 178, 189
prayer-books 136–7, 173; *see also Book of Common Prayer*
Prayer-Book Rebellion *see* 'Commotion'
preaching 86, 111–13, 119, 125, 162, 181, 185
prebends 18, 171
Premonstratensian canons 39, 44, 76

Prest, Agnes, dissenter 179, 181–2
printing 152, 194
prisoners 137–8
processions 25, 28, 60, 127, 129–31, 170, 179, 183
Prust, John, abbot 153, 164

Quinil, Peter, bishop 35, 40, 61, 63, 86, 99, 110, 113–14, 116, 127–8

Rayny family 136
reading, teaching of 144–6
Reformation, the 158–90
relics 18, 140, 182
Reynolds, Thomas, cleric 181–2
Richard I, king 32
Richard II, king 88
Richard III, king 71
Rogationtide 25, 28, 129–31, 183–4
Roman Britain 2–3
Romansleigh 24
Rome 26, 141
rosaries 136
Rousdon 57
Ruan Lanihorne (Corn.) 24
rural deans and deaneries 37, 160
Russell, John, earl of Bedford 168–9, 185

St Giles in the Wood 122
St John, Order of (later Knights of) 36, 39, 45, 52, 76, 104, 141, 167
St Marychurch 15, 20, 36, 60–2, 105
St Mary Marsh, priory 44, 52, 76, 152, 165, 167
St Michael's Mount (Corn.) 88, 138, 141
saints and saint cults 13, 19, 23, 53–4, 67–8, 88, 92, 111–12, 124, 134, 140–1, 156–7, 162–3, 171, 178, 182; *see also* parish churches
Salcombe Regis 36, 59–61
Sampford Courtenay 60, 173–4, 177
sanctuary 158
Sandford 20, 120, 123–4
Sarum, Use of 61, 116
Satterleigh 58, 75
schools 40, 44, 63, 69, 84–5, 91–2, 94, 99, 143–9, 154, 158, 160, 169–71, 189, 193
Seccheville, John, scholar 64
Sellack, William, merchant 111
Shaugh Prior 20, 157
Shebbear 124
Sherborne (Dorset) 4–6, 8–9
Sherford 11–12
Shillingford 55, 75
Shillingford, John, mayor 149
Shirwell 37
Sidbury 19, 23, 36, 60, 141
Silverton 133, 174
Slapton, collegiate church 91, 143, 169
slaves 27
Somerset, Edward Seymour, duke of 2, 170
South Brent 20, 57, 102, 105, 122, 125
South Huish 12
South Milton 12, 124
South Molton 11, 13, 15–17, 22, 98, 114, 122, 134, 136–7
South Pool 53, 124
South Tawton 132
South Zeal 120
Sowton 182
Spain 68, 138, 141, 192
Spreyton 110
Stafford, Edmund, bishop 71–2, 76, 119, 137, 142, 151
Stapledon, Richard, knight 48
Stapledon, Walter, bishop 35, 48, 70–2, 83, 86, 88, 90, 92, 94–6, 119, 146–7, 151
Staverton 36, 60–1
Stephen, king 49
Steven alias Bedeman, Laurence 142
Steyner, Drew, dissenter 142
Stockland 211
Stockleigh English 58
Stoke Fleming 13, 15, 23
Stoke Gabriel 55
Stokenham 12–13, 15, 22–3, 58
stones, inscribed 4
Stonor family 149
stores in churches 132–4, 137, 157, 170, 192
Sutton Coldfield (Warws.) 151, 178
synods *see* councils and synods
Syon (Middx.), abbey 77

Taddiport, hospital 47, 90, 92, 124
Tavistock 1, 174
  abbey 9, 11, 15–17, 19, 22–4, 27, 31, 39, 41, 43, 48–50, 53, 76–83, 152–3, 158–9, 167–8
  church 100, 109
  hospital, hermit, school 47, 93, 146

Tawstock 109, 124, 136–7
'Taxation of Pope Nicholas' 36, 54–7, 74
Templars, Knights 36, 45, 52
Templecombe (Somt.) 210
Templeton 45, 70, 75, 99, 124
Thornbury 157
Thorncombe (now Dorset) 142, 211
Thorverton 59, 122, 131, 158
Throwleigh 132
Tithe Act and surveys 56
tithes 55–6, 65, 168; mentioned 25, 31, 40, 49, 74, 89, 102, 143, 189–90
Tiverton 1, 210
  almshouse, chapels, school 63, 93, 120, 146
  church 12–13, 15, 17, 23, 41, 57, 98–9, 110–11, 157, 161, 171
Toker, John, abbot 153
Topsham 60, 141
Torbryan 111
Torre, abbey 31, 44, 47, 49–50, 76–8, 152–3, 167, 169
Torrington 93, 120, 160, 171, 174
Totnes 37, 178, 181
  chapel, guilds, school 120, 133, 146
  hospitals 47–8, 67, 76, 92, 152
  minster 11, 13, 15–16, 23
  priory 43, 49, 76–7, 152–3, 165
transubstantiation 39, 169, 175, 181
Tregonwell, John, royal servant 165, 167
Tregonwell, Robert, cleric 164
Tremayne family 181
Trinitarian friars 48, 52, 67, 76
Trusham 55
Trychay, Christopher, vicar 154, 180, 182, 185, 221
Turberville, James, bishop 179, 181
Twitchen 57
Tyndale, William, reformer 164

Uffculme *see* Bodmiscombe
Umberleigh 42
unction 102
uniformity 186–7, 189–90
universities 64, 94; *see also* Cambridge; Oxford
Upcott Barton 216
Upottery 36, 60
Upton Hellions 55
Upton Pyne 22
Urswick, Christopher 106

Valor Ecclesiasticus 74, 151–3, 162, 164
'Valuation of Norwich' 36
Veysey, John, bishop 123, 151, 160, 162–3, 176, 178
vicar-general, bishop's 73
Vikings 6, 27
Virginstow 23, 37, 55
visitations 33, 37, 60–2, 64, 78–81, 153, 165, 170, 182
vowesses 93

Wales 4, 23–5, 81
Walkhampton 53, 124, 159
Walsingham (Norf.) 141, 157
Warelwast, Robert, bishop 32
Warelwast, William, bishop 31–2, 37, 41, 44, 49, 88
Warland *see* Totnes: hospitals
Wars of the Roses 71
Washbourne 124
Washfield 179
Washford Pyne 99
Welcombe 75, 120
wells, holy 124–5, 186; mentioned 23, 27, 67
Welsh, Robert, cleric 174–5
Wembury 156
Wembworthy 123
Werrington (now Corn.) 211
Wessex, kings of 5–9, 12, 15
West Alvington 12–13, 15, 22
West Worlington 59, 74
Whitchurch 20, 22, 57, 91, 124
Whitestone 26
Whitstone (Corn.) 141
Whyte, Thomas, abbot 153
Widecombe-in-the-Moor 109, 132
William I, king 31, 49
William II, king 32
Willis, Peter, reformer 181
wills 65–7, 87, 102–4, 132, 137, 141
Wiltshire, countess of 157
Windsor (Berks.) 141, 157, 192
Winkleigh 61, 103, 133
Witheridge 70, 99, 124
wives, church companies of 133, 157

women 27, 67; *see also* children; churching; marriage; nuns
  literacy of 144, 146
  problems caused by 78, 80, 83, 165–7, 181
  religious involvement of 26, 49, 60, 79, 93, 127–8, 133–5, 137, 157
Woodbury 11, 13, 15, 20, 26, 39
Woolfardisworthy West 75
Worcester, William, antiquary 88
Wycliffe, John, reformer 39, 142
Wykeham, William, bishop 90

Yarcombe 72
Yealmpton 11, 13, 15–16, 22
Yeoton 120
Yogge, Thomas, merchant 110
York 13, 129
young men 133–4, 157